ADVENTURES IN
FRENCH COOKING

Adventures in
FRENCH
COOKING

AUTHENTIC FRENCH DISHES FOR
THE MODERN AMERICAN COOK

Myriam Guidroz

ILLUSTRATIONS BY *Barbara M. Shapira*

THE MACMILLAN COMPANY
COLLIER-MACMILLAN LTD., LONDON

The Macmillan Company
866 Third Avenue, New York, N.Y. 10022
Collier-Macmillan Canada Ltd., Toronto, Ontario

Library of Congress Catalog Card Number: 77-101723
Printed in the United States of America

FIRST PRINTING

TO

Harriet G. Guild, M.D.
Sherling T. Lauricella, M.D.
Patsy Phelps, M.D.

Contents

ADVENTURES IN
FRENCH COOKING

Introduction

SAY THE WORDS "French cooking" to a male gourmet and chances are he will immediately visualize something fragrant with wine, delicately coated with cream, dripping with butter, and expensive. In the female of the species, the same words conjure up visions of long hours over a hot stove, endless chopping of improbable herbs and a sinkful of dirty dishes *she* will have to wash.

As far as 49,999,000 Frenchmen are concerned, both visions are wrong at least six days a week! For one thing the French housewife certainly has no more time than her American sister.

Although the large cities of France and Belgium are beginning to have supermarkets, the small towns do not. The daily ritual of shopping can be a delightful experience but very time-consuming. An ordinary meal will require stops at the grocery, the butcher's, the vegetable shop, the pastry and/or bakery, then to the dairy for eggs, butter and cheese and milk. You may still have to make a stop at the druggist's for cleaning supplies and if by now you are foot-sore and weary, you will have to make another call at the pharmacist's for aspirin! The redeeming feature is the people. As you wait to be served you chat or gossip and French shops are the equivalent of Dr. Spock to get advice on child care.

So you may wonder how the French housewife finds time to prepare those fantastically complicated dishes usually known as "French cooking." The answer is, of course, that she doesn't. Slowly simmered dishes, certainly: she can leave them to cook while she shops. On special occasions she will prepare *"un bon petit plat"* and if guests are coming, she will put "little dishes into big ones," the French announcement that you can expect a gourmet meal!

On the whole, French or Belgian family meals are rather simple. A spicy little nothing, such as a few slices of good salami, radishes, or a sardine on a bed of lettuce, will start the meal. This will be followed by a good roast served with its own juices or a carefully simmered cheaper cut of meat. Vegetables with this and, in Belgium, potatoes. A good green salad will follow and the meal will end with a small piece of good cheese and fruit. More elaborate desserts are usually reserved for Sunday dinner.

How then do Belgium and France get their reputation for fine eating? By careful choosing of ingredients, exquisite care in the selection of dishes that go together. Add to that imagination in decorating dishes to make them as appealing to the eye as to the palate and you have the secret of fine cooking.

Although Belgium is France's close neighbor, the eating habits are a little different. The difference lies mostly in quantities. The Belgians love food as fine as the French but more of it. Where the French eat bread, the Belgians have potatoes. The Belgians love bread too, but usually with butter on it. Soups are another difference between the two countries: in Belgium it is served at the start of the noon meal, in France usually at night. The Belgians make and consume enormous quantities of beer and use it in cooking more often than the French. The French may tell you the wines are not as fine in Belgium, but the very best French wines find their way into Belgian cellars!

Family recipes are still closely guarded secrets in both countries and are handed to brides as heirlooms. Cooking is considered a very important part of a happy marriage, as it should be. Few things will make a husband more loving than a good meal. Can you remember as a child being greeted by the scent of cinnamon on your return from school on a cold day? I firmly believe that cinnamon is a great deterrent to juvenile delinquency. As for the budget, you can't move to a cheaper house during lean months or decrease the car payments. But you can use hamburger instead of roast and make the family love it.

Another reason for the careful handing down of recipes in families is that French cookbooks often assume that you can cook. You will be told to dilute something to the right consistency. Fine, if you know what that consistency happens to be. Measurements are usually given by weight with various approximations (a rounded kitchen spoon of flour is about 1 ounce for example). I find American recipes models of clarity and have tried to copy this. Also I have tried to keep to ingredients which can generally be found in any supermarket. There is a French saying that any region which produces a certain food will also provide the ingredients to cook it with and the drink to go with it. I find this true to a great extent although I have still to find a truly great sauce made with American soft drinks. But this country produces fine wines, excellent meat if you know how to choose it, poultry at prices everyone can afford and vegetables and fruit in abundance, unrivaled anywhere in the world. There is no reason why Americans should envy anyone's cooking.

As to my qualifications as a cook . . . I come from a long line of gourmets. I was born in Brussels of a French mother and an English father. Having inherited gourmet taste buds at birth, it is perhaps not surprising that my first words were *"c'est bon"* and *"encore"* during a repast of creamed chicken at the tender age of twelve months. This obviously endeared me to our cook, Maria Malherbes, whose pet I became. This meant I was allowed into her sacrosanct kitchen any time to watch and taste. My younger sister, though, was threatened on sight with Maria's largest skimmer, which was the exact size and shape of her small round derriere.

Maria had me making mayonnaise at seven by pouring oil and vinegar into small bottles I could handle easily. I was poaching eggs at eight, unaware that it was difficult, and by the age of ten, I was quite a good cook without realizing it. I was also rotund and an accomplished *gourmande*, a word untranslatable except as "greedy gourmet."

Came the Second World War and we fled to Britain. My mother was suddenly faced with the problem of keeping house and cooking. Her first effort was spectacular. After a meal of cold cuts she brought out the most utterly beautiful French apple pie I have ever seen. The aroma was exquisite, the thinly sliced apples arranged in picture pretty rows, the edges just delightfully browned. Drooling, we fell to, only to discover that the crust could not be cut. The sharpest knife in the house did not even make a dent in it. The apples, though, were delicious even if not very filling. After several similar experiences, it was decided that I should take over the cooking, a happy arrangement for me as I was excused from doing the dishes, a chore I loathed.

The war years really taught me how to cook. We could not afford failures on the scanty rations we were allowed. After the war I discovered with bliss the wonders of fresh eggs, cream and meats, and cooking became my favorite form of relaxation. After I moved to this country with my American husband I often became furious at the so-called French recipes which came to my attention. So one day, I decided to try my hand at writing down some of our family favorites. Don't be afraid to make changes of your own, that's the way good cooks work. In time I hope some of these recipes will become favorites in your own family!

NOTE: For ease in following the recipes, asterisks have been added to indicate recipes mentioned elsewhere in the book.

1. SOUPS

THE FRENCH AND THE BELGIANS both love their soups but at different times of the day. In Belgium, at home and in restaurants it is the standard beginning of the noon meal. In France, however, soup is usually served at the beginning of the evening meal. In certain country regions, though, soup is served for breakfast! Not so extraordinary when you recall that the standard French prescription for the prevention of hangovers is to end the evening with a big bowl of onion soup at the Halles!

In Belgium soup is soup. The French make a distinction between *soupe* and *potage: soupe* always has bread in it. Bread and milk, for instance, is called *soupe au lait* and anyone with a quick temper will be described as "rising as fast as a milk soup," which is fairly accurate when you think of some people you know!

Some of the best soups I have ever eaten have been nameless, homemade concoctions never to be repeated. There are classic soups, of course, bisques creamy and pungent at the same time, onion soup redolent of toasted cheese, leek and potato soup, which with slight changes is called vichyssoise in this country but which is always served hot in France. Most family soups, though, are made from trimmings of vegetables, leftovers, bits of gravy, sometimes doctored up with a soup mix. Of course, you can always give the soup a name if the family insists on knowing what they are eating. Choose the name wisely, though; 1 teaspoon of leftover chicken gravy is enough for the name "chicken soup," if it is a family favorite—no need to mention the leftover spinach!

Here are a few recipes which should inspire you to create 365 different soups, whether you serve them for lunch, supper or breakfast.

BISQUE

In France a bisque is a cream soup made with lobster, crawfish, or crab or even shrimp. Unlike most cream soups this one is pungent, peppery and only just tamed by the addition of cream. It takes a little time to prepare but will definitely set a gourmet tone to the meal, no matter what you serve after it! What gives bisque its taste is the shell of whatever you are using. If you try to short-cut it by using canned lobster, etc., you will end up with a very good cream of lobster perhaps, but not a true bisque. You can get excellent results with fresh shrimp or crab and· also that can of lobster, if you like, but you need some kind of shell.

FOR 4 PEOPLE:
> 2 baby (1-pound) lobsters OR
>> 6 good-size crabs and/or
>> 1 pound shrimp (with heads, if possible)
> 4 tablespoons butter
> ¼ cup brandy or cognac
> 1 cup dry white wine
> 1 large onion, coarsely chopped
> Salt and pepper
> 1 bay leaf
> ⅛ teaspoon thyme
> 2 tablespoons flour
> 2 small cloves garlic, finely chopped
> 4 tablespoons finely chopped parsley
> 4 tablespoons finely chopped green onions
> 4 tablespoons finely chopped celery (with leaves)
> 1 tablespoon tomato paste
> Worcestershire sauce
> 1 cup heavy cream

With lobster or crabs, start by boiling them in a very small amount of salted water; steaming is more like it. Boil until done, 7 to 10 minutes. Reserve water and proceed.

With shrimp, shell them raw, saving the shells. Around New Orleans, shrimp are often sold with the heads on; save them preciously, they will add a lot of flavor. Remove all the meat from the lobsters or crabs, cracking the claws, legs, etc. Cut into small pieces and set aside for later. Take all the shells, break them into pieces as small as possible, with a hammer if necessary, and place them in a large pot with 1 tablespoon of butter. Shake over high heat until sizzling, pour in the brandy and immediately hold a match to it. When the flames die down, add the wine, the chopped onion and just enough water barely to cover the shells. Season lightly with salt and pepper, add the bay leaf and thyme and the garlic cover and allow to simmer gently for about an hour. Since this is the base of your bisque, stand guard over it or put a sign on it if necessary, because I have known uninitiated barbarians who have peered in while your back was turned, decided the shells were worthless and thrown the whole thing out!

While the shells simmer, melt the remaining 3 tablespoons of butter in another pot. Add to it the raw shrimp, or the crab or lobster meat. Sizzle a few minutes, sprinkle with the flour, stirring well, then add the garlic, parsley, green onions and celery. Cook a few minutes until they wilt but do not let brown.

Line a sieve or colander with a fine cloth. Strain the broth from the first pot (the shell mixture) carefully; you don't want any bits of shell, but press hard to get every last bit of goodness out. Stir this into the second pot and add the tomato paste. You should have about 3 cups of soup now. Add a little water if you have less or leave to simmer, uncovered, if you have too much. Taste and add salt, lots of black pepper and a good dash of Worcestershire sauce. Taste again. This should be a very strong potion, very highly seasoned. Just before serving, reheat, add the cream and do *not* let it boil. Because the shellfish is not puréed it will not be completely smooth, as restaurant bisque usually is, but, oh, my friend, what a flavor!

CRÈME DE PETITS POIS

Cream of Pea Soup

Pea soup is generally thought of as a robust, winter-time soup. Well *crème de petits pois* is as different from split pea soup as corduroy from silk velvet! It is not cheap to make either, but as the beginning of a very special meal in the spring, it is perfect. Even in the cold of winter, it will give you a touch of spring fever, so you might try serving it then. We start with really tiny peas, the smallest you can buy, and don't be fooled by the label. Try a can and see if these are the not quite round, tiny peas. Anything else and you end up with a good pea soup but nothing to write home about.

FOR 4 PEOPLE:

2 1-pound cans very small peas (petits pois)
2 tablespoons butter
1 medium onion, finely chopped
1 small carrot, finely chopped
3 or 4 lettuce leaves, finely chopped
1 slice (¼ pound) boiled ham
2 cups water
Salt and pepper
¼ teaspoon thyme
½ teaspoon tarragon

For garnish:
½ cup heavy cream, whipped
4 slices bacon, fried crisp and crumbled

Set aside about ½ can of peas with their liquid. Heat 2 table-spoons of butter in a large pot and cook the chopped vegetables until the onion is transparent but not brown. Add the slice of boiled ham, the peas along with their liquid and about 2 cups of water. Bring to a boil, season lightly with salt and pepper and the herbs. Tarragon is a must here; use about ½ teaspoon of the dried kind. Leave to simmer for about 30 to 45 minutes.

After this time, remove the slice of ham (you can give it to the cat since all the flavor is in the peas). Buzz the soup in a blender or strain it through a sieve. Return this creamy purée to the pot along with the reserved peas; taste and correct the seasoning to your taste. The soup should be creamy but not too thick. You can thin it down with a little water or milk, if necessary. The whole peas should float around like little gems.

At serving time, whip the cream and lightly season it with a pinch of salt and one-half of the crumbled bacon. Heat the soup to simmer-ing, stirring constantly because pea soup of any kind will burn at the bottom. Pour into bowls and float a large spoonful of cream on top. Sprinkle with the remaining bacon for the crowning touch.

PETITE MARMITE

"*Marmite*" is the French name for those friendly round cooking pots which used to hang over the fire from a long chain in days gone by. The name of this soup is misleading because you need a big pot to cook it in. I would certainly not advise you to make it for only two or three people, but to feed a crowd after a day in the country, an après-ski party, or a ravenous bunch of teen-agers. If you can get a good marrow bone from the butcher, try serving thin slices of toast spread with marrow along with the soup. Freshly ground black pepper on marrow makes it as fine as caviar! With an assortment of cheese and apples to munch before the fire, you should have well-satisfied guests.

FOR 8 TO 10 PEOPLE:
A little fat
2 pounds brisket of beef, in one piece
2 pounds stewing veal, in one piece
Salt and pepper
1 stewing hen (4 pounds)
2 large onions
4 carrots
2 or 3 turnips
1 small stalk celery
4 quarts (approximately) water
1 bunch parsley
Pinch thyme
2 bay leaves
½ small cabbage (optional)
Marrow bone and/or 1 cup grated cheese
French bread

Heat a little fat, a piece of the yellow fat from the hen will do well, in your largest, heaviest cooking pot. Brown first the beef, then the veal on all sides. Season with salt and pepper as you go. Now add the hen, legs neatly tied so it doesn't look ready to fly out of the pot, and the vegetables except the cabbage. Add enough water to cover (approximately 4 quarts), season lightly and flavor with a nice little bunch of parsley, a good pinch of thyme and 2 bay leaves. Bring to a boil, cover and leave to simmer very gently—1½ to 2 hours should be about right. The meats should be tender but not falling to pieces.

If you use the cabbage, and it is very good, cook it separately in a little of the broth for about 30 minutes, drain and add it at the last minute to the pot. Otherwise it will make everything taste like cabbage. Add the marrow bone to the soup during the last half hour if it is in one piece. If the butcher sawed it for you, cook it for 10 minutes or so separately in a little more broth. Now get ready for serving.

Remove the meats from the soup, trim off any fat, skin and bones, and cut into bite-size pieces. Meat cooked in a large chunk will have a much better flavor and texture than if you had cooked it in small pieces. Return all to the pot and keep piping hot. Toast slices of French bread and spread with the cooked marrow or sprinkle with grated cheese. There is no law against having both, if you prefer! Serve in large bowls and pass the bread separately to dunk in the soup or not, as your manners or your appetite dictates. *Bon appétit!*

POTAGE PRINTANNIER

Spring Vegetable Soup

This is a soup which requires a bunch of violets—not to put in the soup, but to place on the table on the first warm spring day after a long winter. This is the soup Parisian housewives make at the beginning of spring when the price of vegetables is beginning to come down. Asparagus may be still too expensive to serve as a whole dish but a few stalks for the soup are not too hard on the budget. Fresh watercress is making its first appearance and, if you are a good customer, the shopkeeper may throw in a handful of parsley and chervil free. Chervil is a delightful, mint-flavored herb, which is not often available here except dried. A good pinch will give true Parisian flavor to this soup.

FOR 4 PEOPLE:

About 2 cups, finely chopped, any or all of the following:
  lettuce leaves, spinach leaves, green peas, asparagus, carrots
Up to 1 cup cooked, left-over vegetables (optional)
2 or 3 green onions, finely chopped
½ bunch watercress, finely chopped
1 small clove garlic, finely chopped
4 tablespoons butter
4 cups beef stock, homemade or canned
Salt and pepper

Place all the raw vegetables in a large pot with half the butter. Season lightly with salt and pepper and cook until wilted but not brown. Add the stock and simmer gently for 30 to 45 minutes. A cupful or so of leftover vegetables can be added to the soup with the stock. Taste and correct seasoning; the salt depends on the stock. At serving time, add a little pat of fresh butter to each serving. This is incredibly fresh-tasting, thanks to the watercress, and full of vitamins, but you need not tell this to your family.

POTAGE PARMENTIER

Potato-Leek Soup

This soup is absolutely delicious and yet no French gourmet would dream of serving it at any time but a family dinner. Good as it is, potato-leek soup is considered strictly an everyday soup, which is one reason why France has such a reputation for good eating. I was much surprised to find this old friend all dolled-up and called vichyssoise in America. A little like finding out that your dowdy cousin twice-removed had come to the United States and become a movie star.

Leeks are sold in great big bunches in French markets. They are often served as a vegetable by themselves and find their way into almost every soup. If they are not as popular in your area of this country you can still make this soup with scallions or green onions. And, if they are out of season, use a large onion and some frozen chives. All are good.

FOR 4 PEOPLE:

4 large potatoes
2 leeks or onions
Salt and pepper
4 tablespoons chopped parsley
1 cup milk or light cream
4 tablespoons butter

The absolute simplicity of this soup belies its flavor. You simply peel and dice the potatoes, clean and chop the leeks, including some of the green part. Put all in a pot with enough water to cover, about 1 to 1½ quarts. Season with salt and a little pepper. Cook until the vegetables are tender, about 45 minutes. Put the soup through a strainer or food mill (a food mill makes this process much easier). Return to the pot, add the parsley and/or the chives if you are using them. Thin down to taste with milk or light cream, add the butter and serve piping hot, well seasoned with additional salt and pepper if necessary. If you want vichyssoise, simply replace the water with chicken stock, and go heavy on the cream. In this case, serve chilled, but Frenchmen like it hot!

POTAGE À LA REINE

Chicken Soup with Almonds

My family loves roast chicken and so do I. Not only for the chicken itself but also for the delicious soup I make with the bones. I also carefully save any bit of leftover gravy and when it is cold, I remove the fat which has hardened on top and use that to baste the next roasting chicken. The jelly-like juices will go into the soup. French chefs make different kinds of stocks from fresh bones and meats, and French housewives often replace these with leftovers and come up with wonderful results.

This soup comes from a very ancient recipe. It required a few bitter almonds, which are practically unobtainable nowadays, and lengthy pounding in a mortar. The combination of chicken, cream and almonds sounded so fine, I decided to try it with a little almond flavoring and blanched, toasted almonds. And it was a great success. But be cautious: the almond flavor should be very subtle; add a drop at a time and taste. The effect should be "What is this delicious flavor?" rather than "Almond soup?!" if you see what I mean.

FOR 4 PEOPLE:

Bones from 1 or 2 roast chickens, including the necks, giblets,
    wings and any leftover chicken and/or gravy
1 small carrot, coarsely chopped
1 small onion, coarsely chopped
1 rib celery, coarsely chopped
1 bay leaf
Pinch of thyme
Salt and pepper
2 quarts (approximately) water
2 tablespoons butter
2 tablespoons flour
½ teaspoon almond extract
2 egg yolks
½ cup heavy cream
4 tablespoons blanched, slivered, toasted almonds

Make a good stock by putting all the bones, chicken, etc., in a large pot with that bit of gravy and the coarsely chopped vegetables, a bay leaf, a pinch of thyme, very little salt and pepper and about 2 quarts of water. Bring to a boil, reduce heat, cover and leave to simmer for about an hour. No need to watch it. After that time, strain and measure. You should have about 1 quart of fine flavored chicken broth. If you have much more, return to the fire and cook down a little. Cream the butter and flour together in a small bowl, add a little of the hot soup to it, stirring well to get smooth, and return all to the pot. Simmer a few minutes, taste and add salt and pepper to taste. Now add drop by drop about ½ teaspoon of almond extract, tasting as you go. Remove the soup from the fire. Beat the egg yolks with the cream in a large bowl or soup tureen and slowly add the soup to this, stirring madly as you go. If you should reheat this soup, be very careful not to let it boil or it will curdle. Serve sprinkled with the toasted almonds.

POTAGE ROSÉ

Pink Soup (Tomato Cream)

Tomato soup is reputedly the largest-selling soup in cans. And yet good as it may be, it is not exactly what you would serve a few gourmet friends, at least I hope not. This recipe is for a soup that has a tomato base. To it we shall add cream and eggs for a velvety smoothness, some celery for a little lift and a good dash of Madeira or red port to take it completely out of the bland category. The goodness of this soup lies in the flavorful broth, so make it as strong and good as you can.

FOR 4 PEOPLE:

4 cups beef broth* or consommé
1 6-ounce can tomato paste
4 tablespoons very finely chopped celery leaves and green onion tops
Pinch thyme
Bay leaf
3 tablespoons cornstarch
¼ cup Madeira or red port
2 egg yolks
1 cup heavy cream
2 tablespoons butter
Salt and pepper

If you use canned beef broth or consommé, use 3 cans of broth to 1 can of water. Just watch the amount of salt; don't add any until you have tasted. To this fragrant broth add the tomato paste, the very finely chopped celery leaves and onion tops, thyme and bay leaf. Bring to a simmer; cover and leave for half an hour or so, so that the flavors can blend.

After this time, mix the cornstarch with a little cold water to make a thin paste, add a little of the hot soup to it, blend thoroughly, and return all to the pot. Pour in the Madeira or red port wine and simmer until the soup has thickened just a little. The cornstarch will make it velvety but still clear. Beat the egg yolks with the cream. Remove the soup from the fire, stir a little of it into the egg-cream mixture, return all to the pot, stirring well. Taste and correct seasoning. Woe to whomever says pass the salt at the table. In France it is (practically) an insult to the cook! Serve with a little pat of butter floating in each bowl.

POTAGE AUX TOMATES FRAÎCHES

Tomato Soup (with fresh tomatoes)

This is a soup to make when you grow your own tomatoes or have a neighbor who does. If your only acquaintance with tomato soup is with the canned kind, be ready for a surprise; this is completely different. This is a gay, fresh soup, full of the flavor of bright sun-ripened tomatoes. It is so popular in France that when you buy tomatoes, the storekeeper will ask you whether you want them for salad or for soup. The soup ones are much cheaper, of course, because they are all those on the point of being overripe or of such odd sizes and shapes that they are not suitable for salads. French tomato salads are very orderly things.

Think of this soup also when you are making stuffed tomatoes. What a wonderful way to use all the juice and pulp you have scraped out!

FOR 4 PEOPLE:

  4 tablespoons butter
  2 pounds (approximately) very ripe tomatoes
  2 or 3 stalks celery with leaves, chopped
  2 large onions, chopped
  Pinch thyme
  Pinch tarragon
  2 or 3 sprigs parsley
  1 small clove garlic
  Bay leaf
  4 cups beef stock, homemade or made from liquid beef extract
  Salt and pepper
  Butter for garnish

Heat to sizzling but not brown 4 tablespoons butter in a large pot. Add to it the tomatoes cut in large pieces, the chopped celery and onions, and a good dusting of thyme and tarragon. Season lightly with salt and pepper. A few sprigs of parsley, the garlic and a bay leaf will each add their particular goodness. Cover and cook until it becomes a kind of thick purée, about 45 minutes. It should start to brown on the edges but don't let it burn. Now pour in the stock and simmer some more, until reduced to about 4 cups, approximately one-half hour. Rub through a sieve or food mill, or buzz in the blender, if you like. Serve with crisp toast and a little pat of fresh butter in each bowl.

SOUPE AU FROMAGE

Cheese Soup

Here is a truly luscious and unusual cheese soup. The base is a well-flavored potato soup. Swiss cheese is added for body and its mild, nut-like flavor. A tablespoon or so of Parmesan would add zip, one of Roquefort will add distinction. A generous dash of white wine makes it a ray of sunshine on a gloomy day.

FOR 4 PEOPLE:

4 medium potatoes
1 large onion, finely chopped
4 cups beef bouillon (from cubes)
½ pound Swiss cheese, grated
1 tablespoon grated Parmesan or Roquefort
1 tablespoon chopped green onion or chives
Salt and pepper
½ cup dry white wine
Chopped parsley for garnish

Peel the potatoes, cut them in small cubes, and cook them with the onion in the bouillon until very soft. Mash well with a fork or, better still, put through a food mill or strainer. Return to the pot and add both kinds of cheese and the green onions or chives. Heat slowly, stirring, until the cheese melts and the mixture is smooth. Season to taste, remembering that the bouillon and cheese are salty, and add the wine at the last moment. Garnish with chopped parsley and serve with plenty of hot, crusty French bread. With a good green salad and fruit, this could be a complete meal.

WATERZOOIE DE POISSON GANTOISE

Ghent Fish Soup

Fish soups are legion: the famed bouillabaisse of southern France, the chowders of the northern United States, the gumbos of Louisiana. This one is Belgian, less well known perhaps, but delicious. The Belgians love their fish, and as the country is quite small, transportation is not much of a problem and the fish is deliciously fresh.

Using the name soup for this Belgian dish is perhaps a little misleading because it's such a thick rich soup it could double as a main dish. If you are going to serve it as a full meal, you should make a side dish of plain boiled potatoes. I find it delicious with part of the fish replaced by crab meat or shrimp. A dash of white wine adds a wonderful something too to the blend of cream and eggs.

FOR 4 PEOPLE:
> 2 *pounds fish (flounder, redfish, snapper, halibut, etc.), fresh*
>   *or frozen*, OR
>   1 *pound fish and* 1 *pound shellfish (shrimp, crab meat*
>   *or scallops)*
> 2 *leeks thinly sliced* OR
>   1 *large onion and* ½ *cup finely chopped green onion tops*
> 2 *large potatoes, diced in* ¼-*inch cubes*
> 1 *carrot, finely chopped*
> 1 *stalk celery with leaves, finely chopped*
> 4 *slices bacon*
> 1 *stick (*¼ *pound) butter*
> 3 *cups (approximately) water*
> *Salt and pepper*
> *Pinch thyme*
> *Bay leaf*
> 4 *egg yolks*
> 1 *cup heavy cream*
> ½ *cup dry white wine (optional)*
> 1 *lemon*

If you use fresh fish and it is not filleted, skin and bone it. Peel the raw shrimp. Cut these into bite-size pieces and set aside.

Fry the bacon in a large pot. Remove most of the fat, add half the butter, and when it is melted, the vegetables. Cover and cook a few minutes; do not let the vegetables brown, just allow them to wilt and absorb the butter flavor. The French call this making the vegetables sweat.

Now pour in about 3 cups of water or what you judge will be necessary just to cover the fish when you add it. Bring to a boil, seasoning well with salt and pepper, a pinch of thyme and the bay leaf. When boiling, add all the fish (including any shellfish) and the rest of the butter. Add the wine also if you are using it. Cook quickly over high heat just until the fish is done. It should take only 15 to 20 minutes at the most. Taste and add more salt if needed. It should already taste wonderful.

Beat the egg yolks with the cream in a large bowl or soup tureen. Pour a little of the hot soup over them, stirring like mad, then add the rest of the soup. Stir in a good squeeze of lemon juice as a final touch. Serve in large bowls. Succulent is a good word for this meal.

2. HORS D'OEUVRES

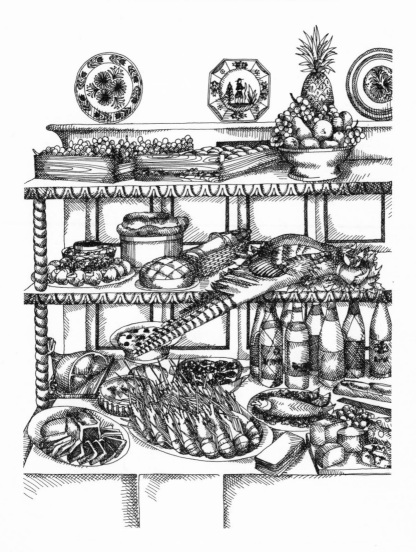

OPEN A FRENCH MENU and the first thing on the list is "Hors d'Oeuvres." If you want to make a French headwaiter really miserable, refuse to select anything and say that you will wait for the main dish you have ordered. His powers of persuasion will be put to the test and he will do anything, except perhaps stand on his head, to make you change your mind. You will never hear more delightful descriptions of tempting morsels as when he tries to coax you into choosing something. In fact, if you were a fussy eater as a child, he will probably remind you of your mother. Unlike your mother, however, he does not have solely your health in mind. In a good restaurant, the dish you select will often have to be prepared for you and, if you are hungry, the delay will make you cross. Hence the hors d'oeuvre.

In France this generally delightful small dish is eaten at the table. In this country, the name hors d'oeuvre is usually applied to those little things you nibble on while waiting for dinner to be served, usually in the living room. I find this a delightful custom, particularly if you are short of help in the kitchen. Also, it keeps your guests amiable while waiting for a late arrival. I am, therefore, all for it, except when the tidbits consist of dozens of little salty things which spoil your appetite and dull your taste buds. Whether at the table or in the living room, the hors d'oeuvre should be a well-planned part of the meal. It's better to have only one delightful concoction which will herald the good things to come. Leave the choice of many things for cocktail parties. If your first course is to be eaten at the table, keep the nibbling to a minimum and serve dinner promptly.

The hors d'oeuvres in this chapter can usually be served either French or American fashion. Vary the size and you can even make them perfect for cocktail parties or luncheons. If you want to go really very French, you can serve at the table a large dish of "hors d'oeuvres variés." In this case you must use your imagination more than a cookbook. Select a variety of sardines, anchovies, herring fillets, olives, tomatoes, cucumbers, small salami slices, etc. Arrange all this on lettuce leaves, with little bunches of parsley and slices of lemon here and there. A large silver tray is perfect for this and quite impressive. The portions should be quite small, this is just a teaser.

Another delicious French beginning to a meal is simply radishes served with butter and salt. Hot crusty French bread goes with it, of course. Simply wash the radishes, trim the root end but leave a few leaves on if you can as they make a wonderful handle to hold the radish. You place a little pat of fresh, hard butter, salted or not, on the radish, dip in a little salt and eat. The butter tones down the pepperiness of the radish and a bite of bread clears your taste buds for the next radish. This is so simple and good you will want to have it often after the first try, although you will probably get stares at the supermarket when you walk out with 2 and 3 bunches of radishes!

Other good hors d'oeuvres consist of a few good slices of *saucisson*, the best salami you can buy. Or herring fillets marinated in wine sauces. Pass butter and French bread and keep the portions small; you'll see what a nice way it is to start a good meal and good conversation.

BEIGNETS PIGNATELLI

Ham and Almond puffs

This is something just pleasantly different to serve as an hors d'oeuvre. Little puffs of chou pastry, to which you add chopped ham and toasted almonds, are deep-fried until golden brown. If you must, you could even make them early in the day and reheat them in the oven without losing much flavor. Be sure to make them small and very crisp.

Another good way to serve them is with a clear hot bouillon or consommé or hot tomato juice. Après-ski or après anything outdoors in cold weather. Après cocktail party also. In France, hot consommé with something to nibble on is usually served at the close of a cocktail or evening party. Try it, it is a pleasant and safe way to have one for the road.

FOR 3 TO 4 DOZEN PUFFS, DEPENDING
ON SIZE:

1 recipe chou pastry* made with:
½ cup water
4 ounces (1 stick) butter or margarine
½ cup unsifted flour
3 eggs

Salt and pepper
3 thin slices boiled ham, chopped
1 tablespoon butter
4 ounces blanched slivered almonds
Oil for frying

First make the chou pastry. Heat the water and butter together until the butter is melted and the water boiling. Add the flour all at once and stir vigorously until you have a ball of soft dough which leaves the sides of the pan. Remove from the heat, cool a little. Beat in the eggs one by one, beating until each is completely mixed in before adding the next one. Season this dough with salt and pepper and mix in the chopped ham, trimmed of all fat.

Heat the butter in a skillet, add the almonds and shake and stir them over medium heat until golden. They burn very easily, don't go away. Drain them on a couple of paper towels for a minute and stir them into the dough.

Heat at least an inch of oil in a deep skillet or use a deep fryer at 375°F. Drop half teaspoonfuls of the dough into the hot oil and fry until golden and crisp on both sides. These generally turn over by themselves when done on one side; if not, give them a gentle push with a fork. They swell considerably so don't try to fry too many at one time. Drain on paper towels, sprinkle with a little salt and serve immediately.

To reheat these puffs, arrange them on a cooky sheet and pop into a 375°F. oven for about 10 minutes or until piping hot.

GOUGÈRE

When the French want to say that something is so simple it is almost stupid, they say *"c'est bête comme chou,"* as simple as cabbage. This is certainly true of *"Pâte à Choux,"* the stuff éclairs are made of.

Éclairs are well known in this country but the pastry is seldom filled with anything but sweets. And yet, once you have mastered this simple art, you will find that it makes all kinds of delicious hot or cold hors d'oeuvres. The *"gougère"* is an old country-style recipe, simply a large ring of chou pastry with little bits of ham and cheese added to it. I suspect that its original purpose was to fill people up a little before the more expensive meat dish was served, somewhat on the order of Yorkshire pudding in England.

In any case, what a delightful way to cut one's appetite! You can serve the *gougère* in the traditionally large ring and cut it in pieces, or for a party bake it in small puffs. These take very well to being reheated in the oven, especially since there is no filling to worry about.

FOR 12 TO 18 SMALL PUFFS OR
1 LARGE RING:

>   *1 recipe chou pastry**
>   *4 ounces Swiss cheese, cut in small cubes*
>   *2 thin slices boiled ham, finely chopped*
>   *Salt and pepper*

Make the pastry as directed and after adding the eggs, beat in the cheese, cut in small (¼ inch or smaller) cubes and the finely chopped ham. Taste and season well with salt and pepper. Grease a cooky sheet and bake as follows: For a large ring: pre-heat the oven to 475°F. and bake for 10 to 15 minutes or until risen and golden, then finish cooking for 25 minutes at 325°F.

For small puffs: Use the same temperatures but cut the time to about 7 minutes and 15 minutes at the lower temperature to finish cooking.
>   Serve hot.

CREVETTES

Shrimp

Shrimp make delicious hors d'oeuvres by themselves or combined in sauces. In order of preference you can get fresh shrimp, shrimp frozen in the shell, shelled and cleaned frozen shrimp and lastly the canned ones. Canned shrimp are generally tasty but unfortunately rather soft. It is a good idea to chill the can several hours before draining and using the shrimp.

New Orleanians have developed cooking shrimp to a fine art. They use something called "crab boil," which is a mixture of many different herbs and spices with a lot of fiery red peppers. If this is not available in your area, mixed pickling spices will do well. Where-ever fresh shrimp are sold, each cook is likely to have her pet recipe to cook them. Some use lots of spices and drain the shrimp quickly, some use less and leave them to soak for a while. This last is my favorite method and, being a French cook, I add white wine. Here are the various ways I cook shrimp, depending on the kind I can get.

Fresh Shrimp

If you have a choice of fresh shrimp with or without heads, un-hesitatingly choose the first. The heads add a lot of flavor.

AS HORS D'OEUVRES FOR 4 PEOPLE:
- 1 quart water
- 2 tablespoons salt
- 1 tablespoon crab boil or mixed pickling spices
- ½ cup dry white wine (optional)
- 1 stalk celery with leaves
- 1 onion, cut in two
- 2 whole cloves garlic
- 1 lemon
- About 1 pound shrimp with or without heads

Bring the water to a boil with all the ingredients except the lemon and the shrimp. Simmer for 5 minutes, then add the shrimp. Wait for the water to come to a boil again. If the shrimp are small, turn the fire off as soon as the boiling starts. For larger shrimp count between 3 and 5 minutes. Test a shrimp: if it is opaque and milky white all the way through, it is done, further boiling will only make it tough. As soon as the shrimp are done, cut the lemon, squeeze the juice onto the shrimp and drop the peel into the pot. Leave the shrimp to soak in their fragrant broth for at least an hour and up to 2 or 3 hours, if convenient, before draining and peeling them.

Shrimp done this way are so good by themselves that adding any sauce is almost like gilding the lily!

Shrimp Frozen in the Shell

Let the shrimp thaw completely and proceed exactly as for fresh shrimp.

Peeled Frozen Shrimp

These little peeled beauties undoubtedly save you a lot of work. Unfortunately you lose a bit of flavor and the texture is apt to be rubbery, particularly if you follow instructions which say "drop in boiling water." The only way to make these shrimp tasty is to cook them while frozen but starting in *cold* liquid. For use especially in prepared dishes calling for cooked shrimp. For 2 cups of shrimp, try this way:

1 pound peeled, frozen shrimp
1 quart water
1 tablespoon salt
1 teaspoon crab boil or pickling spices tied in cheesecloth
1 stalk celery with leaves
1 small onion
1 clove garlic
½ cup white wine
½ lemon

As the seasonings penetrate these naked shrimp very easily, you need much less of them. Place the still frozen shrimp and all the ingredients except the lemon, in a pot. Bring to a boil over medium heat. As soon as the mixture is bubbling hard, test one shrimp; if it is opaque, turn heat off. Squeeze in the ½ lemon and drop the peel into the pot. Leave to cool in the water; drain and serve or use in shrimp dishes such as the Shrimp Patties.

TOMATES AUX CREVETTES

Shrimp-filled Tomatoes

In Belgium, practically every restaurant features these shrimp-filled tomatoes on the hors d'oeuvres list. Belgian shrimp are tiny and you need a lot of patience to peel enough of them to fill a number of tomatoes. The job is much easier over here.

This very simple dish attains perfection if you choose good ripe tomatoes, make your own mayonnaise as described in the sauces and cook the shrimp as indicated in the hors d'oeuvre section.

FOR 4 PEOPLE:
 4 medium-size round firm red tomatoes
 Salt and pepper
 1 cup cooked shrimp*
 ½ cup homemade mayonnaise*
 Parsley or lettuce for garnish

Peeling the tomatoes adds a lot to the flavor and makes them so much easier to eat. Place them in a bowl and pour boiling water over them, count to seven and drain them. More simply, hold them with a long fork over a flame for a few seconds. Either way, the skin will slip off easily.

Cut off and reserve the stem end of each tomato. Carefully scoop out the seeds and pulp with a little spoon, sprinkle a little salt and pepper in each tomato and turn it upside down to drain for an hour or more if you have the time. The salt will make a lot of water ooze out of the tomatoes.

Mix the shrimp with enough good firm mayonnaise to coat them generously and fill the tomatoes with this mixture. Replace the little caps at an angle to let the shrimp show tantalizingly. They should give the impression that the tomatoes are simply bursting with shrimp.

Serve well chilled with a little parsley or lettuce for garnish.

BOUCHÉES AUX CREVETTES

Shrimp Patties

A *bouchée* in French means a mouthful. These are delicious mouthfuls of shrimp in a delicate sauce, spiked with a little sherry, served in the most brittle and crunchy pastry shells. You can buy these patty shells frozen and ready to bake in most supermarkets. The pastry is puff pastry, that triumph of French cooking which is practically impossible to duplicate at home. In France we usually buy these shells already baked from the pastry shop, but I find the frozen ones a complete success if you follow faithfully the instructions on the box.

FOR 6 PATTY SHELLS:
> *1 pound fresh or frozen shrimp, cooked*
> *1 box frozen patty shells*
> *2 tablespoons butter*
> *2 tablespoons flour*
> *6 tablespoons water shrimp were cooked in*
> *¾ cup light cream*
> *1 tablespoon tomato paste*
> *1 teaspoon Worcestershire sauce*
> *2 tablespoons sherry*
> *1 tablespoon lemon juice*
> *Salt and pepper*

A well-meaning soul once tried this recipe with canned shrimp, evaporated milk, margarine, bottled lemon juice and no sherry. She found it nothing to write home about and I wasn't particularly surprised! This becomes a gourmet dish if you treat the shrimp with tender loving care from the first. See the recipes for plain boiled shrimp.

Bake the patty shells according to the instructions on the box, remove the centers and set them aside.

Make the sauce by melting the butter in a small pan. Stir in the flour and cook until frothy but not brown. Add the shrimp broth, stirring quickly and thoroughly with a French wire whisk, then the cream. Cook until thickened a little. Stir in the tomato paste, the Worcestershire sauce, the sherry, and then, judiciously, tasting as you go, add the lemon juice. It should need little or no salt (the shrimp broth being quite salty) and just a little pepper. The sauce should be very smooth and silky. Add the shrimp and stir.

At serving time, heat the shrimp in their sauce until piping hot, fill the patty shells and pop them in the oven at 425°F. just long enough to get them thoroughly hot (about 5 minutes). Handle carefully, crystal is robust compared to these shells. If you prefer, you can heat shells and shrimp separately and fill just before serving. This is the best method if your guests are notably unpunctual, as the shells should on no account be allowed to get soggy.

CHAMPIGNONS À LA GRECQUE

Mushrooms (or other vegetables) à la Grecque

Champignons à la Grecque are crisply tender mushroom caps in an aromatic sauce, not quite a pickle, not quite a salad. The ingredient which gives the sauce its particular flavor is coriander. Many supermarkets have it on the spice shelf or you can look in Spanish and Mexican stores. If you cannot find any, you can remember that it is one of the ingredients in curry powder and use that instead, not quite the same but still very good.

With or instead of the mushrooms, you can prepare in the same way pearl onions, tiny cauliflowerets, artichoke hearts, cucumbers, or any tender young vegetable your fancy dictates. These vegetables may be fresh, frozen or canned. The canned vegetables will have to cook very little, just a minute or so, the others only until crisp tender. If you cook several vegetables, simply cook one batch in the liquid, remove when done with a slotted spoon, and cook the next lot in the same liquid. Taste and add a little more seasoning if necessary.

FOR ABOUT 2 CUPS VEGETABLES:
> *2 large juicy lemons*
> *1½ cups dry white wine*
> *½ cup olive oil*
> *3 tablespoons white vinegar*
> *1 teaspoon whole coriander*
> *Salt and pepper*

Cut the lemons, squeeze the juice into a small pan and scrape out as much as you can of the pulp, without any of the white or membranous part. Add this pulp to the juice along with the wine, olive oil, vinegar, coriander and a seasoning of salt and pepper.

Bring the mixture to a boil and simmer for about 5 minutes to bring out the flavors. Add the vegetables and cook until barely tender. Pour into a bowl or wide-mouth jar, cover and refrigerate at least until the next day. Canned vegetables particularly will taste even better after two or three days, provided you can resist the temptation to nibble at them and you don't let the family discover them.

CROISSANTS ET ALUMETTES AU FROMAGE

Cheese Matches and Rolls

My world as a child was almost completely separate from that of adults. Two of the grown-up customs I most envied were the delightful tidbits served with before-dinner drinks and the tiny sandwiches and cheese rolls served at grown-up afternoon teas. I really looked forward to becoming old enough to be allowed to share in these goodies beyond an occasional snitching when no one was looking. Times have changed! My children and yours now partake freely of whatever is served, so you may have to use ingenuity to save enough of these delicacies for the grown-ups. They go delightfully with soups, a welcome change from packaged crackers.

The cheese rolls are simple but delicious. Take ready-to-bake croissants and unroll the dough as directed on the package. Sprinkle each little triangle generously with grated Parmesan cheese before shaping into crescents. To be even daintier, you can cut each triangle in two if you like. Sprinkle the tops with more Parmesan and plenty of freshly ground black pepper. Bake as directed on the package.

The cheese matches or straws are delicious this way:

FOR ABOUT 2 OR 3 DOZEN STRAWS:
  1 stick (¼ pound) butter or margarine
  2 egg yolks
  1 cup grated cheese, preferably sharp, aged Cheddar
  1½ cups (approximately) flour
  Salt and pepper

Cream the butter or margarine (but butter is definitely better here) with the egg yolks and the cheese. Work in the flour, a little at a time until you get a dough you can roll easily. The exact amount varies as cheeses vary, so I cannot give you an absolutely exact measurement; it should be like pie dough. Add a little salt and plenty of pepper. Taste the dough—any child will tell you raw dough tastes fine—and season really sharply. Roll out on a well-floured board to ¼ inch thickness. With a sharp knife cut out in narrow strips about the size of a pencil and 4 inches long. If you want to be quite fancy, form every sixth strip into a ring; I'll explain later.

Bake at 375°F. on well-greased cooky sheets for about seven minutes or until the little strips and rings are crisp and pale gold. Cool. Now push gently and carefully as many strips as you can into each ring and serve your straws in neat little bunches. This is silly, but most people will think you baked them that way and wonder how you did it! Just smile and stuff a straw into the mouth of your five year old before he gives you away.

CROQUE MONSIEUR AND CROQUE MADAME

Belgians will munch their way contentedly through a movie and then repair immediately to the nearest café or restaurant for sustenance. A great favorite, which will be served at any hour of the day or night even in the smallest café, is the *Croque Monsieur*, a delicious ham and cheese sandwich deep fried to a crisp golden brown. For the faint-hearted there is the *Croque Madame*, which omits the ham. These sandwiches are really wonderful with beer or a hot drink or, if you make them tiny, as a fast disappearing appetizer.

FOR 4 SMALL SANDWICHES OR
8 APPETIZERS:

4 slices white sandwich bread
A little mustard
8 thin slices cheese
4 thin slices ham
Fat for frying

Trim the crusts off the bread, spread each slice thinly with mustard. Dijon mustard is especially good with this. The cheese can be thinly sliced Swiss or Cheddar but not processed cheese; it melts too quickly. Layer bread, cheese, ham, cheese again and bread; press down firmly with your hand to make it all stick together a little. Cut each in two or four and deep fry, or fry in a skillet with at least ½ inch of oil, until golden brown on both sides. Drain on paper towels. Fried quickly in very hot oil these "snacks" will not be greasy, but the oil must be smoking hot and you have to watch, of course, so they do not burn.

Don't eat too many just before bedtime unless you are still in your teens.

CROUTES AUX CREVETTES

Shrimp Toast

This recipe could very well come under the heading of "Little nothing to win a man's heart"! Oh! You can make these toasts small and serve them at a cocktail party, but they are most effective served on the spur of the moment. For instance, when you come home from that first long walk together, hungry but not wishing for a crowd? Or that blissful moment when the children are all asleep and you are suddenly hungry for something special. All you need is a can of shrimp, lobster or crab meat on the pantry shelf.

FOR 4 TOASTS:
>   2 tablespoons butter
>   2 tablespoons flour
>   1 cup milk
>   2 slices processed cheese, cut in pieces
>   1 6-ounce can shrimp or crab meat or lobster
>   1 egg yolk
>   Salt and pepper
>   Lemon juice
>   4 slices toasted bread

To make the sauce, melt the butter in a small pan, add the flour and cook a minute until frothy. Stir in the milk and cook until thickened. Add the cheese, the drained seafood and the egg yolk. Stir well until the cheese is melted and season to taste with salt, pepper and a few drops of lemon juice. Trim the crusts off the slices of toast, place them in a flat baking dish and pour the sauce over them. Place under the preheated broiler until bubbly and beginning to brown. If you are not afraid of a few extra calories, you can butter the bread generously and toast it under the broiler before pouring on the sauce. Excellent but very, very rich!

FONDUES AU FROMAGE

Belgian Cheese Fondue

Every Belgian restaurant I have ever been in features *Fondues au Fromage* on the list of first courses. These are sometimes superb, sometimes simply excellent, but never bad. This dish bears no resemblance to French or Swiss fondue, to the great surprise of some tourists. It is more like a croquette, a deep gold fried morsel. Cut into it and a velvety, deep yellow cheese oozes out. One bite and you will understand why Belgians are so fond of it!

FOR 4 PEOPLE:

¼ cup (½ stick) butter or margarine
4 tablespoons flour
1½ cups milk
4 ounces sharp cheese, grated
4 egg yolks
Salt and pepper
1 egg, bread crumbs and flour for coating
Oil for frying
Parsley for garnish

Make a very, very thick white sauce. Heat the butter until bubbly and blend in the flour. Cook over medium heat a few minutes, being careful not to brown. Heat the milk in a separate pan, and add it gradually to the butter and flour, stirring like mad with a wire whisk. Cook until very thick and bubbly, then add the grated cheese and stir until it is melted. Cool slightly and stir in the egg yokes one by one. Now is the time to taste and add salt—but remember that the cheese is already salty—and plenty of pepper. Grease a flat dish generously and pour the mixture into it. Cover with waxed paper or plastic film and chill. When it is cold and firm, take spoonfuls of this dough and, with well-floured hands, shape it into little balls the size of walnuts for appetizers or make slightly larger little sausages for a luncheon dish. When all are shaped, roll each in beaten egg and then in bread crumbs. There is a trick to this which saves getting both hands full of goo; simply never let your right hand know what your left is up to. Take two plates, one with the beaten egg, the other with the bread crumbs. With your left hand, dip the fondue in egg, lift it out and place it in the bread crumbs. With your right hand, push crumbs over the fondue, then roll and shake it gently. When all are done, return to the refrigerator to chill thoroughly before cooking.

At serving time, use a deep fryer or a skillet with at least half an inch of oil in it. Heat to 375°F. and fry the fondues a few at a time. Turn them gently with a spoon and on no account pierce or prick them. When they are deep brown remove and drain them on paper towels. Serve garnished with plenty of parsley.

If you prefer, you can fry them ahead of time, refrigerate them until the next day and reheat them in the oven at 375°F. for 10 to 15 minutes. They are almost as good this way.

These little fondues freeze beautifully, by the way. You can freeze them after coating them with bread crumbs. In that case, freeze them on a tray or cooky sheet until hard, then package them in plastic bags. Let them thaw a little before frying. Nice to have on hand for impromptu parties during the holidays.

TARTE AU GRUYÈRE

Swiss Cheese Pie

In this country the word pie usually conveys visions of desserts. The French, being very precise, have several words for pie. There is the *tarte* or open pie, the *tourte*, which has a cover of dough, and the *flan*, which usually has a thick creamy filling. However by any other name this pie is just as good. Serve wedges as a first course or bake it in tiny shells for appetizers. With a green salad, it makes a perfect luncheon dish.

Swiss cheese gives this pie its particular mild flavor, but there is no law against using Cheddar if you prefer.

FOR ONE 9-INCH PIE:

> 1 recipe for 9-inch piecrust*
> 4 eggs, separated
> 3 tablespoons flour
> 2 cups milk
> Salt and pepper
> Nutmeg
> 6 ounces Swiss Gruyère Cheese, grated
> 2 tablespoons mayonnaise

Line a well-greased pie pan with pastry and flute the edge. Set aside the egg whites and beat together the yolks and the flour in a small pan. Gradually add the milk, salt and pepper and just a dash of nutmeg. Cook, stirring all the time, over low heat until thickened. This is like a salty custard, but you don't need to use a double boiler because the flour will keep things smooth if you use low heat and stir. Stir in the grated cheese, reserving a couple of spoonfuls for the top, and pour into the unbaked pastry shell. Bake in preheated oven at 375°F. for 35 minutes or until the pastry is a nice deep gold around the edges and filling is set.

Add a good pinch of salt to the egg whites and beat them as for meringue, stiff enough to make peaks but not dry. Very gently fold in the mayonnaise, season with a little pepper, and swirl on top of the pie so that it extends to the edges. Sprinkle with the reserved grated cheese. Return to the oven, now set at 450°F., just long enough to brown the meringue slightly, 2 or 3 minutes.

You can put this pie together early in the day and even bake it with the exclusion of the meringue. In such a case, reheat the pie at 325°F. for 10 or 15 minutes while you beat the egg whites and proceed.

TARTE AUX OIGNONS (OU AUX POIREAUX)

Onion (or Leek) Pie

Leek or onion, you can have no idea of the flavor they add to food until you try to do without them, as we had to during the war at times. Served in small pieces, this country dish is sure to be a hit at a party. It is different from the better-known Quiche Lorraine, but in the same family.

FOR ONE 9-INCH PIE:

    1 recipe pastry for 1 piecrust* (omit sugar)
    4 large onions or leeks
    4 tablespoons butter
    Salt
    2 tablespoons flour
    1 cup milk
    4 slices bacon or Canadian bacon
    3 eggs
    3 tablespoons cream or evaporated milk
    Pepper
    A little grated nutmeg
    Grated cheese (optional)
    2 cups dried beans

Line a deep pie plate with your favorite piecrust, made without sugar of course. Line it with foil and fill it with dried beans, just as they come from the package. Bake piecrust until dry and crisp but not yet brown on the edges. The beans keep it in shape and French cooks keep them in a jar for just that purpose; they can be used many times over. Other cooks keep dried cherry pits for the purpose but they are harder to come by!

Slice the onions or leeks thinly and cook them in 4 tablespoons butter until they are soft and limp. Season with a little salt as you go. When they are just beginning to brown, sprinkle the flour over them, mix well and then stir in the milk, a little at a time to get a lump-free sauce. Cool while you fry the bacon crisp, drain and crumble it.

Beat the eggs with the cream and stir into the onion mixture along with the crumbled bacon. Taste and season well with salt and pepper. Tasting is important because some bacons are saltier than others. Pour into the piecrust and dust just a little nutmeg over it. Bake in preheated 375°F. oven for about 40 minutes, or until a knife inserted near the middle comes out clean. The French very rarely add cheese to this recipe but I find that a little, sprinkled over the pie before baking, makes a deliciously brown "gratin" over the pie. If you use cheese, omit the nutmeg; they are not very good friends.

OEUFS POCHÉS À LA ROYALE

There was a restaurant in Brussels a few years ago which had the most impressive quantity of hors d'oeuvres I have ever seen or heard of. I think the total number, including both hot and cold dishes, was 125. Many people including myself, would order the "Hors d'Oeuvres" specifying "without anything to follow." This meant that you would be charged the price of a standard three-course meal but were welcome to sample any or all of the hors d'oeuvres.

And believe me, sample you did! You barely had time to spread out the thick and shiny cloth napkin over your lap when the first waiter made his appearance with a two-tiered cart. This would be the fish: you pointed out to the headwaiter the smoked salmon, diverse sardines and herring fillets you desired. He might then press you to try the anchovies or stuffed olives and smoked eel. When you were quite sure there was nothing else on the cart you wanted to try, a quick change of plates and the next cart would appear. This was covered with dishes of salads, eggs, cold hams, tongues and salami. And the list would go on, pâtés, hot little cheese things and curried meat balls, with the headwaiter hovering by solicitously, pressing you to try this and that, until gasping, you admitted defeat and practically begged him to take it all away! The standard joke of the waiters was that any customer able to taste all the hors d'oeuvres was given an engraved gold watch to commemorate the occasion. Nothing was said about a first class funeral, which, I am sure, would have been in order.

One hors d'oeuvre on the menu which I found delicious was the cold poached eggs. They make a very good lunch on a hot summer day, if you do this:

COUNT ONE OR TWO EGGS PER PERSON
AND FOR EACH EGG:
> 2 to 3 tablespoons tarragon vinegar
> 1 thin slice boiled ham
> Boston lettuce leaves
> 1 slice tomato
> Homemade mayonnaise*

Poach the egg(s) in salted water to which you have added 2 to 3 tablespoons tarragon vinegar. This is a little more than usual but will flavor the eggs deliciously. Cool and trim the eggs neatly. Wrap each egg in a thin slice of ham, place on a bed of tender lettuce leaves, Boston lettuce if possible, and garnish with the slice of tomato. Chill in the refrigerator, 2 hours or longer.

Spoon a wide ribbon of mayonnaise across the neatly rolled ham and pass more mayonnaise separately.

The soft yolk of the eggs will mix with the mayonnaise as you cut into them for a marvelous combination. Make sure all is well chilled and serve with bread or toast and a cool bottle of white wine, and a hot summer day will become infinitely more pleasant.

3. EGGS

QUICHE LORRAINE

This French pie is often a subject of controversy. There are almost violent discussions about exactly what it should contain, a bacon and custard (unsweet, of course) baked in a pastry shell. Some will add a little cheese, some a little onion, others will use ham. The basic difference, and it is a minor one, lies in the bacon. The French use "lard," not the shortening but a kind of unsmoked bacon, drier than salt meat. If you can find slab bacon, it will do very well. Have a slice about ½ inch thick and proceed. If your taste runs to a little cheese or onion, add it, you don't have to be like everybody else!

FOR 4 PEOPLE:
  1 recipe pastry for 1 piecrust,° pre-baked
  1 thick, ½-inch slice bacon or ¼ pound regular bacon
  4 eggs
  1 cup rich milk or, preferably, light cream
  Salt and pepper

Pre-bake the pie shell, and set aside. If you are using the thick slice of bacon, cut it into small cubes, place them in a bowl and pour a little boiling water over them. After 5 minutes, drain them and fry them until golden. With regular bacon, cut the slices in small strips and fry until not quite crisp. Drain and arrange evenly in the pastry shell.

Beat the eggs with the cream and season well with salt and pepper. Pour over the bacon in the pie shell and bake at 375°F. for about 35 minutes or until well browned and set. Let it stand for 5 minutes or so before serving; this should be warm rather than hot to savor it at its best. Small slices make a wonderful first course. With a good green salad, this makes a perfect lunch.

BOULETTES AUX OEUFS

Egg Meat Balls

This is a good recipe to remember just after Easter when you are absolutely loaded with hard-boiled eggs and feel like committing mayhem on the nearest chicken!

At other times, you may want to fix it when you want to stretch a pound of hamburger or ground lamb for unexpected guests or simply because it tastes very good. I prefer it with lamb, the chutney and curry go so well with it, but it's also very good made with beef and chopped pickles and mustard instead of the chutney and curry.

FOR 4 TO 6 PEOPLE:
   1 onion
   1 stalk celery
   2 sprigs parsley
   1 pound ground lamb
   1 raw egg
   Salt and pepper
   4 hard-boiled eggs
   Chutney to taste, 2 or 3 tablespoons
   A little fat
   2 tablespoons flour
   1½ cups water
   1 beef bouillon cube
   1 tablespoon curry powder

Chop the onion, celery and parsley finely. Mix with the ground meat and the raw egg, seasoning well with salt and pepper. Cut the hard-boiled eggs lengthwise, mash the yolks with chutney to taste (1 or 2 tablespoons), fill the whites with this mixture and then cover the whole half egg with meat, pressing it in place with your fingers to form a neat, tight little package.

Heat a little fat in a skillet and gently brown the meat balls in it on all sides. Handle them gently at first, so they will not break. When they are well browned all over, push them to one side, spoon out all but 2 or 3 tablespoons of the drippings. Stir 2 tablespoons of flour in the fat which remains in the skillet and let it get golden. Now pour in about 1½ cups of water into which you have crumbled a bouillon cube. Stir well and season with very little salt (the cube is very salty already) and pepper and as much curry powder as you prefer. I like about 1 tablespoon, which gives a fairly strong curry taste but is not burning hot.

Cook for about 10 minutes so the flavors will blend well into the meat. Just before serving, stir in a tablespoonful of chutney. Serve with rice, of course, and a cucumber salad goes beautifully with it!

OEUFS BROUILLÉS

Scrambled Eggs

Scrambled eggs can be sheer delight or absolutely abominable, varying in degrees from a gourmet experience to simply fuel! I am thinking in particular of hospital scrambled eggs usually served for breakfast at an ungodly hour and which arrive looking and tasting like partially set concrete. I suppose they have a therapeutic value— they certainly make you want to get well and go home!

The scrambled eggs of French cuisine are delicate, fluffy, pale gold flecked with creamy white. Eggs, except perhaps soft-boiled occasionally, are not a breakfast food in France. Scrambled eggs are regarded as an *entrée* before a main course, a delicate supper or luncheon dish. They are worthy of the finest accompaniment, truffles perhaps, fine pastry shells, delicate mushrooms or herbs. And plain scrambled eggs, properly prepared, can be an epicurean feast all by themselves!

There is perhaps no other preparation in which the true flavor of the egg is as apparent as in scrambled eggs. It is worth shopping around until you find a brand or store where the eggs are fresh and have a good flavor. The taste depends, I think, on the feed the chickens receive. I lived on a farm for some years during the war and I remember that at one time when chickens were fed some kind of fish meal, the eggs tasted almost like cod-liver oil!

So having bought the best eggs money can buy, get some fresh creamery butter, unsalted if you can, and proceed to make scrambled eggs:

FOR 4 PEOPLE:
10 eggs
1 stick (¼ pound) butter
Salt and pepper

If the number of eggs startles you, rest assured that there won't be too much. Two scrambled eggs per person is really very little when prepared this way and you may have to scramble some more for seconds! Break the eggs in a large bowl. Don't beat them yet, wait!

Take what one of my ancient cookbooks refers to as "a delicately clean" saucepan. A 2-quart one should be just right. Melt 4 tablespoons of butter in it, over low heat; don't let it sizzle too hard or brown. Take a spoon, French cookbooks usually specify a silver spoon but I think a stainless steel one will do! Stir the eggs in the bowl just enough to break the yolks and blend them a little with the whites but not enough to mix them thoroughly. Season with salt and pepper. If you are very particular, you can use white pepper so that no black flecks will mar the color of the eggs. Pour the eggs into the saucepan over the butter and stir, over a very low heat, scraping the bottom of the pan as soon as the eggs set. Keep adding little dabs of butter to the mixture as it cooks until you have added the whole stick. Remove the eggs from the fire just before they are done. I know this sounds silly but it is true: the eggs will go right on cooking in their own heat until the first mouthful; if they are done when you take them off the fire, they will be overdone by the time they are eaten!

You may have to experiment a little to find the exact degree of softness you like best of all. You can now serve the eggs with toast, in little pie shells with a large mushroom on top for a glamorous occasion, or any of dozens of ways. Here are a few:

Scrambled eggs on toast or fried bread, criss-crossed with anchovy fillets.

Scrambled eggs with mushrooms cooked in butter and added just before the eggs are set.

Thinly sliced truffles, heated in a little butter, added to the unbeaten eggs and left in the refrigerator for a couple of hours so their aroma can permeate the eggs. Truffles are all aroma, they have actually little taste, hence the delay. This is really grand and expensive!

Scrambled eggs served with (not mixed with) tiny green peas in butter or asparagus tips.

Scrambled eggs with . . . you name it!

OEUFS CHASSEUR

Hunter's Eggs

Here is a good recipe for eggs you may find handy if you need a quick lunch other than a sandwich. In a pinch, on a day when you come home too late to defrost the roast, you can serve it with rice or mashed potatoes and you will have a quickly prepared meal.

You can cut the preparation time even more if you use canned tomato sauce. Really though, this sauce is so quick to make that I like to start from scratch. It does give one the impression of "having cooked something for dinner" and removes some of the guilt you may feel if you stayed out with the girls too long. This recipe is called "Hunter's Eggs" because of the sauce, tomatoes with mushrooms. It supposedly was invented by a disgruntled hunter who had missed everything he shot at one day. So he threw away his rifle, picked mushrooms instead and concocted this delicious sauce!

FOR 4 PEOPLE:
  8 *hard-boiled eggs*
  2 *tablespoons butter or olive oil*
  1 *large onion, coarsely chopped*
  1 *stalk celery, coarsely chopped*
  1 *6-ounce can tomato paste*
  6 *ounces mushrooms, frozen or canned*
  Pinch of herbs: thyme or sweet basil, tarragon or oregano
  1 *to 1½ cups water*
  Salt and pepper

Put the eggs to boil. Melt the butter in a large skillet, add the onion and celery and cook a few minutes until beginning to brown. Add the tomato paste and cook until it loses its bright red color. Add the mushrooms along with their liquid, the herbs, and 1 to 1½ cups water, depending on how thick you like your tomato sauce. Season with salt and pepper and leave to simmer while you shell the eggs, which are done by now.

Cut the eggs in four lengthwise and add to the sauce. Leave them to get thoroughly acquainted while you set the table.

Tell the story about the hunter as you sit down to eat and no one will wonder what happened to the roast you were supposed to cook.

OEUFS À LA CHIMAY

Eggs Chimay (with mushrooms)

A nice casserole dish which can be prepared in advance and popped in the oven at the last minute is always a boon to any busy housewife. And show me the housewife who is not busy! This one combines eggs, mushrooms and onions. You can add grated cheese if you are fond of it, for flavor and protein. Served with a good green salad and plenty of hot French bread, this can be quite a memorable meal.

FOR 4 PEOPLE:
    8 *hard-boiled eggs*
    1 *6-ounce package fresh or frozen mushrooms*
    2 *tablespoons butter*
    4 *tablespoons chopped onions or scallions*

For the cream sauce:
    4 *tablespoons butter*
    4 *tablespoons flour*
    2 *cups milk* OR
        1½ *cups milk and ½ cup dry white wine*
    Salt and pepper
    Grated cheese (optional)

Shell the hard-boiled eggs, cut them in two lengthwise and remove the yolks to a small bowl.

Clean and chop fresh mushrooms and cook them in 2 tablespoons butter or cook the frozen ones according to package directions, then chop them. Fry the onions or scallions slowly in the same butter until pale gold. Add onions and mushrooms to the egg yolks.

Make the cream sauce by melting the butter in a small pan; add the flour and cook until frothy. Gradually stir in the milk and cook, stirring, until bubbly and smooth. Add the wine only after the sauce has thickened, if you are using it, then bring to a boil the second time. Season well with salt and pepper.

Mash the egg yolk-mushroom-onion mixture with just enough of the white sauce to bind all together. The mixture should be quite stiff and hold its shape. Season very generously with salt and pepper, hard-boiled eggs need a lot of salt.

Fill the whites with this mixture, piling it rather high. Arrange the stuffed eggs in a well-buttered baking dish and pour the rest of the white sauce over them. Dot with a little butter and place in a hot 425°F. oven for 10 minutes or so or under the broiler until thoroughly hot and flecked with brown. You can cover the dish with plastic film or wax paper and refrigerate it for several hours before baking, taking into account that it will take a little longer to get good and hot all the way through. Allow about 20 to 25 minutes at 375°F.

OEUFS À LA CRÈME

Eggs in Cream

These creamed eggs are a wonderful way to enjoy the full flavor of tarragon. It has a slightly minty flavor all its own and goes wonderfully with creamed dishes and chicken. This is definitely an aristocratic herb. It loves the company of cream, brandy, mushrooms, almost anything luxurious and expensive. Although it is one of the most expensive herbs, a jar which lasts a long time costs under a dollar. So live a little. . . .

FOR 6 SERVINGS:
   1 cup heavy cream
   Salt and pepper
   1 teaspoon tarragon
   A little butter
   6 eggs

Heat the cream in a small pan with salt and pepper and the tarragon. Do not let it boil, just get hot. Set aside for 10 or 15 minutes so that the tarragon can release its full flavor.

Butter generously small custard cups, one per egg, and share the cream between them. Break a fresh egg into each cup with cream, season it lightly with salt and pepper and bake in preheated 375°F. oven for about 10 minutes or until the eggs are soft set. Delicious with plenty of hot buttered toast.

OEUFS FARCIS AU THON, SAUCE AUX CAPRES

Eggs Stuffed with Tuna, in Caper Sauce

Caper sauce and fish is one of those marriages made in heaven. I am often surprised to find that many people have never tried those little flower buds pickled in vinegar. They have a piquant flavor that can turn a plain white sauce into something quite special. Delicious too when added to the gravy of roast lamb.

I never see any recipes for fresh tuna in this country, and I wish I knew why it is not even available frozen, only in cans. It is a delicious firm fish, the texture almost more like meat than fish. In France and Belgium we often have a tuna roast, something like a veal roast, served with tiny green peas. And eggs stuffed with canned tuna, covered with a delicate sauce, and served with tiny sweet peas and French fried potatoes make a superb meal.

FOR 4 PEOPLE:
> 8 *hard-boiled eggs*
> 1 *small can (4 to 6 ounces) tuna*
> 2 *tablespoons mayonnaise*
> ½ *teaspoon mustard*
> *Dash Worcestershire sauce*
> *Dab ketchup*
> 2 *tablespoons capers*
> 1½ *cups medium white sauce*
> *Salt and pepper*

Shell the hard-boiled eggs and cut them in two lengthwise; remove the egg yolks and cut a very thin slice off the bottom of the whites so they will sit still and not go slithering in all directions. Arrange them in a buttered baking dish.

Drain the tuna and mash it with the egg yolks not too finely. Season well with the mayonnaise, mustard, Worcestershire sauce and ketchup. The mixture will be highly seasoned and contrast well with the bland whites. Refill the whites.

Add the capers and a little of their juice to the white sauce. Pour over the eggs, making sure that each egg is covered with a film of sauce. Season with salt and pepper. The sauce will run to the bottom of the dish but that is as it should be.

Bake in the oven, preheated to 400°F., just long enough to get the eggs piping hot and flecked with brown on top (about 10 to 15 minutes).

Substitute chopped olives, stuffed or ripe ones, for the capers in the sauce. Also very good.

OEUFS POCHÉS SAUCE AURORE

Poached Eggs Aurora

Poached eggs are practically always served on croutons of fried bread in France. The contrast in textures is what makes this so delicious. The egg poacher must be an Anglo-Saxon invention, I did not know they existed until I came to this country. I know they make the job somewhat easier but to me the eggs don't have a poached taste. French cooks always add a few drops of vinegar to the water eggs are poached in and this gives them a particular taste. The simmering directly in water also affects the texture.

The vinegar in water has a practical reason; it makes the whites coagulate more quickly. There is no particular trick involved. Many cooks break the eggs directly into water. You may find it easier at first to break the egg into a saucer and slide it in gently. The most common reason for failure, however, lies with the eggs and not the cook! To get really pretty poached eggs, looking just like slightly flattened eggs in the shell, they have to be absolutely fresh. If you break an egg onto a flat plate or saucer, you will see what I mean. If the egg is fresh, it will still retain its shape—not completely, of course, but you will see a high rounded yolk with the white clinging thickly to it. There will be very little liquid spreading all over the plate. If the egg is not as fresh, though still good for other uses, the yolk will flatten out and there will be a lot of liquid. When this happens in the simmering water, you will have a poached egg fluttering off in all directions no matter how careful you are!

Poached eggs are delicious served with many things. A classic is a thick mound of fresh spinach, creamy with butter, surrounded by poached eggs and little triangles of fried bread. The eggs, resting on croutons or toast, if you are calorie conscious, can be covered with many sauces. Here is one, so easy to make a child can do it and yet, absolutely delicious. The name comes from the dawn pink color of the sauce.

FOR 4 PEOPLE:

4 slices day-old bread
Butter
1 cup light cream
4 ounces grated Swiss cheese OR,
    even easier, 4 slices processed Swiss cheese
2 to 3 tablespoons ketchup
1 teaspoon Worcestershire sauce
Salt and pepper
8 fresh eggs
1 tablespoon vinegar

Trim the crusts off the bread, cut in two, and fry the "croutons" in butter until golden on both sides. This admittedly takes quite a lot of butter; you can use half butter, half oil, if you prefer. Keep warm on a serving dish.

Place the cream in a small saucepan and add the cheese to it. Heat gently, stirring until the cheese has completely melted. Processed cheese does this in no time, grated takes a little longer. Be careful not to let the mixture boil. Season with ketchup, Worcestershire sauce and salt and pepper if necessary. Keep warm also while you cook the eggs.

Poach the eggs in gently simmering water in a large skillet. There should be at least an inch of water to bathe the eggs well. Season it with salt and about a tablespoonful of vinegar. Tarragon vinegar is a nice touch. Don't cook too many eggs at once and keep pushing the whites back in place with a spoon as they cook. About 3½ minutes will give you well-set whites and soft yolks. As the eggs are done, remove them gently with a slotted spoon and place them in very warm but not boiling water to keep hot while you do the others.

Drain the eggs thoroughly before placing them on the croutons. I find the easiest way to do this is to take a clean towel folded several times in my left hand and gently place each egg onto it as I remove it from the warm water with a slotted spoon. Trim the edges neatly and quickly with the edge of the spoon, and plop the egg back in the spoon and onto the crouton. Pour the sauce over the eggs and serve immediately.

Unlike toast, the fried bread prevents this dish from getting soggy from the sauce. If you find it really too rich, you can use lightly buttered crisp toast and pass the sauce separately. But be sure to drain the eggs thoroughly. I can't think of anything sadder than soggy wet toast with poached eggs!

OEUFS EN MEURETTE

Eggs in Red Wine Sauce

This is a really fine way to serve eggs, fit for the most discriminating guest. A meurette is a pungent red wine sauce, which originated in Burgundy and is well seasoned with bacon and garlic. Eggs are poached in this sauce and served on fine "croutons" of bread fried in butter. This dish makes an excellent appetizer for an elegant dinner or makes a glamorous lunch. Maybe it tastes best of all served at the beginning of an intimate little candlelit supper for two. . . .

FOR 4 SERVINGS:

½ pound lean bacon, unsliced if possible or ½ pound slice ham
2 tablespoons butter
1 small shallot or onion, finely chopped
2 cups good red wine, a Beaujolais, or any full-bodied red wine
1 10-ounce can consommé
2 whole cloves
1 clove garlic, minced very finely
Bouquet garni: 2 sprigs parsley, 1 bay leaf and ⅛ teaspoon thyme
Salt and pepper
1 teaspoon sugar
4 slices day-old bread
2 tablespoons butter
4 very fresh eggs
2 tablespoons flour
2 tablespoons butter

If possible use unsliced bacon and cut it into ½ inch chunks. Put them in a small bowl and pour enough boiling water over them to bathe well. Let stand a few minutes, drain and dry the bacon on paper towels. If you use ham, simply dice it and proceed.

Heat 2 tablespoons of butter in a small pan, add the bacon pieces to it, the shallot or onion and cook, stirring once in a while, until the onion turns pale gold. Now pour in the wine, the undiluted consommé, add the cloves garlic and the bouquet garni tied together in a piece of cheese cloth. (If you grow your own parsley, you can add a parsley root to the bouquet garni.) Season very lightly with salt (the bacon and the consommé have already added salt), add pepper and the sugar. Bring to a simmer and leave for about 1 hour. It should reduce by about half and fill the house with a heady aroma! Strain the sauce into a skillet, remove the bouquet garni but save the pieces of bacon and set them aside. This part of the recipe can be prepared ahead of time.

Near serving time, trim the crusts from the pieces of bread, fry them in hot butter until golden on both sides and keep them warm on a dish in a low oven.

Heat the wine sauce until just simmering in the skillet and poach the eggs directly into it. Break the egg in a saucer and gently slide it into the liquid; push the white back toward the yolk with a spoon or spatula until set. The fresher the egg, the better it will stay together. Cook the eggs for 3 minutes and gently lift them out with a slotted spoon. Place them on the fried bread. Return the bacon to the sauce and thicken it as follows: Mix 2 tablespoons flour with an equal amount of butter. Drop a teaspoon at a time of butter-flour mixture into the hot liquid, stirring as you go. Add a few at a time and stop as soon as the sauce is glossy and slightly creamy, not pasty and thick. You may not need all of it. Taste and correct seasoning if necessary; pour sauce over the eggs and serve.

OEUFS AU NID

Eggs in a Nest

This is a good, simple family dish and, if you have small children, you'll find they like this very much. It takes little time to fix, and you can serve it plain or with a good mushroom or tomato sauce.

Also, if you have a small amount of leftover chicken, fish or meat, you can hide it with impunity in this dish.

On a really harried day, you can even use instant mashed potatoes. A raw egg beaten in after you have added the potatoes to the milk and water mixture does absolute wonders for the taste. So does a little grated onion and/or grated cheese.

FOR 4 PEOPLE:

   3 cups mashed potatoes, whipped with milk and butter
   Salt and pepper
   Pinch grated nutmeg
   1 cup finely minced ham, chicken, cold meat or fish
      (optional)
   2 to 3 tablespoons butter
   4 eggs
   4 tablespoons grated Swiss or Cheddar cheese

Make the mashed potatoes fluffy and rich with milk and butter, season them well with salt and pepper and just a whiff of grated nutmeg. If you are using the meat or fish, mince it finely and add to the mashed potatoes.

Generously butter a baking dish and arrange the potatoes in it evenly. With a large spoon make deep holes for each egg. Place a little dab of butter in each and break a fresh egg over it. Season each egg with salt and pepper. Use a fork to make circles of deep grooves around each egg to make the nests. Sprinkle grated cheese over all. Bake in preheated 400°F. oven for about 15 minutes or until the eggs are set to your liking. Pass any sauce or gravy separately.

OEUFS À LA RUSSE

Eggs in Mayonnaise

Go to any French restaurant, from the best known to the smallest café, and chances are you will see *"Oeufs à la Russe"* in the list of hors d'oeuvres. They are practically always good and a favorite first course in summer. The goodness lies mostly in the mayonnaise: if it is spicy and yet mellow, well seasoned, it blends with the hard-boiled eggs in a truly tasty combination. These eggs are usually served on small individual plates on a bed of *Salade Russe,* which is simply diced mixed vegetables in mayonnaise. Fresh lettuce surrounds this and a bit of parsley and the whole is thoroughly appetizing and cool to eat.

Salade Russe was a great favorite of ours when I was a child. Maria did not make it as often as I requested it, though, and when I started to cook and discovered how long it took to dice all those vegetables, I understood why! Maria was also very exacting on the matter of cooking the vegetables. She insisted that each be cooked separately, so the flavors would contrast nicely. Truly, this is the very best way, but so time consuming that I settle very happily for the frozen mixed vegetables available at the supermarket. Cook these until just done, still somewhat crisp. Drain thoroughly and mix with mayonnaise. Arrange the hard-boiled eggs, cut in two lengthwise, over the vegetables and garnish with more mayonnaise, lettuce, parsley, radishes, etc., as your fancy dictates.

Maria added ham to her Oeufs à la Russe, in a way that I have never eaten anywhere but home. Try it, it is truly sensational:

FOR 4 SERVINGS:

    4 hard-boiled eggs, cooled
    1 (½-inch thick) slice boiled ham
    *½ cup homemade mayonnaise**
    Salt and pepper
    Lettuce for garnish

Shell the hard-boiled eggs and cut them lengthwise. Remove the yolks and place them in a small bowl. Dice the ham in tiny ¼-inch cubes. I mean this literally; you cut the slice into ¼-inch strips and cut these across again. The cubes of ham make all the difference, since they keep their juicy flavor and texture better than indiscriminately chopped ham!

Mash or sieve the yolks so there are absolutely no lumps. Beat in enough mayonnaise to get a fluffy mixture which hold its shape. Taste and season with salt and pepper if necessary; then fold in the ham cubes and mix well. Heap this high into the egg whites and serve, well chilled, on a bed of lettuce. The contrast between the spicy mixture of yolks and the bland coolness of the whites is unforgettable!

OEUFS À LA TRIPE

Eggs à la Tripe

Don't let the name of this recipe confuse you, it has nothing to do with tripe. The name comes from the fact that the dish resembles tripe in white sauce. It is an extraordinary example of what a difference one ingredient can make to the taste of a dish. In this case: sugar! When you first read this recipe, it sounds quite ordinary, hard-boiled eggs in a cream sauce with a little onion added. But believe me, you have to taste it to find out how good it is.

The secret is adding the sugar to the barely wilted onions and NOT letting it brown. It changes the taste completely. This is a delicious first course served in scallop shells with a border of mashed potatoes. Or in little individual dishes with plain toast. With a good green salad, a most satisfying lunch!

FOR 4 PEOPLE:
    8 hard-boiled eggs
    5 tablespoons butter or butter and oil but no margarine
    4 or 5 little green onions OR
    3 tablespoons chopped yellow onion plus 2 tablespoons chives
    Salt
    1 tablespoon sugar
    3 tablespoons flour
    1½ cups milk
    Freshly ground pepper
    Parsley for garnish

Cut the eggs in two, remove the yolks carefully without breaking them and cut the whites into long thin strips.

Melt the butter in a saucepan large enough to hold both the eggs and the sauce. Cook the chopped onions until soft and transparent but do not let them brown. Add a little salt and the sugar. Cook until the sugar has dissolved, stirring all the time, a few seconds. Stir in the flour and make a white cream sauce the usual way. Add the milk gradually, stirring well, and cook until bubbly and thickened. Add the eggs to the sauce, mixing gently, and season well with salt and plenty of freshly ground black pepper.

Pour into a shallow dish or dishes and brown quickly under the preheated broiler. Garnish with parsley.

OEUFS AUX TOMATES

Eggs in Tomatoes

Here is a simple and quite pretty dish which requires very little time. You might have it for lunch or a light supper, it requires about 20 minutes in the oven. It is quite a gourmet's delight, and you could serve it happily for a delightful Sunday brunch along with slices of Canadian bacon or lightly fried slices of ham.

On the other hand, if you add mashed potatoes and a good salad, you can have a meatless main dish at very little cost. The secret once again is the judicious use of herbs. Tomatoes have an affinity for sweet basil, so try that, with the merest touch of garlic. Tarragon is good by itself and chives add pungency.

FOR 4 SERVINGS:
   4 large, round tomatoes
   Salt
   Pepper
   A pinch of herbs
   4 thin slices cheese, processed or block cheese, Swiss or
      Cheddar
   4 eggs

Cut off the stem end of the tomatoes, scoop out the pulp and seeds carefully with a small spoon. Save this for soup or gravy. Season the tomatoes inside out with salt and turn them upside down to drain while you butter generously a baking dish. Choose a dish in which the tomatoes will fit quite snugly.

Rub a little pepper and a tiny pinch of herbs into each tomato. Cut the cheese into strips about an inch wide and fit these into the tomatoes; if the cheese is at room temperature, it will line the cavities quite neatly. Break a nice fresh egg into each "cup" so formed, season it with salt and pepper to taste. The baking time will depend upon how you like your eggs: 375°F. for 15 to 20 minutes. Peek in and see once in a while. If you like your eggs soft, be sure to serve them immediately as they continue to cook after you take them out of the oven.

OMELETTE AU JAMBON, AU LARD, ETC.

Omelet with Ham, Bacon, etc.

So much has been written about omelets that most people in this country regard them as something very difficult to make. In France, a bride may not be able to boil an egg but you can be sure she knows how to make an omelet!

Omelets are as popular in France as hamburgers are in America. Any small café will fix you one quickly if you say you are too hungry to drive on to a restaurant. They fry a couple of slices of country ham or bacon, which has a deliciously smoky flavor, make the omelet, right on the ham, and with a glass of wine and French bread, you will be entirely satisfied.

All you really need to make a good omelet are eggs and a skillet. It is easier to make several small omelets than a large one. I find that two eggs and an 8-inch skillet make the very best omelets; next best are four eggs and a 10-inch skillet. With all the new Teflon-coated pans, you don't have to worry about sticking. However, any good thick frying pan will do. If a pan has been scoured by mistake, treat it as a new one by rubbing it with a little oil and letting it get really hot. Wipe the grease with paper towels before using it.

Eggs should be fresh because the beating is important: more omelets are ruined by over-beating than not enough. Use a fork and beat only until the mixture is uniformly yellow. With a fork, the eggs will not get really frothy, but will make large bubbles. They will still have some body to them and this is what ensures a fluffy omelet.

Now the cooking itself. Even with a non-stick pan, an omelet needs butter for flavor. I like to heat the pan, then add a good lump of fresh butter, about a tablespoon, which will sizzle as soon as it touches the pan. The French call this making the butter sing; it is a very happy sound. Tilt the pan this way and that so it will be evenly covered with frothy butter. Pour in the eggs, beaten and seasoned, and swirl them around a little. I like to cook omelets over a very high fire, holding the pan an inch or so above it. This allows the omelet to cook evenly as you move the pan back and forth. Lift the edges as they cook and let some of the runny top part run under. As soon as the top stops running but is still very moist, the omelet is done. It will be golden on the bottom and soft inside, light as a feather as a good omelet should be. To fold an omelet like a chef: Hold the pan in your left hand, fold the left-side third toward the center with a spatula. Slip the right-side third off the pan and onto the serving dish, still with the help of the spatula. Now just flip the whole skillet upside down and the omelet will be neatly rolled onto the dish!

To make ham or bacon omelets, the French cook the ham on one side, turn it and pour on the eggs immediately. It continues to cook with the eggs and the blend of flavors is really delicious. You can do this also with slices of tomato. Or fry cold boiled potatoes and pour the omelet on them for an "Omelette Paysanne" with a little chopped onion added to the eggs.

Chopped mushrooms, very finely chopped herbs and shrimp can all be beaten right into the eggs. As a last touch, a little butter on the hot dish you slide the omelet onto, and/or a little more butter placed inside the omelet before folding, add enormously to the mellow texture, particularly if it has to stand a few minutes before serving.

Now we can look at a few very special omelets.

OMELETTE DE BREDA

There was a small restaurant on the Belgian coast which was famous far and wide for its absolutely marvelous food. The chef died during the Second World War but people still talk about him. When you try this omelet you will understand why! His secret was the tiny croutons of fried bread which he added at the last moment. Their delightful crunchiness in the soft, creamy omelet was as delicious as unexpected. This omelet is one of the very first dishes I cooked without Maria's direction. Chefs guard their recipes jealously as you probably know, but somehow M. Breda must not have suspected me when I innocently wandered into the kitchen and watched him, as I did Maria.

FOR 4 PEOPLE:
8 thin slices bacon
4 tablespoons chopped green onions
4 tablespoons chopped parsley
5 tablespoons butter
2 slices day-old bread
8 eggs—2 of which are separated
Salt and pepper

Cut the bacon into ½-inch pieces and fry them until crisp. Push them aside and fry the onions until pale gold. Spoon all this into a bowl with the chopped parsley. Add a tablespoonful of butter to the drippings in the pan and fry the bread, cut into tiny ¼-inch cubes, until golden and crisp. Keep stirring so they brown evenly. Drain on paper towels and set aside.

Place 6 eggs and 2 yolks in a large bowl. Beat the remaining 2 whites until stiff but not dry in a separate bowl. Beat the whole eggs plus the extra yolks as explained for a plain omelet; season with salt and pepper and add the onion, parsley, bacon mixture. Now gently and carefully fold in the whites (mixing well without beating hard).

Two smaller omelets are easier to make than one large one, so proceed this way. Wipe the pan you used for frying the bacon, etc. You don't want any crumbs to burn and spoil the appearance of the omelet but a slight flavor will remain. Heat the pan, add 2 tablespoons of butter and when it sizzles merrily pour in HALF the egg mixture. Immediately sprinkle over the omelet half the croutons and cook as explained before for the plain omelet. Keep this omelet very, very soft, as though, it will continue cooking a little while you make the second one unless you decide not to stand on protocol and serve 2 people while you and the other one wait! The omelet will puff considerably due to the beaten whites. Don't try to get the top thoroughly cooked, it should be still a little runny and ooze out of the folded omelet slightly as you serve it.

OMELETTE MALINOISE

Omelet with Asparagus

This is a stuffed omelet, a delicious thing to make when you want to combine the flavor of the omelet with something else quite separate and distinct—in this case, asparagus.

FOR 4 PEOPLE:
  1 pound asparagus, fresh preferably, or frozen or canned
  1 cup thick white sauce*
  Salt and pepper
  3 tablespoons butter
  4 eggs
  Parsley for garnish

Cook the asparagus, drain it well and choose a few of the nicest tips for garnish, half a dozen or so. Cut the rest of the asparagus into ½-inch pieces and mix them with a cupful of thick white sauce, well seasoned with salt and pepper. Keep warm while you make the omelet. Heat the reserved tips with a spoonful of butter in a small pan.

Make a four-egg omelet, keeping it *moelleuse*, a French word which means downy and creamy at the same time. A 10-inch skillet and 2 tablespoons of butter sizzling merrily will take care of that. See recipe for plain omelet. Pour the asparagus and sauce onto the center of the omelet just before folding and sliding it off onto a warm dish. Arrange the reserved spears at one end, as if just peeking out of the omelet, and garnish the other end with parsley. Serve immediately.

PIPERADE BASQUAISE

Red and Green Pepper Sauce

The Basque region of France is near the Spanish border and its food specialties are faintly reminiscent of Spanish cuisine.

This piperade is a wonderful sort of sauce, very thick, red and fragrant with tomatoes and peppers, both green and red. If you can't get sweet red peppers by the way, use a can of pimientos. Piperade is usually served with eggs. Sometimes it is folded into an omelet, sometimes it is used in a sort of scrambled egg mixture, the latter being the true country version. My preference goes to eggs scrambled separately to a golden creamy delight with the piperade poured over them.

FOR 4 PEOPLE:

4 large ripe tomatoes
2 large sweet green peppers
2 large sweet red peppers OR
1 4-ounce can pimientos, drained
4 tablespoons olive oil
2 tablespoons chopped onion
Salt and pepper
Pinch thyme and/or sweet basil
½ large clove garlic, finely chopped

The best way to make piperade is to peel not only the tomatoes but also the peppers. Hold them over a flame with a long fork or place under the broiler until the skin turns completely black. Rinse with cold water and the black will peel right off. The difference in taste is quite spectacular.

Chop the tomatoes and the peppers coarsely, removing all the seeds from the latter. If you are using pimientos, drain them before chopping. Heat the oil and cook the onion in it until soft and transparent. Add the tomatoes and peppers, a good seasoning of salt and pepper, a pinch of thyme and/or one of sweet basil and the chopped garlic.

Simmer, covered, until all is reduced to a sort of thick purée. It will take 20 to 30 minutes. Serve with a regular omelet, placing most of the piperade inside the omelet before folding it and pouring just a little on top after, as a garnish; or beat 8 eggs right into the piperade and cook as you would scrambled eggs. I prefer scrambling the eggs separately and pouring the piperade over them. This makes a fabulous Sunday brunch and you can prepare the piperade the day before.

4. VEGETABLES

THE UNITED STATES IS BLESSED with a great variety of climates and quite a formidable choice of vegetables. Add to that all the frozen foods and the choice is excellent, just about all year round. France is much smaller and yet produces quite a bountiful choice also. The French love their vegetables and very often serve them by themselves as a separate course so that their full flavor can be appreciated.

Fresh vegetables should be used whenever possible. I know that frozen ones are very convenient but really fresh ones in season will always have a subtle (or not so subtle) difference. The texture of fresh vegetables is different, for one thing. If you cannot use fresh vegetables, use the frozen ones and, except for tomatoes and little green peas, canned vegetables only as a last resort.

Regarding canned vegetables, I have never been able to figure out why canned mushrooms in this country have hardly any taste. Canned mushroom soup, on the other hand, has an excellent flavor and I use it frequently in creamed dishes. In fact, if I had to make a list of the types of mushrooms in order of preference, it would run something like this:

1) Fresh mushrooms
2) Frozen mushrooms
3) Imported canned French mushrooms (outrageously expensive)
4) Dried mushrooms
5) Mushroom soup
6), 7), 8), 9) NOTHING!
10) Canned mushrooms! And then only for looks and not for flavor.

So much for mushrooms! A word about onions: if you have ever had to do without onions, you know how much flavor they add to anything. The French are very fond of a small purplish one called eschalot. It also goes by the name shallot in some parts of the country but is not the green onion or scallion. It has a flavor all its own and it is worth looking for. There even exists a sort of "shallot of the month" club which will mail you a supply; inquire at Gourmet Food stores. They can be used by themselves or mixed with onions; for real Béarnaise sauce, they are a must.

The beauty of French vegetables lies in their absolute perfection in the raw state. For example, green beans are picked when much smaller than in America, when they are still quite tender and young. One really doesn't need to do anything to them besides cooking them in a very little salted water. Add a pat of butter and a little chopped parsley and you are done. Peas and carrots get the same treatment with equally pleasing results.

If you have children who dislike practically all vegetables, try serving them raw. Most kids who turn up their noses at cooked vegetables will nibble contentedly on raw carrots, celery, even white turnips. Arrange them attractively on a dish with a small bowl of mayonnaise as a dip. Even the usual holdouts will feel very sophisticated and probably enjoy them.

Another delicious way to prepare vegetables is to cook them until barely tender in salted water, drain them thoroughly, and pour French dressing over them while hot. Then chill and serve as a salad. Carrots, cauliflower, broccoli, small cabbage wedges, green beans are all delicious this way.

French potato salad, by the way, is made differently from American. Cook the potatoes until tender in their jackets in salted water. Peel them while hot, cube them and pour over them about ¼ cup dry white wine for about 4 cups cubed potatoes. Make a French dressing with 2 parts of oil to 1 part of vinegar, salt and pepper, 1 teaspoon prepared mustard and plenty of chopped parsley and onion. Pour over the potatoes while still warm and chill for several hours before serving. This makes a light potato salad, much less filling and cloying than the usual one. It is particularly good served with little pickled herring fillets or with canned salmon, sardines, tuna, etc.

Another delight is a South of France dish called *Aioli*. This is often served with plain boiled fish or, as I prefer, with hot, plain boiled vegetables: potatoes, carrots, onions, turnips, leeks, cabbage wedges, all those cooked in plain salted water, left whole and arranged steaming hot in a large dish. With them pass a good mayonnaise (preferably homemade; see Index) flavored with what seems an incredible amount of finely mashed garlic. Use 2 or 3 large cloves of garlic for about 1½ cups of mayonnaise. The mayonnaise melts and seeps into the vegetables as you eat and the taste is out of this world.

Many vegetables can also be served by themselves in *beignets* or fritters. Artichoke hearts, cauliflowerets, salsifies (oyster plants—a root vegetable somewhat like a white carrot with vague oyster flavor and available in cans), can all be served this way. For *beignets* vegetables should be cooked until barely tender, drained thoroughly and dipped in fritter batter (see the batter recipe for apple fritters). Then deep fry until brown, drain on absorbent paper, and serve piping hot and crisp, just sprinkled with salt. These are quite glamorous when served as hors d'oeuvres and you can serve large shrimp or pieces of sweetbreads prepared the same way right along with these fritters.

When a Frenchman is broke, he'll say he has not a radish! When the budget has to be trimmed, remember that vegetables with eggs and/or cheese can make wonderful meals.

ARTICHAUX BARIGOULE

Artichokes must be one of the most glamorous vegetables and a plain boiled artichoke, either hot or cold, is one of the easiest to serve. However, you can achieve a truly festive dish if you remove the feathery choke that covers the heart and then fill the center with shrimp, crab meat, pâté or any number of rich fillings—a delightful luncheon dish which needs little else.

In this recipe the artichokes are filled with a mixture of ham and mushrooms and reheated in a rich tomato sauce. Serve them by themselves or with baked ham or pork roast.

FOR 4 PEOPLE:

4 large artichokes
1 lemon
1 eschalot or small onion
4 slices boiled ham
½ pound fresh or frozen mushrooms
3 tablespoons butter
Salt and pepper
Tarragon
2 tablespoons tomato paste
½ cup white wine
1 tablespoon liquid beef extract
1 teaspoon flour, if needed

Trim the stems off the artichokes, rinse them well under running water. Parboil them in a little salted water to which you have added the juice of a lemon. By parboil, I mean cook them until not quite done; they should be still a little too firm to eat, 25 minutes or so depending on the artichoke.

Take them out of the water and drain them upside down. When cool enough to handle, trim the first two or three rows of leaves about halfway down with kitchen shears. Grab the center leaves firmly and pull them off with a twisting motion. Scrape out the choke with a silver or stainless spoon, a grapefruit spoon does very well.

Chop finely the eschalot or onion, the ham and the cleaned mushrooms. Cook in 2 tablespoons butter until the onion is limp and transparent. Season with very little salt because of the ham, pepper and a little pinch of tarragon. Spoon the mixture evenly into the artichoke hearts.

Melt the remaining spoonful of butter in a pot large enough to hold the artichokes upright. Add the tomato paste and cook it until it loses its bright red color. Stir in the wine, the beef extract and just enough water to bathe the bottom of the artichokes. Season lightly with salt because of the beef extract this time, pepper and a little more tarragon. Place the artichokes in this fragrant brew and bring to a simmer. Cover the pot and leave to cook until the artichokes are quite tender. Check once in a while; the juices should be just plentiful enough to prevent burning. Add a little water or more wine if needed.

At serving time, place the artichokes on a dish. If the sauce seems a little thin, you can thicken it with a teaspoonful of flour mixed to a thin paste with a little water. Boil up and pour over the artichokes.

ARTICHAUX AU GRATIN

Artichokes in Cheese Sauce

Although fresh artichokes are a seasonal delicacy, the small canned or frozen artichoke hearts are available all year round. The canned ones are cheaper than the frozen ones but some brands are better than others. The frozen ones are uniformly tender and small although sometimes I find that they contain a little too much citric acid or something like an imitation lemon flavor which is rather unpleasant. So shop around for the best and remember the brand name.

In this recipe, use either frozen or canned artichokes. For a quick, light gourmet meal, try serving them with a dish of creamy, smooth scrambled eggs. This makes a marvelous combination. Swiss cheese in the sauce adds a nutty flavor which goes particularly well with the artichokes; you can grate it or simply use processed cheese, which melts very quickly.

FOR 4 PEOPLE:

2 10-ounce boxes artichoke hearts
4 tablespoons butter
3 tablespoons flour
½ cup light cream
Salt and pepper
2 ounces Swiss cheese, grated, OR
    2 thick slices processed Swiss-type
½ clove garlic
4 tablespoons dried bread crumbs

Cook the frozen artichokes according to package directions, drain and reserve the liquid; or, with canned artichokes, simply drain and reserve liquid. Measure this liquid and add water if necessary to make 1 cup.

Melt 3 tablespoons butter in a small pan, add the flour and cook until frothy, without letting it brown. Stir in the artichoke liquid gradually, cooking until thickened and bubbly. Now add enough light cream to make a sauce the consistency of heavy cream. Season well with salt and pepper and the grated cheese, stirring until it has melted.

Arrange the cooked artichokes in a baking dish. Pour the sauce over them evenly. Chop or mash very finely the ½ clove garlic and mix it with the dried bread crumbs. Sprinkle this over the artichokes and dot with the remaining butter. Place the dish under the preheated broiler or in a hot oven until bubbly and flecked with brown. You can of course prepare this well in advance and bake it at the last minute.

ASPERGES À LA FLAMANDE

Asparagus

Fresh asparagus is a specialty of Malines, not far from Brussels in Belgium. There it grows, or rather, is grown, in thick white and tender stalks to the delight of Belgian epicures. The season is much too short for everybody; asparagus makes its appearance at fancy prices and as soon as the price comes down, it is over! Great bunches tied with bright purple or orange ribbons appear in the market stalls signaling the last bunch picked by the grower; the shopkeepers call your attention to the fact that this is your last chance to enjoy this delicious vegetable for another year.

The Belgians being thrifty as well as gourmets, the housewives get two delicious dishes out of a bunch of asparagus: one is the vegetable itself, the second is a soup made from the water they cooked in.

The French and Belgians prefer a sauce mousseline with asparagus to the classic hollandaise. This is simply hollandaise to which is added about one third of its volume of whipped cream. Makes it lighter, creamier and . . . heavenly!

Another favorite, as pretty as it is good, is a cold asparagus dish. Individual bunches are wrapped in a slice of good boiled ham with the tips peeking out temptingly. A ribbon of homemade mayonnaise* is placed across the ham slice and more mayonnaise is passed separately. Garnished with parsley, the combination of tastes and colors is memorable.

To serve asparagus the Flemish way, proceed this way:

FOR 4 PEOPLE:

  2 pounds fresh asparagus
  Salt
  4 hard-boiled eggs (hot)
  1 cup finely chopped parsley
  ½ pound (2 sticks) butter
  Pepper

Break the asparagus about halfway down. Save the ends for soup,* along with a few tips. With a very sharp knife or potato peeler, scrape each stalk thinly, starting about 2 inches below the tender tip. This makes a lot more of the asparagus edible. Tie the stalks in neat little bunches.

Take a pot just large enough to hold the asparagus upright, for example, the bottom of a double boiler or a coffeepot. Fill it with enough water to come about halfway up the asparagus, salt it and bring it to a boil. Stand the little bunches in this and cover. The tips will steam instead of boil and remain whole and pretty.

Hard-boil the eggs, shell them and keep them hot in water. Chop the parsley finely and melt the butter. Drain the asparagus thoroughly. Arrange it in the center of a long dish. Some people place a couple of slices of day-old bread under it; this is not eaten but drains the asparagus like a blotter. Arrange the hard-boiled eggs, cut in two lengthwise at one end of the dish with a mound of chopped parsley at the other. Pour the melted butter in a warmed bowl or sauceboat.

Each guest helps himself to eggs, asparagus and parsley, mashes the eggs with a fork, drenches them in butter and seasons them with plenty of salt and pepper and parsley. The asparagus is dipped in this sauce as you eat it, an absolutely marvelous combination.

For the soup:

FOR 4 PEOPLE (ABOUT 1 QUART SOUP):

  A few asparagus tips for garnish
  Asparagus trimmings, including a few tips
  Asparagus water
  2 beef bouillon cubes or 1 tablespoon beef extract
  2 tablespoons butter
  2 tablespoons flour
  Salt and pepper
  1 cup heavy cream
  Chopped parsley

Save the few asparagus tips to garnish the soup; it looks pretty and advertises the fact that this is indeed asparagus soup! Set them aside, raw.

Place all the trimmings and ends in a pot with enough water added to the cooking water to make about 1½ quarts. Add a couple of bouillon cubes to this or good beef extract and leave it to simmer until it has reduced by about half. Don't add salt until later; bouillon cubes are notably salty. Put this through a strainer or food mill, pressing out as much as you can of the good juices.

Melt the butter in a 2-quart pot, add the flour and cook until frothy but not brown. Gradually add the asparagus broth, stirring well so there are no lumps. Add the reserved asparagus tips and cook, simmering until they are quite tender. Taste and season quite highly with salt and pepper; the cream will dilute it. Just before serving, pour in the cream and garnish with the asparagus tips and freshly chopped parsley. Except for the cost of the cream, this soup is practically free!

CAROTTES ET PETITS POIS À LA FLAMANDE

Carrots and Green Peas the Flemish Way

The Flemish have a particular way with carrots which is delicious. Try serving a dish of them with *Carbonnades*, that other Flemish specialty, and you are in for a treat. Thyme is a key ingredient. It makes all the difference between just carrots and a special treat! You can serve the carrots all by themselves or, as is often done in Belgium, combined with an equal amount of little green peas. Together this way, they make a vegetable fit for the most discriminating company.

FOR 4 PEOPLE:
> 1 pound tender young carrots
> 1 pound fresh green peas OR
>   1 1-pound can small green peas
> ¼ pound (1 stick) butter
> Salt and pepper
> 1 bouillon cube
> 1 cup water
> Thyme
> 1 teaspoon sugar

Scrape and clean the carrots and cut them in very thin slices. If you are using fresh peas, shell them. I know it takes time but the taste is rewarding. Drain canned peas but reserve the liquid. Melt half the butter in a pan, add the carrots and fresh peas and cook gently over low heat until the vegetables have absorbed some of the butter. Don't let them brown. Season with very little salt, pepper and pour on 1 cup of water into which you have dissolved a bouillon cube. Cover the pot tightly and cook gently until the vegetables are tender and the water almost completely evaporated. The amount of thyme you add to flavor the dish depends on your particular taste; I like a good pinch, about ¼ teaspoon. If you are using the canned peas, add them when the carrots are beginning to get tender. Add water or the juice from the peas only as needed to prevent burning. Just before serving, taste and add salt and pepper as needed, about 1 teaspoon of sugar and the rest of the butter. Stir until the butter is melted and serve.

CÉLERI AU JAMBON

Cooked Celery with Ham

I am surprised that celery is not served cooked more often in this country. In France and Belgium, it is considered quite a glamorous vegetable. Besides it has quite a reputation. (I'll tell you about it if the children are out of the room: served to husbands who have become slightly inattentive, it rates on a par with French perfume and black lace; just try all three at the same time!)

Served in a cheese sauce, the celery is first wrapped in a slice of ham. Then the whole thing is popped under the broiler until appetizingly flecked with little gold and brown spots. It is marvelous when served with more ham, or just by itself. Depending on the size and the whiteness of the celery, you will need two large or 4 small hearts. Try this:

FOR 4 PEOPLE:

2 large or 4 small celery hearts   *3 tablespoons flour*
Salt   *1 cup milk*
4 slices boiled ham   *3 ounces grated cheese*
  Pepper

1 cup cheese sauce made with:
  3 tablespoons butter

Trim the outer stalks of celery and cut off all the leaves. You can keep them either for soup or for seasoning various dishes. Cut· the hearts in two if they are large and cook them until just tender in a little boiling salted water. Drain them well and wrap each in a slice of ham. Arrange in a well-greased baking dish.

Make the cheese sauce by melting the butter, adding the flour and cooking until frothy. Gradually pour in the milk, stirring like mad. Add the cheese, stir until melted, then taste and season with salt and pepper. Careful with the salt, the ham and cheese both add some. Pour the sauce over the celery and pop under the preheated broiler or in a hot (450°F.) oven until sizzling hot and flecked with brown.

CÉLERI À LA MOELLE

Celery with Marrow

Another delicious way to serve celery cooked is on toast, or better still, on fried bread in a delicious marrow-flavored sauce. This is a real delicacy served as a first course. Plan something light after it, though; it is extremely rich.

FOR 4 PEOPLE:
2 small celery hearts
1 tablespoon liquid beef extract
Salt
6 to 8 slices marrow bones, about 1 inch
4 slices fresh crisp toast or fried bread
Freshly ground black pepper

Trim the celery hearts of leaves and tough outer stalks. Cut them in two lengthwise so you have four pieces. Cook them in very little water to which you have added the beef extract. By the time the celery is tender there should be barely any liquid left. Add salt cautiously, the extract is usually salty enough.

With a sharp pointed knife, circle the marrow next to the bone and push it out. Cut it in little ½-inch cubes and add these to the celery when it is almost tender. The marrow will almost melt entirely and make a sort of flavorful sauce with the celery juices. Serve on crisp toast or fried bread with lots of freshly ground black pepper. An epicure's delight and a calorie counter's nightmare!

CÉLERI-RAVE TARTARE

Celeriac Tartar

A vegetable that is seldom seen mentioned in recipes in this country is celeriac, or root celery. It looks like a rather round, brownish turnip but the taste is unmistakably celery. This is quite a good vegetable cooked as other roots, in boiling salted water until tender and seasoned with a cream sauce. At other times you may want to peel them, scoop out the inside until you have about ½-inch shell left and stuff this with meat. Cook in bouillon to come about halfway up the celeriac until it is tender. Thicken the gravy with a little flour before serving.

The most usual way to serve celeriac in France, though, is in a salad, as a relish or hors d'oeuvre. If you can't find celeriac, this recipe goes well too with stalk celery. Just be sure not to overcook it!

FOR 4 PEOPLE (AS A RELISH):
   1 large celeriac or celery
   ½ cup dry white wine
   ½ cup beef bouillon (from a cube)
   Salt and pepper
   1 hard-boiled egg
   ½ cup homemade mayonnaise*
   2 tablespoons chopped pickles and/or capers
   1 teaspoon chopped onion
   Lettuce leaves

If you are using celeriac, peel it, slice it thinly (about ¼ inch) and cut the slices into julienne strips, i.e., little strips about ¼ inch thick. With fresh stalk celery, simply divide the head into 4 or if it is really large, 8 pieces. Trim off the leaves and tough outer stalks and save for flavoring dishes.

Bring the wine and bouillon to a simmer, add the celeriac with little salt, plenty of pepper. Cook the root celery 10 minutes but less time is required for regular celery. Both should be barely cooked and still crisp. Drain thoroughly.

Make a tartar sauce by mashing the hard-boiled egg very finely and mixing with mayonnaise. Season highly with chopped pickles and capers and chopped onion. Mix the celery with this sauce and store in the refrigerator for several hours or overnight for the flavors to blend. Delicious served on lettuce leaves.

CHICORÉES DE BRUXELLES

In this country endive is often served raw in salads, but its full flavor comes out in cooked dishes. Maybe you have to eat Belgian endive from an early age to like it since it has a faintly bitter taste. However, if the bitterness is too much for you, you may enjoy it with a few tricks to tone it down. Endive is less bitter if cooked in hardly any water. Melt a little butter or bacon fat in a pot, add the endive with just the water which clings to it after you have washed it. Leave it whole if small, cut in two if large. Season with salt and cook, well covered, until it is tender. It will give off a lot of juice at first and gradually reabsorb it. True devotees of endive will tell you that it should almost burn, the outer leaves slightly brown when it is done.

Another trick to reduce bitterness is to take out a small cone-shaped wedge from the root end of the endive with a sharp pointed knife. Most of the bitterness hides there. Once the endive is cooked as explained above, you can do many things with it: cover it with a white cream sauce, a cheese sauce, or wrap it in slices of ham, cover it with cheese sauce and then bake it until browned. This last is a whole meal in a dish and delicious.

Another good way to serve it is stuffed this way:

FOR 4 PEOPLE:
    8 large endive
    Salt
    2 slices day-old bread
    1 egg
    1 pound ground pork
    1 onion, finely chopped
    4 tablespoons chopped parsley
    Pepper
    Pinch thyme
    A little butter or bacon fat

Wash the endive quickly without letting them soak in the water. Trim a thin slice off the root end. Plunge them in boiling salted water for about 5 minutes, take them out and drain them well.

Make the stuffing by dipping the bread in cold water and squeezing it dry. Place it in a bowl with the egg and beat until no pieces of bread remain; add the meat, the onion and parsley and a good seasoning of salt and pepper. Add a pinch of thyme for flavor. Mix this well. Gently open and pull back the leaves of the endive, somewhat like opening up a tulip, and place little dabs of stuffing down into the petals. Press back together and twist a little white thread around them to keep them in shape. Melt a little butter or cooking fat, such as bacon drippings, in a large pot, arrange the endive in it, season with a little salt and pepper, cover the pot and leave to cook in its own juices for about 1 hour. Look in once in a while and add water only if necessary to prevent burning.

At serving time arrange the vegetables on a serving dish, boil down the juice a minute with an extra pat of butter if you like, pour over the endive and serve. In Belgium, boiled potatoes would go with this dish but if you prefer French fries . . . be cosmopolitan, they go very well too!

CHOU FARCI

Stuffed Cabbage

Stuffed cabbage is one of those country dishes which taste so good once in a while, particularly after rich and delicate meals. Such dishes bring us back to earth, somehow, and when well prepared can be immensely satisfying.

For this recipe you can use red or green cabbage, as you prefer. With green cabbage, you may find that the gravy is even more delicious with the addition of a little tomato paste. For the red cabbage, though, try a few spoonfuls of applesauce. Tomato does nothing for the taste of red cabbage and the clash of colors is enough to cut your appetite, unless you happen to be on a psychedelic trip.

FOR 4 TO 6 PEOPLE:
> 1 *medium head cabbage*
> 2 *slices day-old bread*
> 1 *egg*
> 1 *pound ground beef or beef and pork*
> 4 *tablespoons chopped parsley*
> 4 *tablespoons chopped onion*
> 4 *tablespoons chopped celery with leaves*
> 1 *small clove garlic, finely minced*
> *Salt and pepper*
> *Pinch thyme*
> 4 *slices bacon*
> 2 *tablespoons liquid beef extract or 2 bouillon cubes*
> 2 *cups water*
> *Tomato paste or applesauce (optional)*

Trim the cabbage of any bruised or decayed outer leaves, cut the stalk close to the leaves but don't cut it all off. Plunge the whole head into boiling water and leave it for about 5 minutes. Drain and rinse it with cold water. Now you should find it quite easy to separate the leaves and push them open, but don't break them off the stalk. When you come to the center, which will be quite raw, cut it out with a sharp knife and save it for slaw. It should be about the size of a tennis ball.

Now for the stuffing: dip the bread in water and squeeze it. Place it in a bowl and beat it with the egg. Add the meat, parsley, onion, celery, and garlic. Season with salt and pepper and a pinch of thyme. Fry the bacon in a pot large enough to hold the cabbage, take it out and crumble it into the stuffing. Mix well. Place a ball of stuffing in the center of the cabbage, fold a layer of leaves over it, and then push more stuffing between the leaves, working your way outward. Fold the largest leaves back in place and tie the whole cabbage together with a few twists of white thread. Do this loosely, you don't want the thread to cut into the leaves as the cabbage cooks.

Place the cabbage into the bacon fat remaining in the pot. Mix the beef extract with 2 cups of water and pour into the pot. Season with a little pepper and thyme but don't add salt until later, the extract is quite salty. Cover the pot and leave to simmer gently for about 2 hours. Add more water if it needs it, and turn the cabbage gently with two large spoons once in a while. It doesn't need much watching.

At serving time, take out the cabbage carefully. Remove all the thread or string. Thicken the gravy with a little tomato paste for green cabbage and a few tablespoons of applesauce for red. Or simply leave it plain! Pour over the dish and serve with mashed potatoes.

CHOU ROUGE

Red Cabbage

If you like coleslaw, try red cabbage slaw made with mayonnaise, it is just slightly different and delicious.

Red cabbage has quite a different flavor from the regular green variety. It goes marvelously with roast pork or ham. One of the beauties of red cabbage is that the more it cooks the better it is, leftovers warmed up the next day always taste better! Maria believed this and always started her red cabbage at least one or two days before she planned to serve it. When it finally did appear at the table, it was a deep wine red, fragrant with apple and spices, glossy with thick juice. Here is the recipe for it.

FOR 4 TO 6 PEOPLE:

1 large head red cabbage
2 apples
1 large onion
4 tablespoons pork drippings or lard
4 slices bacon
¼ cup dry red wine
Salt and pepper
Pinch thyme
Bay leaf
1 or 2 cloves
1 tablespoon sugar

Wash the cabbage and slice it very thinly. The easiest way to do this is to quarter it, remove the thickest part of the stalk and just slice with a large sharp knife. You obtain what seems an unbelievable amount of cabbage but it will cook down amazingly!

Peel and slice the apples and chop the onion. Heat the pork drippings or lard in a large heavy pot with a good lid. Add the onion and apple and cook until the onion is transparent and the apples soft. Add the bacon, cut into small pieces, and the cabbage. Keep stirring it into the hot fat until you can get it all in. Pour in the wine, season with salt and pepper and a nice little pinch of thyme. Drop in the bay leaf and the cloves. If you are very particular, you can tie these in a little piece of cheesecloth so that you can find and remove them later or you can substitute powdered cloves.

Cover and cook over a very low fire. At first the cabbage will render quite a bit of juice. Don't add any water. When it cooks down and the cabbage seems to be getting dry, add water sparingly, just enough to bathe the bottom of the pot. The fat will keep the cabbage from burning. Just keep on cooking it, stirring once in a while to mix well, for about 2 hours. At that time the cabbage is beginning to get good! Taste and season it with salt and pepper if necessary and about 1 tablespoon of sugar. To get the cabbage to the peak of perfection, however, you should now refrigerate it until the next day. Then cook again for at least another hour, adding only enough water to prevent burning. If you are cooking a pork roast to go with it, you can add a little more pork drippings to the cabbage. The result will be what the French call *confit*, which does not mean comfy but something more like preserves and is unbelievably good!

CONCOMBRES À LA POULETTE

Cooked Cucumbers

Americans are often teased for making remarks about how everything is bigger in the United States than in Europe. Well! I have news for you: French and Belgian cucumbers are about three times as long as the average American ones! They are no bigger around but incredibly long compared to the ones I have seen here. Until recently, though, the French and Belgian ones had to go through a bit of preparation to remove a certain bitter taste. In England, the cucumbers grow long but not bitter. I suppose the differences have something to do with climate.

Although you may have enjoyed French cucumber salad, with the cucumber soft and wilted, it is not regarded as a culinary achievement: to remove the bitterness, the cucumbers have to be covered with salt for several hours. They are then rinsed in lots of cold water and seasoned with vinegar, oil, salt and pepper. American cucumbers do not need this treatment but if you enjoy the texture of soft cucumber salad, and it *is* more digestible, you can proceed this way: Peel and slice the cucumbers very, very thinly. Some graters have a slicer and this gives perfect paper-thin slices. Sprinkle a little salt over the cucumbers and leave for several hours or overnight in the refrigerator. Rinse, drain and squeeze the slices in a dish towel to remove as much water as you can. Place them in a bowl and season to taste. I find 1 part vinegar, 2 parts oil, salt and pepper to taste, and perhaps a little chopped parsley, just about right.

When cucumbers are plentiful and cheap or when your neighbors grow some, you can make a delicious dish of cooked cucumbers. Concombres à la Poulette are made with a cream sauce with lots of chopped parsley, which does a lot for the cucumbers.

FOR 4 PEOPLE:
4 large cucumbers
Salt
2 tablespoons vinegar
3 tablespoons butter
2 tablespoons flour
1 cup beef bouillon (from a cube)
4 tablespoons finely chopped parsley
2 egg yolks
½ cup light cream or rich milk
Salt and pepper

As American cucumbers are not acrid in flavor, you may omit the first step of this recipe although I find the slight tang of vinegar which remains very tasty. Peel and slice the cucumbers about ¼ inch thick. Sprinkle them with salt and vinegar and leave to stand for about 1 hour. Drain and rinse with cold water.

Melt the butter in a saucepan, add the flour and blend but do not let it get brown. Gradually stir in the bouillon. Let this come to a boil, stirring, then add the cucumbers. Cook for about 20 to 30 minutes, stirring once in a while. You should not have to add any water because cucumbers are a watery vegetable, but don't let it burn. Stir in the chopped parsley. Just before serving, bring the cucumbers to a rolling boil. Remove from the fire and stir in the two egg yolks beaten in the cream. Taste and correct seasoning if necessary. The cucumbers must not boil after the cream and eggs are added, so if you have to reheat it, do so gently. This is a delicious vegetable with fish or chicken.

ÉPINARDS AUX OEUFS POCHÉS

Spinach with Poached Eggs

Spinach is regarded as an expensive vegetable reserved for special occasions by many French people. Although the spinach itself is quite reasonably priced, it is not considered perfect unless served with an immense quantity of fresh creamery butter. In fact, the expression *"Ça va mettre du beurre dans les épinards"* (that's going to put the butter in the spinach) means something is going to be lucrative.

If you want spinach at the absolute peak of gourmet perfection for this recipe, you will need to buy an extra amount of it: after a first brief cooking, it will be strained finely, removing all the stalks and fibers. If you enjoy the slight rough feeling of the stalks on your tongue, you can get by with the lesser amount.

FOR 4 PEOPLE:

> *2 or 3 pounds fresh spinach*
> *½ cup water*
> *Salt*
> *½ pound (2 sticks) fresh butter, unsalted if possible*
> *Pepper*
> *Nutmeg (optional)*
> *8 fresh eggs, poached and warm*
> *Croutons (4 slices day-old bread and butter and oil for frying)*

Wash the spinach thoroughly in several waters. Remove all the tough stalks. Bring half a cup of water to a boil in a large pot, salt it lightly and add the spinach with just the water which clings to the leaves. You will have to press it down as it wilts to get it all in. Cook uncovered, as this keeps the spinach a pretty green, for only about 5 minutes or until the leaves are completely wilted and soft. Cool a little so that you can touch it. Taking a handful at a time, squeeze out as much water as you can with your hands. Spinach retains an incredible amount of water so squeeze carefully. Put the spinach through a food mill, discarding the tough stalks as they accumulate. This is admittedly fairly wasteful and there will be little purée in comparison to the amount of spinach but it will taste incredibly fine. If you prefer, you can simply chop the spinach very, very finely.

Return the spinach to the pot. Add a large piece of butter and toss the spinach over high heat. More water will come out with the heat. Keep stirring and tossing the spinach until the water evaporates, adding more butter as it is absorbed by the spinach. Season to taste with salt and pepper and just a whiff of nutmeg. Keep the spinach hot.

Have the poached eggs ready. Keep them hot in water if you want to. Make croutons by trimming the crusts from 4 slices of bread and cutting them in four. Then cut each little square into two triangles. Heat just enough oil to cover the bottom of a skillet with about ¼ inch. When it is hot, add about 4 tablespoons butter. After it has melted, fry the little croutons, a few at a time until golden on both sides. Drain on paper towels.

Mound the spinach in the middle of a large round dish. Arrange the poached eggs around the base of the mound, garnish with a circle of croutons and stick more croutons like a crown in the spinach. As pretty as it is good.

Note: Spinach cooked this way is the base of all dishes described as "à la Florentine," such as fish fillets, sliced turkey, etc. The cooked meat is arranged on a bed of spinach, and a cream sauce poured over it. This spinach deserves royal treatment.

FLAN AU ÉPINARDS

Spinach Pie

This is almost a spinach soufflé, creamy and light, baked in the tenderest crust you can concoct. Served with ham, particularly if the ham is in Madeira sauce, it is an epicure's delight. Forget all about potatoes or any other starch—the crust takes its place to establish your reputation as a gourmet cook!

FOR ONE 9-INCH PIE, FOR 4 PEOPLE:
>   2 cups cooked spinach (2 1-pound cans)
>   4 tablespoons butter
>   3 tablespoons flour
>   1 cup milk
>   Salt and pepper
>   Pinch nutmeg
>   2 eggs, separated
>   1 recipe pastry for 1 piecrust,* pre-baked
>   4 tablespoons grated Parmesan cheese

Or start if you are using fresh spinach, which is better still, washing it well to get ALL the sand out and cooking it quickly with very, very little water. Don't be afraid to buy 2 pounds, it will shrink down to what you need. You may remove all the stems before cooking it, but personally, I rather like their texture; remove the largest ones, though, they could be tough.

Drain and cool the spinach and I mean drain! Actually to get this drained enough, you will have to take handfuls of it and squeeze as much water out as you can. Then chop it finely, a little at a time, and return it to the pan. Add 1 tablespoon of butter to it and shake and stir over high heat until you have no juice left. I bet you never thought there could be that much water left in it after all your squeezing!

Make a cream sauce by melting the remaining 3 tablespoons butter in a pan, adding the flour and cooking until frothy. Gradually stir in the milk, beating well, and cook until bubbly and thick. Add this to the spinach and season well with salt and pepper and just a whiff of nutmeg. Nutmeg has a definite affinity for spinach; use enough to notice the difference but not so much as to realize it's nutmeg. Stir in the egg yolks.

Beat the egg whites with a pinch of salt until they hold soft peaks but are not dry. Gently fold them into the spinach mixture and pour into the prepared piecrust. Smooth the top and sprinkle generously with grated Parmesan cheese. Bake in preheated 375°F. oven for about 30 minutes or until the filling is puffy and the cheese a dark brown. Serve immediately.

HARICOTS VERTS À LA LIÉGEOISE

Green Beans Liégeoise

Green beans ;o under several names in French, depending mostly on their size. The true *haricot vert*, like *petits pois*, is picked long before it reaches anything like maturity. I have always wanted to grow my own green beans in this country, just so I could pick them at that tender flavorful moment, when they are no bigger than my little finger and yet a deep dark green. Such beans need to be cooked in very little boiling salted water, seasoned with a large piece of fresh butter and served with chopped parsley. If you grow your own beans or know someone who does, try it. You'll never again wait until they grow big!

When beans get a little bigger, about the size they are generally sold here, they go by the name of *haricots princesse*. They are then considered much less fine and need preparation to be good. Then there are the large flat green beans, a different variety, called Italian here, which are the only kind to be sliced or "Frenched."

In this recipe, we usually use *haricots princesse*, so fresh beans are perfect. You can make it also with the frozen, and the result is still very good even if not as fresh tasting.

FOR 4 PEOPLE:

2 pounds fresh green beans
2 cups water
Salt
4 or 8 eggs
4 slices thick bacon
4 tablespoons butter OR
  2 tablespoons butter and 2 tablespoons oil
4 croutons (2 slices day-old bread or toast, fried)
2 tablespoons finely chopped parsley
1 small clove garlic, finely minced
2 tablespoons vinegar
Pepper

Cut off the ends of the beans and say a little prayer of thanks for the man who changed the name of green beans. These used to be known as string beans, you know! And it certainly took a lot longer to clean them! Don't slice them unless they are very large. Bring about 2 cups of water to a boil in a large pot, toss in the beans, season with salt and cook them until they are just tender but not mushy. If you don't cover the pot, the beans will be a brighter green but you may have to use more water. The flavor is better with less water and darker beans.

Drain the beans thoroughly and keep them in a warm place. Poach the eggs, counting one or two per person depending on your appetites. Keep them warm also in a little hot water. Cut the bacon in small pieces, fry it until crisp and add the drained, crisp bits to the beans. Drain all but 4 tablespoons of bacon fat.

Now prepare the croutons. You can substitute toast if you are very calorie conscious. Heat just enough oil (or butter) to cover the bottom of a skillet, add about 2 tablespoons butter and when it has melted, fry the slices of bread, halved and trimmed of their crusts. These are to go with the eggs. Assemble the dish:

Place the green beans in the center of a large round dish. Surround them with the poached eggs, well drained on a dish towel, each placed on its little crouton or toast. Add the parsley and garlic to the bacon fat remaining in the pan. Add vinegar and just a little pepper. Heat this to simmering, pour over the green beans and serve. A delicious kind of hot salad! Excellent for a summertime supper.

LAITUE À LA CRÈME

Creamed Lettuce

Cooked lettuce is too little known in this country, and yet it is one of the very finest green vegetables. The French don't have iceberg lettuce; *laitue* is always Boston lettuce, which is much more tender. However, Boston lettuce is usually more expensive than iceberg which can also be cooked. So let your purse and what is available at the market be your guide. But if you have a choice Boston lettuce is finer. And you can do what French housewives do—use the hearts in a salad and serve the large green leaves cooked.

When lettuce is cheap, remember to use it for soups (see recipe for Potage Printannier) and also *braisées*. This last means simply cooked in a little butter in a well-covered pot. You can also stuff lettuce. (See the recipe for stuffed Belgian endives.) The procedure is the same but you don't have to parboil the lettuce. Tarragon and lettuce make a love match; try using some in any lettuce dish. In this one, we use tarragon, a touch of garlic, parsley and green onions and come up with something extraordinarily good.

FOR 4 PEOPLE:
>   2 *large heads Boston lettuce with as many green leaves as possible*
>   4 *tablespoons butter*
>   4 *or 5 small green onions or 1 large yellow onion, finely chopped*
>   4 *tablespoons finely chopped parsley*
>   1 *very small clove garlic, minced*
>   1 *teaspoon dried tarragon*
>   *Salt and pepper*
>   1 *tablespoon sugar*
>   2 *egg yolks*
>   ¼ *cup heavy cream*

Wash the lettuce thoroughly in lots of cold water. Boston lettuce is often sandy, so let it rest in the water a few minutes so that the sand can sink to the bottom. Then rinse it some more. Drain it in a colander for a few minutes. If the heads are really very large, you may keep the hearts for salad.

Take a few leaves at a time, roll them together and slice very thinly; this gives you thin strips without any trouble. Melt the butter in a large pot, and add the onion with some of the green, the parsley, garlic, and the tarragon. Season with a little salt and pepper and sugar. Cook gently over low heat until the onions are soft and transparent but not brown. Add the lettuce with just the water which clings to the leaves; it will shrink considerably, so add it a little at a time if you have to, stirring. Season with a little more salt, cover the pot and cook over very low heat. You will probably be surprised, but lettuce takes about 35 minutes or more to get tender. During the last 10 minutes or so, inspect the lettuce carefully: there should be hardly any liquid left, the lettuce must be just good and juicy. If there is too much liquid, remove the lid for a while.

When the lettuce is quite tender and almost dry, beat the egg yolks with the cream. Take the lettuce off the fire, stir in the eggs and cream. It will thicken almost immediately. Taste and correct seasoning if necessary.

If you like spinach, try fixing it this way too. It really is good!

PETITS POIS À LA FRANÇAISE

Green Peas with Lettuce

French *petits pois* are famed the world over. I am amused to find labels on cans indicating that the contents are *petits pois* peas, which literally means "little peas peas." The only secret of these tender peas is that they are picked long before reaching maturity. If you shell them yourself, the shells are still flat looking, the little peas hiding inside. Unless you grow them yourself, they are not available fresh here. For the finest flavor you had better stick with the smallest, tiniest peas you can buy in a can, as the frozen ones are generally much too large.

In addition to the peas you need a couple of lettuce leaves, the large green ones you usually discard anyhow. Boston lettuce will taste best.

FOR 4 PEOPLE:
>   *2 or 3 large lettuce leaves*
>   *4 tablespoons butter*
>   *4 tablespoons chopped parsley*
>   *1 small green onion, chopped*
>   *Salt and pepper*
>   *1 teaspoon (scant) sugar*
>   *2 1-pound cans tiny green peas*

Wash the lettuce and chop it finely. Melt about half the butter in a saucepan, add the lettuce with just the water that clings to it, the chopped parsley and onion. Season with a little salt and pepper and the sugar. When the lettuce is wilted, add the drained peas and cook only until they get thoroughly hot. Stir in the rest of the butter and serve. Simply delicious.

If you want to prepare fresh peas this way, follow the same procedure but add just a little water when you add the peas. By the time the peas are tender, most of the water will have evaporated. So add a little at first and a little more later if the peas need it.

PETITS POIS ET POMMES DE TERRE À LA CRÈME

Creamed Peas and Potatoes

This is a very simple dish: little new potatoes and tiny green peas in a mushroom sauce. The sauce is made from a can of mushroom soup so you really don't have much work to do. This is a dish fit for company, delicious with fish for instance, and the bonus is that small children usually go for it in a big way.

When the new potato season is over, you can make it with large potatoes cut into small pieces. Or in the spring, when tender baby carrots make their appearance, you can add a few of them too. The combination is delicious and pretty to look at.

FOR 4 PEOPLE:

*About 12 small new potatoes or equivalent amount
    larger ones, peeled and cut
Salt and pepper
Pinch tarragon
2 or 3 green onions or 1 large yellow onion
1 1-pound can peas, petits pois
1 10-ounce can undiluted mushroom soup*

Scrape or peel the potatoes, depending on their age, and put them to cook in water to cover with salt, pepper and a pinch of tarragon. Add the onions cut in ½-inch slices, including some of the green part. When the potatoes are tender but not mushy, drain them thoroughly. Add to them the drained peas, the undiluted mushroom soup and stir gently to mix. Heat until piping hot and serve.

POMMES DE TERRE FRITES

French Fried Potatoes

Although the French resisted eating potatoes when they were first introduced from the New World, they finally did accept them and applied the same inventiveness to preparing them as they have to most other foods. Even boiled potatoes are given special treatment by adding a good dab of butter mixed with chopped parsley and a few drops of lemon juice. And perfectly prepared French fries are one of the best recipes. They should be crisp and golden on the outside, mealy and tender inside. To get them that way you must follow a few rules.

*1 medium white potato per person
Vegetable oil
Salt*

The potatoes have to be of good quality, firm and mealy when cooked. You can't make good French fries with new potatoes. Wash the potatoes before peeling them. Cut them in strips a little less than ½ inch thick. Dry these strips on dish towels or paper towels. It is important that the potatoes be as dry as possible. Use a deep fryer and enough oil to cover the potatoes. Cook them first at about 375°F. until they are soft and mealy inside but not yet golden. They should be covered by a thin fried layer, somewhat like a skin. Now lift them out of the fryer and leave them to cool and drain. You can do this quite a bit in advance. At serving time, get the fat or oil really hot, close to 400°F., add the potatoes, which will get golden in just a few minutes. Drain thoroughly, salt and serve.

Note: Frozen French fries, prepared just as though you had done the first frying yourself, can be practically as good as fresh fried potatoes. To get the full flavor, though, you have to let them defrost before adding them to the very hot oil.

POMMES DE TERRE RÔTIES

Pan-roasted Potatoes

This is a very simple way to prepare potatoes but absolutely delicious when done well. Perfect with a good roast, for instance. Here is what you need:

FOR 4 PEOPLE:
8 or 10 small potatoes the size of a small egg
Cooking oil
4 tablespoons butter
Salt and pepper
Pinch thyme

If you cannot get enough small potatoes (these are not new potatoes), cut some larger ones and trim them so they are the size and shape of small eggs, with no flat side. This is important!

Pour enough cooking oil in a very heavy skillet or pot with a good lid to cover the bottom with about ¼ inch of oil. Wipe the potatoes well with paper towels to get them as dry as possible. Place them in the hot oil and cook them uncovered over medium heat until they are golden on all sides. The centers will not be cooked at all.

Pour off as much oil as you can, add the butter and season with salt and pepper and thyme. Cover the pot tightly and cook over a low fire until the potatoes are tender. This will take from 45 minutes to 1 hour. Don't peek in too often, just shake the pan once in a while so the potatoes will roll around. If you do turn them over with a fork, don't pierce them. Potatoes well done this way will be golden outside and tender and mealy inside. If you don't want to use butter, you may leave just a little oil in the pan. Don't use margarine—it burns and spoils the dish entirely. With a little practice, you will be able to shake the potatoes without opening the lid at all. The reward will be potatoes that absolutely melt in your mouth!

POMMES DE TERRE À LA NORMANDE

The French like the combination of leeks and potatoes very much, and if you have ever tasted vichyssoise, you can easily understand why. In this recipe, a leek or two are added to the thinly sliced potatoes for a marvelous flavor. You can, if you prefer, cook this dish in the oven, but, particularly in summer, the top of the stove will do quite well.

FOR 4 PEOPLE:
>   *2 pounds potatoes*
>   *3 tablespoons butter or cooking oil*
>   *½ cup finely chopped leeks or green onions, including some*
>   *of the green*
>   *1 tablespoon flour*
>   *3 cups scalded milk*
>   *Salt and pepper*
>   *Nutmeg*
>   *Thyme*
>   *1 bay leaf*
>   *½ cup light cream (optional)*

Peel the potatoes and slice them thinly. Héat the butter or oil in a very heavy pot, add the chopped leeks or green onions and cook until wilted and transparent but not brown. Dust flour over them, stir, and gradually beat in the scalded milk. Season generously with salt and pepper, just a whiff of nutmeg, a little thyme and a bay leaf. Add the potatoes, cover the pot and cook over very low heat for 20 to 25 minutes until the potatoes are quite tender. Stir only occasionally and then gently so as not to break the potatoes too much.

If you want an even richer dish, pour in about ½ cup cream just before serving. These potatoes go marvelously with fish.

POMMES DE TERRE PAYSANNE

Country-Style Potatoes

This is a very simple country-style dish that will take care of itself in the oven on a busy day. There is no basting, hardly any watching and yet it can come under the heading of "Meat and Potatoes" if your man is the type who feels he has not eaten unless he has meat!

Try serving this with a good green salad, well seasoned with a little garlic. With cheese and fruit for dessert, you will have an excellent meal.

FOR 4 PEOPLE:
> 4 to 6 large potatoes, depending on size
> 1 pound ground pork or bulk sausage
> 1 small onion, chopped
> 4 tablespoons chopped parsley
> 1 clove garlic, finely minced
> Pinch thyme
> 1 egg
> Salt and pepper
> 4 tablespoons (approximately) packaged bread crumbs

Scrub the potatoes but don't peel them. Choose them of as even size as possible. Cut them in two lengthwise and scrape out some of the center to hollow them out slightly.

Mix all the other ingredients except the bread crumbs and add also the scraped out potato centers. Fill the potatoes with the well-seasoned meat mixture, rounding it on top like large meat balls. Sprinkle the tops with bread crumbs, preferably the Italian-style seasoned crumbs.

Arrange the potatoes in a greased baking dish, cover with aluminum foil and bake them in a preheated 350°F. oven for about 1 hour or until the potatoes are tender. Remove the foil about 10 minutes before serving so that the tops can brown. If you want to, you can serve tomato sauce with the potatoes, but they are delicious just plain.

SAVARIN DE POMMES DE TERRE

This elegant way to serve potatoes is very easy to prepare. Into the center of a ring of potatoes, golden and crisp on the outside, we pour a sauce made with cheese and port wine which is tangy, mellow and creamy.

These potatoes go well with almost anything but are particularly delicious with a fine steak. You can start very simply with frozen French fries, but there's no doubt that the dish is better if you start with fresh potatoes, peeled and cut into very thin strips, a little thinner than the usual French fries.

FOR 4 PEOPLE:
  6 *large potatoes* OR
  1½ pounds (approximately) frozen French fries
  ¼ pound (1 stick) butter plus 2 tablespoons
  Salt and pepper

  For the sauce:
  4 tablespoons flour
  2 cups rich milk
  4 ounces grated cheese such as aged Cheddar
  ¼ cup dark rich port wine
  Salt and pepper

Peel, slice and cut into strips the fresh potatoes or let the frozen ones thaw. Butter generously a 1-quart ring mold. Set aside 4 tablespoons butter for the sauce. Arrange the strips of potato in the mold, packing them in tightly and adding little dabs of butter and salt and pepper on each layer as you go. Real butter is the secret here, don't use margarine. Press the whole thing down firmly and bake the ring in a preheated 375°F. oven for about 45 minutes or until the potatoes are tender inside and golden. Turn them out on a serving dish and pour over them the following sauce:

Melt 4 tablespoons butter in a saucepan and stir in the 4 tablespoons flour. Cook until frothy but not brown. Gradually stir in the milk, cook until bubbly and smooth. Stir in the grated cheese and keep stirring over a very low heat until it melts. Season with salt and pepper; taste it though, cheese is salty already. Last of all stir in the wine. If you wish, you can make the sauce early in the day and cover it with wax paper so that no skin forms as it cools. Stir in the wine when you reheat it.

The aroma alone will go to your head!

PURÉE DE POMMES DE TERRE

Mashed Potatoes

With a large family, I use instant mashed potatoes quite often. Once in a while I make the real thing and realize how much we have been missing. Fresh, creamy mashed potatoes, fluffy and light as a cloud, are indeed worth the effort. The rules are fairly simple and you have to start with good mealy potatoes:

FOR 4 PEOPLE:
> 5 large potatoes
> Salt
> 6 tablespoons butter
> 1 cup (approximately) hot rich milk
> Pepper
> Nutmeg
> 1 egg

Peel and boil the potatoes in salted water. Leave them whole, they will taste even better. As soon as they are tender, drain them thoroughly and return them to the fire, shaking the pan for a few minutes so that the potatoes can dry completely. Immediately put them through a ricer or mash them with a potato masher. Speed is of the essence and you must not pound them, the idea is actually to break them into dust! Place this back on the fire, add 4 tablespoons butter in small pieces and about half the hot milk. Beat thoroughly but lightly, lifting the potatoes so air can get trapped in them and make them fluffy. If you stir they will get heavy. Add more milk as needed to make them light and fluffy to your taste, still beating well. Taste and season them with salt and pepper and just a whiff of nutmeg. Beat in the whole egg at the last moment. These potatoes should be served with speed for the most delightful consistency. If they have to wait a little, dab the top with 2 tablespoons butter, beat again just at serving time. The whole beating procedure should be done over the fire so the potatoes never get a chance to get cold. These are really mashed potatoes! Trouble is, the family may not like the instant kind later!

PURÉE DE POMMES DE TERRE INSTANT

Instant Mashed Potatoes

Instant mashed potatoes vary a lot depending on the brand. I find the potato flakes the best. With the right additions, these can be quite good. First of all, I usually substitute at least ¼ to ½ cup of extra milk for the amount of water indicated on the package. Then I let the potatoes' stand for a few minutes before beating so that they have time to absorb the liquid. Finally, I add a whole egg to the hot potatoes, as the French often do with regular mashed potatoes, and this does wonders for the taste.

Here are a few recipes for which instant mashed potatoes are particularly suited:

Pommes de Terre Duchesse

Prepare the potatoes as directed on the package but decrease the amount of water by 3 tablespoons for each four servings. Let stand a few minutes and then beat thoroughly. Add 1 whole egg plus an extra yolk for each 4 servings. These potatoes can be used for the decorative and tasty borders of many creamed dishes. You can pipe them around the dish or simply spoon them around it and make little dents with a fork. Brush with melted butter and bake or broil until the top of the potatoes turn a rich brown. These potatoes keep their shape well when baking so you can use them to make a border on scallop shells for instance so that the filling will not run out.

Pommes de Terre Duchesse can also be spooned or piped in attractive shapes on a well-buttered cooky sheet and baked until golden. Remove them carefully with a large spatula. The French often add just a touch of nutmeg to these mashed potatoes; it should be barely perceptible, but it does make them finer.

Pommes de Terre Dauphine

This is one of the most delicious ways to serve potatoes but it does require a little work. Make instant potatoes with ¼ cup less milk than called for on the recipe for 4 servings. Add 2 egg yolks, a dash of nutmeg and 4 tablespoons butter and mix well. Mix 2 cups mashed potatoes with 1 cup chou pastry,* folding it in thoroughly. In vegetable oil deep fry small spoonfuls of this mixture, about the size of a pecan, until golden and crisp on the outside. Drain on paper towels. These can be kept warm in the oven for a reasonable amount of time or even reheated if necessary. Really quite fancy served with something in a good sauce.

Purée de Pommes de Terre

You can, of course, use instant mashed potatoes for . . . mashed potatoes! Although they are not as fine as the freshly cooked ones, they can be quite acceptable, particularly if you add a little minced green onion and a pinch of thyme to the heating water. You can also season them with a little grated cheese or Parmesan. A delicious combination is to add about ½ cup of finely chopped watercress and a little onion to the hot potatoes. One of our family favorites is to add 1 chopped green pepper, 1 peeled, seeded and chopped tomato, a few green onions and a pinch of thyme to the hot potatoes. You practically don't need another vegetable and this is delicious with cold cuts.

Vichyssoise

If you add a few finely chopped green onions or leeks to the water for instant mashed potatoes and allow them to cook until soft, you have the beginning of vichyssoise. Add the potatoes and thin down with as much milk as you need to reach soup consistency. The fresh onions or leeks make this much better than the prepared mixes.

SOUFFLÉ DE PATATES DOUCES

Sweet Potato Soufflé

Sweet potatoes or yams are not often used in France and practically unknown in Belgium. I have found them delicious, particularly when served with game birds or turkey in place of the French *purée de marrons*, or chestnut purée. However, chestnuts are not always available in some parts of this country, and sweet potatoes, due to their taste and texture, can be used in their place. It is better to use very little sugar; I find that candied sweet potatoes or those concoctions involving marshmallows are a little too reminiscent of gooey desserts to serve with meats.

In this recipe, I use only 3 tablespoons of sugar for 2 pounds of yams. If your taste runs to something sweeter, add a little more.

FOR 6 TO 8 SERVINGS (DEPENDING ON
WHAT ELSE YOU SERVE):
   2 pounds canned or freshly cooked sweet potatoes
   4 tablespoons butter
   4 eggs, separated
   3 tablespoons brown sugar, or more to taste
   ½ teaspoon grated orange peel
   Pinch cinnamon and/or nutmeg
   Salt

Start by heating the canned yams in their juice or with hot freshly cooked ones. Drain and mash them very, very well. Add about 3 tablespoons of butter and beat in the egg yolks while the yams are still hot. Sweeten to taste and season with the orange peel, cinnamon, and nutmeg.

Beat the egg whites until they stand in soft peaks but are not dry, as for meringue. Adding a pinch of salt to the whites at room temperature hastens the job and gives greater volume. Fold into the sweet potato mixture very gently, pour into a greased baking dish, dot the top with the remaining tablespoon of butter and bake in preheated 375°F. oven for about 40 minutes or until puffy and golden. This is not a real soufflé in the sense that it will not fall if not served immediately, but it is nevertheless very light and delicious. If you are planning to serve it with turkey and are not blessed with two ovens, you can place the sweet potatoes on the lower shelf during the last hour of cooking the bird.

MACÉDOINE DE LÉGUMES

Mixed Vegetable Salad

This is a delightful salad to serve instead of potato salad. It tastes good and looks as pretty as jewels as the colors of the vegetables contrast nicely. One version is simply to use the mixed frozen vegetables available at the supermarket. Simply boil them until just tender, drain thoroughly and season with mayonnaise as indicated below.

For the finest taste, though, you should use as many fresh vegetables as you can and cook them separately. Each retains its flavor that way and you do get a finer salad. Cut the vegetables in nice even cubes and watch them carefully so that none over-cooks.

FOR 4 PEOPLE:
½ *cup diced potatoes*
½ *cup diced carrots*
½ *cup diced green beans*
½ *cup diced turnips*
½ *cup tiny cauliflowerets*
   (All the above cooked in salted water and drained.)
½ *cup drained canned peas*
1 *tablespoon tarragon vinegar*
½ *cup mayonnaise*
1 *or 2 small green onions*
4 *tablespoons chopped parsley*
Lettuce for garnish

Place all the vegetables in a large bowl, drizzle the tarragon vinegar over them and chill thoroughly. Chop the little green onions finely, including some of the green part. As close to serving time as convenient, mix the onions, 2 tablespoons of parsley and the mayonnaise with the vegetables.

Arrange a few lettuce leaves, the tender pale green ones, all around a pretty platter or shallow bowl, heap the salad in the middle and sprinkle with the rest of the parsley.

RATATOUILLE

In the South of France this dish is often eaten cold, and it has a wonderful cool tanginess. We like it hot also, sometimes with rice in Louisiana fashion. It is excellent with fish and even the lowly hamburger takes on glamor when served with this.

The quantities for ratatouille are plentiful and perhaps you will have enough left over to serve cold. Don't really count on it though. As they say in France, *"Ça se laisse manger"*—this lets itself be eaten without effort.

FOR 4 TO 6 PEOPLE:
> *2 or 3 eggplants, small to medium*
> *3 large very ripe tomatoes* OR
> *1 1-pound can whole tomatoes*
> *3 green sweet peppers*
> *1 zucchini or cucumber*
> *2 large onions*
> *3 cloves garlic*
> *A handful parsley*
> *4 tablespoons olive oil*
> *Salt*
> *Pinch thyme and/or sweet basil*
> *Pepper*
> *2 tablespoons tomato paste*

Wash all the vegetables. Slice the eggplants into ½-inch slices and cut these into cubes. Set aside. Cut the tomatoes, the green peppers (removing the seeds), the zucchini or cucumber into small pieces. No need to peel any of these vegetables except the cucumber if it is large and thick-skinned. Chop the onions, keeping them separate from the other vegetables. Finely mince the garlic and parsley, and set aside about 3 tablespoons for later use.

Heat the olive oil in a large heavy pot and cook the onions in it until they begin to brown. Add the eggplant with a dusting of salt and leave it to absorb the oil and with it the onion flavor. Eggplant is a glutton for oil. Now add the other vegetables and stir to mix them all very well. If you are using canned or very ripe tomatoes, you should not have to add water at all. The vegetables will render enough to cook themselves. Sometimes, though, you may have to add a little, but do this a few drops at a time, just so things don't scorch. Add the garlic and parsley and a little pinch of thyme and sweet basil. Salt and pepper generously, cover, and leave to simmer gently.

When the vegetables begin to get tender, about 30 minutes or so, add the tomato paste, enough to color and thicken the juices. Simmer some more, stirring gently once in a while. When all the vegetables are tender and reduced to a sort of thick purée, pour into a dish and sprinkle with the reserved parsley and garlic mixture for a last fragrant touch.

LES BELLES TOMATES

Beautiful Tomatoes

When I arrived in the United States, I was most unhappy with the tomatoes I found in the supermarkets, bemoaning their lack of flavor. Then came the season for vine-ripened beefsteak tomatoes and my love affair began. I should really call them by their ancient name of love apple: I love them raw, cooked, stuffed, plain, in soups, sauces, any way you can name. So, if you share my delight in tomatoes, here are a few ideas.

A French classic, *tomates à la provençale* is delicious as a light first course by itself or as a vegetable with meat. Cut nice round tomatoes in two across. Arrange them, cut side up, in a lightly greased baking dish. In a small bowl, mix fresh bread crumbs, torn from day-old bread, with plenty of finely chopped garlic and parsley. Season generously with salt and pepper, pile and press on top of the tomatoes. Drizzle with a little olive oil or dot with butter. Bake in a hot (450°F.) oven until the tomatoes are tender and the bread browned, about 10 minutes. Simple and delicious.

One of my favorites: slice thickly two or three large tomatoes. Heat a little butter or better still, bacon fat, in a large skillet. Season the tomatoes with lots of salt and pepper and brown them gently on one side. Turn over carefully with a spatula. Sprinkle them liberally with chopped fresh herbs. I use what I happen to have on hand: green onions, chives, parsley, finely minced garlic, sweet basil or tarragon. Serve as soon as tender. With hot buttered toast and crisp Canadian bacon, this is the perfect summer breakfast or brunch.

SALADE DE TOMATES

French Tomato Salad

Let us not forget that simple but delicious treat, French Tomato Salad:

FOR 4 PEOPLE:
4 to 6 medium tomatoes
Salt and pepper
2 tablespoons finely chopped onion
4 tablespoons finely chopped parsley
1 tablespoon vinegar
2 tablespoons oil

Do peel the tomatoes, they have a much better flavor that way. Hold them over a flame at the end of a long fork for a few seconds on each side or pour boiling water on them, drain after 5 seconds. In either case the skin will peel off with a minimum of trouble.

Slice the tomatoes fairly thinly. If the core is strong and deep, remove the hard pieces as you slice. Season the tomatoes with plenty of salt and pepper as you arrange the slices in a dish. Mix the onions and parsley together and spread a thick layer of the mixture over the tomatoes. Mix the vinegar with the oil and drizzle over the dish. Allow it to stand for at least an hour so the flavors will permeate the tomatoes. Serve as a first course with hot and crusty French bread and fresh butter. You could almost make a meal of this!

TOMATES MONTAGNARDES

Mountain Tomatoes

Whether the name of this dish comes from the fact that the cheese is heaped in a mountain on top of tomatoes or that Swiss cheese makes one think of mountains naturally, I can't say! But the combination of cheese and tomatoes has always been what the French call *un mariage heureux* (a happy marriage) and as such each makes the other a little bit better.

These tomatoes again make a good and rather glamorous lunch-eon dish or can be used as a vegetable with meat, especially with ham.

FOR 4 PEOPLE:
4 large tomatoes
Salt
2 tablespoons butter
2 tablespoons flour
1 cup milk
2 ounces Swiss cheese, grated or shredded
Pepper
Nutmeg
2 eggs, separated

A word about the cheese. You can also use a good aged Cheddar or a combination of Swiss cheese with a tablespoonful of grated Parmesan added.

Cut the tomatoes in half crosswise, scoop out some of the center and press out the seeds. Salt them lightly and turn them upside down to drain while you make the sauce.

Melt the butter in a small saucepan. Add the flour and cook until frothy. Gradually stir in the milk and cook until thickened. Add the cheese, remove from the heat and stir until it has melted. Stir in the egg yolks and season well with salt and pepper and just a dash of nutmeg, it brings out the cheese flavor particularly well. Beat the egg whites until stiff but not dry and fold gently into the cheese mixture. Butter a baking dish generously, arrange the tomatoes in it, and mound the cheese mixture in the tomatoes. Bake in preheated 375°F. oven until the cheese is puffed up and golden, about 15 to 20 minutes. Serve immediately.

TOPINAMBOURS

Jerusalem Artichokes

Jerusalem artichokes look like crazy mixed-up potatoes that did not know which way to grow. In France, they are so plentiful they are used as cattle fodder and therefore not regarded as highly as they merit. Although they are not related to the artichoke, their flavor is almost exactly that of artichoke hearts and they deserve good treatment.

They are a bit of a nuisance to peel, protruding in all directions as they do, so arm yourself with a sharp knife and patience. Scrape and peel carefully and you will produce nice white-looking vegetables. Drop them in water to which you have added the juice of a lemon so that they won't turn black.

To cook them, place them in plenty of boiling salted water and after 10 minutes start prodding. Some of these artichokes have a tendency to cook much faster than others. To be at their best, they must not overcook and get soggy with water. When they are done take them out and drain thoroughly.

You can serve them several ways. Simply roll them in a little butter and parsley and they will then take the place of potatoes most deliciously. Or, you can make a good cheese sauce, pour it over the artichokes and bake them in a preheated 375°F. oven for 25 minutes or until bubbly and brown. They are delicious either as a luncheon dish or as a vegetable.

Lastly, you can serve them cold as you would potato salad with a good homemade mayonnaise.* Their artichoke flavor is more pronounced when they are cold, and you can use them with cold cuts for quite a glamorous summer supper at a fraction of the cost of artichoke hearts.

Add a few well-mashed or strained Jerusalem artichokes to cream of chicken soup and they will give a very delicate and completely different flavor. Thin it down with milk or cream until you reach the desired consistency.

PÂTES

The French do wonders with most foods except one: Macaroni! They make delicious noodles, though, and different kinds of *gnocchi*, which are both kinds of pasta. But macaroni and spaghetti should only be eaten in a true Italian restaurant while you are in France. In French homes macaroni is usually boiled to almost a mush and served with a rather thin tomato sauce which contains no meat. Over this is sprinkled a little grated Swiss cheese. True, most French families consider this a Lenten dish and I suppose that it is generally eaten with a strong feeling of doing penance!

Sometimes, boiled macaroni is added to cubed chicken in a

creamy mushroom sauce as a filling for a *vol au vent,* that feathery pastry. As such, it is quite good, it absorbs readily the mushroom flavor and acts as a sort of filler. Remember it when you are preparing a rather scanty bit of leftover chicken.

Fresh homemade noodles, on the other hand, are really delicious. Simply buttered they go excellently with many dishes. Creamed chicken, roast veal with a little of the gravy poured on the noodles, are really a gourmet treat. So here is the recipe for Noodles:

FOR 4 PEOPLE:
　　2 *eggs*
　　2 *tablespoons water*
　　2 *tablespoons oil*
　　Salt
　　1 *cup (approximately) flour*
　　4 *quarts boiling water*

In a large bowl, beat together the eggs, water, oil and a pinch of salt. Add about ½ cup of flour and mix well. Now add enough flour to make a soft, pliable dough you can work with your hands. Knead well but lightly with well floured hands for several minutes. The dough must be very soft to roll out thinly later. Slightly dampen your table or a counter so that your pastry cloth will not slide. Pick a spot where you will be able to leave the dough to dry for several hours. Spread out the cloth or a large, coarse dish towel. Dust the cloth well with flour and also the rolling pin, and roll out the dough paper thin. This amount of dough should give you a rectangle roughly 18x22 inches, so be sure the dough is soft. Roll the dough like a jelly roll after leaving to dry for at least an hour. With a sharp knife, slice it in ¼-inch strips, unrolling the strips as you go.

You now have raw noodles. Dry them a little longer if you don't intend to cook them at once. You can then store them in a tightly closed container in the refrigerator for several days.

To cook the noodles: bring a large pot of salted water (4 quarts) to a boil. Add the noodles and cook for about 7 minutes or a little longer if you like your noodles soft. They should be a little more chewy than the packaged kind, though.

When the noodles are done they can be seasoned simply with pepper and fresh butter. They are also delicious with a cheese sauce or other creamy sauce or in casseroles.

An Alsatian trick with noodles is to reserve a few raw noodles and boil the rest. Chop the raw ones finely and fry them until golden in a little butter or butter and oil mixed. Sprinkle over the freshly cooked noodles or a casserole. Crunchy and delicious.

GNOCCHI

The French make two kinds of gnocchi, entirely different. One is made with chou pastry and the other with farina, called Gnocchi à la Romaine. Both are rather good. To make the usual Gnocchi:

1 recipe chou pastry,* unbaked
Salt
1 cup cream or cheese sauce
6 small baked pastry shells* OR
  1 large baked pie shell (optional)*
Grated cheese or butter

Make a batch of chou pastry and put it in a pastry bag or a large paper cone. Fit a smooth round tip or clip the tip of the paper with sharp scissors.

Have a large shallow pan or a skillet filled with gently boiling salted water. Drop little strips of chou paste, about the thickness of a pencil and an inch long, directly from the pastry bag into the water. Just press and snip off the paste with the tip of a knife or your finger. Cook 4 or 5 minutes until firm. Lift out with a slotted spoon and place in a buttered dish. Don't try to cook too many at one time or crowd them.

When all the little strips are cooked, mix them gently with a cream sauce or cheese sauce. You can now fill baked pastry shells or a large pie shell with them, sprinkle grated cheese over the top if you like or dot with butter. Or simply omit the pastry shell and bake in a buttered dish. Bake for 10 minutes in preheated 450°F. oven or until the gnocchi are piping hot and golden on top. In the pastry shells, gnocchi are usually served as a first course. They have a delicious, noodle-like flavor.

GNOCCHI À LA ROMAINE

Gnocchi à la Romaine are made with farina as a base. This is then shaped in little round slices and baked with a covering of grated cheese and butter until sizzling hot and golden. Delicious with many dishes instead of rice or potatoes.

FOR 4 PEOPLE (OR MAYBE 6!):
  3 cups milk
  ½ cup farina
  2 eggs
  1 cup grated Cheddar OR
    ½ cup grated Romano or Parmesan
  Additional ½ cup grated Romano or Parmesan
  Salt and pepper
  Butter

Bring the milk to a boil and sprinkle in the farina, stirring well to avoid lumps. Cook 5 minutes or until very thick. Beat the eggs, add a little of the hot farina to them, then stir back into the farina, mixing well, and off the fire. Beat in the cheese, reserving the other ½ cup of Romano or Parmesan for later. American Cheddar grates much coarser than Italian cheese, so you need more. Season to taste with salt and pepper, watching the salt as the cheese already adds a lot.

Pour the farina onto a well-buttered flat dish or cooky sheet, spreading it to about ½-inch thickness. Brush a little melted butter on top so that no thick skin will form, and leave to cool or chill until quite firm.

Cut this dough into small rounds with a pastry or biscuit cutter, or more simply, just cut it into small 1½-inch squares. Dip each piece in remaining ½ cup grated Romano or Parmesan cheese on both sides —it will stick to the dough—and arrange them, slightly overlapping, in a well-buttered baking dish, just as you would scalloped potatoes, but only one layer deep. Drizzle a little melted butter over all. Sprinkle any remaining grated cheese over the top and bake 10 to 15 minutes in preheated 450°F. oven until bubbling hot and golden all over. Fit for a king!

5. FISH AND SHELLFISH

POISSON POCHÉ

Basic Poached Fish Recipe

You can vary this recipe in thousands of ways and vary the name accordingly. It is the basic recipe for such delights as Fish Marguery, Normande, aux Champignons, etc. The French say, with reason, that it is the sauce which makes the fish. In the great restaurants, to make these delicious sauces, they start with *fumet de poisson,* a fragrant fish broth. The French housewife poaches the fish in a well-seasoned stock called a court bouillon and uses this stock to make the sauce. Once she has got that far, her imagination and her well-developed sense of economy take over and she finishes the sauce with whatever is at hand, is cheap or is the most likely to get her what she wants. This can, of course, go all the way from truffles for a very special occasion to that piece of leftover Swiss cheese which is only fit for grating anyway!

Practically any fish can be prepared in this manner, a large fish left whole, smaller individual fishes and even frozen fish fillets. The time of cooking is the only thing which differs. To cook a really large fish whole, the French usually have a *turbotière.* This fish kettle has a sort of slotted tray at the bottom which makes it easy to drain the fish without breaking it. You can get as good results by using a large roaster with an ordinary heat-proof dish. Place one or even two dish towels, depending on the size of the dish, under the dish and fold them over the fish. When things have cooled off a little, you can grab the ends of the towel and lift out the fish firmly and securely on its dish.

Always remove the skin and/or the bones before the fish cools. This makes the job very easy. You can then return these trimmings to the stock to cook it down and get a really strong base for your sauce.

I give you a detailed recipe for 4 trout; from there on use your imagination:

FOR 4 PEOPLE:
1 large onion
2 ribs celery with leaves
1 carrot
Bay leaf
Pinch thyme
2 or 3 sprigs parsley
Parsley root (optional)
1½ to 2 quarts (approximately) water
1 cup dry white wine
Salt and pepper
1 slice lemon
4 trout

For the sauce:
1 cup fish stock
¼ cup (½ stick) butter
3 tablespoons flour
3 egg yolks
1 cup heavy cream
Salt and pepper
Lemon juice

Start by cooking the fish. In a large kettle, place the onion, celery, carrot, a bay leaf, a good pinch of thyme, and a few sprigs of parsley. The French often add a parsley root and you can too if you grow your own. Add enough water to cover the trout, about 1½ to 2 quarts, and the cup of wine. Season lightly with salt and pepper and drop in a thick slice of lemon. Bring to a boil and leave to simmer for about 20 minutes.

Wipe the trout and gently place them in the simmering liquid. Trout are pretty firm and you should not need the dish and towel combination for this. Let them cook in barely simmering liquid. A really low simmer allows the fish to absorb the flavor of the broth and still retain their firmness. They will be done after 10 to 15 minutes. Take them out gently with the help of a large slotted spoon and pancake turner. Remove the skin and place the trout in a well-buttered baking and serving dish while you make the sauce.

Return any skins and heads or tails, etc., to the pot and let the whole boil fast, uncovered, for about 45 minutes. You only need 1 cup of this brew for the sauce; strain that much and discard the rest. Melt ¼ cup of butter in a saucepan, stir in 3 tablespoons of flour and cook until frothy and not brown. Stir in the reserved fish stock—a French wire whisk is practically a guarantee there will be no lumps —and cook until thick and smooth. Beat the egg yolks with the cream, stir a little of the hot sauce in them, return to the pot and stir well. You can gently reheat this sauce but because of the egg yolks and cream, it must not boil. Season well with salt and plenty of freshly ground black pepper, and a touch of lemon juice.

Now taste the sauce. You will probably find this absolutely delicious as is. To vary your sauce, you can add to it cooked shrimp, cooked oysters or mussels, mushrooms cooked in butter, grated cheese, and a dash of white wine or sherry. If you add all but the cheese, you practically have a Sauce Normande. Add just the cheese and you can have a Sauce Mornay. A lot of chopped parsley turns it into a Sauce Poulette, which is absolutely excellent.

Pour the sauce over the fish and place the whole in a preheated 400°F. oven, just long enough to heat the fish entirely about 15 minutes. The sauce will be lightly flecked with brown. For really glamorous occasions, try piping a border of mashed potatoes into which you have beaten an egg, all around the dish.

POISSON AU FOUR

Baked Fish

Here is a fine lazy way to prepare almost any kind of fish. Although it is ridiculously simple, it makes for fine eating. A large fish left whole, or individual fish, can be used. Trout, large perch, any fresh fish will do fine, except perhaps flounder or sole, which tend to dry too quickly, being flat. Fresh fish is best and if you have a fisherman husband you are in luck, particularly if he will clean the fish for you.

FOR 4 PEOPLE:

4 trout or perch or any good-sized fish, about 3 to 4 pounds
2 large onions
4 lemons
6 tablespoons butter
Salt and pepper
½ cup dry white wine (optional)

Clean the fish well. In France we always leave the head on, the cheek of the fish being considered the tastiest morsel imaginable. If you can't stand the thought of a cooked fish staring you in the face, you can always cover its eye with a piece of parsley or a slice of lemon.

Generously butter the bottom of a dish large enough to hold all the fish in one layer. Peel and slice thinly the onions and two of the lemons. The lemons should be peeled *à vif* (to the quick) as the French say, so that not a scrap of the white pith remains. Place about half the slices of lemon and onion at the bottom of the dish, arrange the fish on this and cover it with the remaining onion and lemon. Dot with butter and season generously with salt and pepper. Squeeze the 2 remaining lemons and sprinkle the juice over the whole dish. Bake in preheated 375°F. oven for approximately half an hour; the fish is done when you can lift the meat from the bones easily. Do this with a pointed knife along the backbone so that you don't spoil the appearance of the dish. As the fish cooks, baste it occasionally with a little wine or water—just enough to keep it moist. There should be just enough juices to bathe thinly the bottom of the pan. Serve directly from the baking dish.

Baked potatoes don't have to be reserved exclusively for steak, they go marvelously with this fish.

POISSON AU FOUR À LA GRECQUE

Baked Fish à la Grecque

This is a dish fit for the gods of Mount Olympus although I am not quite sure whether it is authentically Greek. So if you have a Greek ancestor and this is not the way she fixed fish, don't write and tell me, I suspect as much. This is delicious, though, so why worry?

FOR 4 PEOPLE:

    3 tablespoons olive oil
    2 cups coarsely chopped onions
    Pinch thyme
    Salt and pepper
    1 1-pound can whole peeled tomatoes
    2 cloves garlic, minced
    2 1-pound boxes frozen flounder fillets, thawed, OR
      about 2 pounds filleted fish
    12 ripe olives, chopped

Heat the oil in a saucepan, add the onions and dust them with a little thyme and salt and pepper. Cook until golden, then add the peeled tomatoes, the garlic, and simmer until the tomatoes are broken up and practically melted and the whole thing rather thick.

Pour half this sauce in a baking dish. Arrange the thawed fish over it and sprinkle with the chopped ripe olives and a little salt and pepper. Pour the rest of the sauce over all and bake in preheated 375°F. oven for about 30 minutes or until the fish flakes easily. Serve with rice.

POISSON GRATINÉ AUX TOMATES

Baked Fish with Tomatoes

The French are so fond of food that many of their expressions reflect it. Take *gratin* for instance, that golden, fragrant crust covering the top of cheese dishes. For a long time it has meant, in popular slang, society people, the upper crust!

This dish is a fine way to prepare frozen fish fillets for the family. Although it is not very grand, it's marvelously wholesome and usually well liked by children. They seem to enjoy the combination of tomato and cheese and, also, the frozen fillets are ideal for children as they have almost no bones.

FOR 4 PEOPLE:

4 tablespoons butter
2 tablespoons chopped onion
4 tablespoons chopped parsley
Pinch thyme
1 bay leaf
Salt and pepper
2 1-pound cans whole tomatoes OR
  2 pounds fresh (about 6 medium tomatoes)
2 1-pound boxes frozen fish fillets, thawed
1 clove garlic, minced finely
½ cup fine bread crumbs
4 tablespoons grated Parmesan, Swiss or Cheddar cheese

Melt half the butter in a large skillet, add to it the onion, parsley, pinch of thyme, the bay leaf and a dusting of salt and pepper. When beginning to brown, add the tomatoes along with their liquid and cook, uncovered, until the juice has almost completely evaporated. Don't let them burn, of course, but they don't require much watching. Shake the pan once in a while rather than stir, to keep the tomatoes whole if possible. During the tomato season, use fresh ones, the really large ones cut in thick slices.

When the tomatoes are done, spoon them gently into a large baking dish. Arrange the fish over them and season with salt and pepper. Mix the garlic with the bread crumbs and the cheese. If the children are small, they seldom like Parmesan, so you can use Swiss or Cheddar if you prefer. Sprinkle this mixture evenly over the fish and dot with the remaining butter.

Bake in preheated 375°F. oven for about 30 minutes or until the fish flakes easily and the top is an appetizing golden brown. Buttered corn, practically unknown in France, goes beautifully with this.

BARBECUE À LA FRANÇAISE

Barbecued Fish the French Way

When I first came to America I had never heard of barbecues. It seemed like such fun, however, that I promptly wrote home giving detailed instructions on how to build a barbecue pit. I was sure that the numerous teen-agers in the family would enjoy it. A short time later my mother sent me French recipes for barbecuing fish.

Some of the French recommendations would be rather hard to follow in this country. For instance they recommend using grapevine stumps instead of charcoal as they give the fish a wonderful flavor, but unless you live next to a vineyard, you may find this a little too *recherché*. Here is my version of one of the sauces.

FOR 4 PEOPLE:

> For the sauce:
> ½ *cup olive oil*
> 2 *cloves garlic, finely minced*
> 6 *anchovy fillets, chopped*
> 1 *tablespoon tomato paste*
> 1 *teaspoon paprika*
> A *few drops red pepper sauce or Tabasco sauce*
> *Salt*
>
> 4 *to 8 perch, trout or other fish, depending on size*
> *Whole thyme or rosemary* OR
>   2 *tablespoons thyme leaves*
> *Fresh butter*
> 3 *lemons*

Make the sauce with the oil, garlic, anchovies, tomato paste and paprika. Add a few drops red pepper sauce and very little salt—the anchovies have already added that. Set aside for an hour or so to let the flavors marry.

Heat the coals for the barbecue. Wipe the well-cleaned fish, brush it with the sauce and cook it over hot coals, the grill set not too high, turning and basting it several times with more sauce as it cooks. For an extra fine flavor, try wetting a few sprigs of thyme or rosemary and placing them on the coals as you turn the fish. If you cannot get whole sprigs of thyme, mix a couple of tablespoons of thyme leaves with water and sprinkle that on the coals.

When the fish is done depends on its size and the heat, so just poke it along the backbone with a knife to see if the flesh separates from the bone easily. If so, serve it immediately. Pass separately fresh butter, cold and hard, to melt on the hot fish, and cut lemons to squeeze on each mouthful.

POISSON GRILLÉ AU FENOUIL

Broiled Fish with Fennel

Fennel can be found in good supermarkets or in stores specializing in Italian fruit and vegetables. It looks like a short fat celery with very fine green feathery leaves. It has a deliciously fresh mildly anise flavor; try nibbling on a few raw pieces, cut thin.

For this recipe pick a fennel bulb with plenty of green leaves. Place the leaves on the hot coals, and they will burn slowly, giving off a deliciously fragrant smoke.

FOR 4 PEOPLE:
   1 bulb fennel
   2 to 3 pounds fish such as red snapper, trout, flounder
   Salt and pepper
   2 cloves garlic, crushed or minced finely
   ½ cup olive oil
   3 lemons
   2 or 3 very large onions
   Fresh butter

Chop the fennel finely, reserving the green leaves or tops, and stuff the cavities of the fish with it. Season with salt and pepper as you go.

Mix the crushed garlic with the olive oil, the juice of 1 lemon, and salt and pepper. Brush the fish with this. Slice the onions, but not too thinly so that they do not separate into rings.

If you are using a broiler with the heat from above, place some of the onion slices on top of the fish, or under it on an outdoor grill. Keep turning the fish, brushing it with oil and changing the onion slices for fresh ones as they burn.

Wet the fennel leaves and throw them on the hot coals as the fish cooks to give it a smoky taste. When the fish is done, from 8 to 15 minutes, depending on size, serve with fresh pats of butter and cut lemons. You don't have to eat the fennel if you don't want to. It has already flavored the fish.

POISSON EN DAUBE

Fish in a Pickle

When I was a child, this fish preparation was undoubtedly my favorite. Maria usually made it for skate, a flat fish with a sort of gelatinous bone. I have made it for other kinds of fish and find it very good. It is almost a pickle, very sharp and sour.

Don't be afraid to use fish with lots of bones. If you cook this dish very slowly, you will find that the bones almost disappear, as they do in canned fish. Fresh herring is perfect, or trout, perch, mackerel, depending on what is available.

FOR 4 PEOPLE:
   ½ cup cooking oil
   ½ cup vinegar
   1½ cups dry white wine
   2 cloves garlic, minced
   2 onions, sliced and separated into rings
   1 lemon, peeled and sliced
   1 bay leaf
   Salt and pepper
   4 to 6 medium to small fish
   Parsley for garnish

If you have a glass baking dish with a tight lid, use it. If not, make a lid with foil. But don't use a metal baking dish, I find it gives a slight taste.

Mix all the ingredients in the baking dish except the parsley and add the fish. The liquid should barely cover it. If not, add a little water. Cover tightly and bake in a slow preheated oven, 275°F., for at least 2 hours. Leave it for as long as 4 hours if you want the bones to disappear. Peek once in a while and add a little water if it seems dry. Let cool in the marinade and chill. Garnish with parsley. Makes a delicious snack or luncheon with buttered, crusty French bread.

FILETS DE POISSON À LA CRÈME

Fish Fillets in Cream

Fish and cream and mushrooms is a mouth-watering combination, and this dish is extremely easy to prepare. You can do everything well ahead of time and pop the dish into the oven as soon as your guests arrive. By the time they have finished their drinks, the fish is ready to serve. Fillet of sole is of course the most delicious fish to use. Frozen flounder fillets are cheaper, more readily available and very good also. Your budget and what is available will help you decide.

Tiny frozen potato puffs go very well with this, and they can heat in the oven while the fish is cooking. I like to add a dish of the tiniest green peas imaginable, simply warmed with a dollop of butter, a sprinkle of tarragon and ½ teaspoon of sugar. Serve a bottle of chilled dry white wine and you have an elegant dinner.

FOR 4 TO 6 PEOPLE:

12 fillets of sole OR
    2 1-pound boxes frozen flounder fillets, thawed
½ pound fresh mushrooms OR
    2 6-ounce boxes mushrooms frozen in butter
A little butter to cook fresh mushrooms
1 lemon plus wedges for garnish
Salt and pepper
4 tablespoons chopped parsley
1 teaspoon cornstarch
2 tablespoons French Dijon mustard
2 cups heavy cream
4 tablespoons bread crumbs

Cut the thawed fillets lengthwise so that you have strips about 2 inches wide. Roll each, starting from the narrow end, and stand them side by side in a well-buttered baking dish that can come to the table.

Either clean and cook the fresh mushrooms in a little butter or prepare the frozen ones according to the directions on the package. Use them to stuff the little rolls, pushing them into the centers with your finger or a spoon, keeping a few of the nicest ones to place on top of each roll. Sprinkle all with juice of 1 lemon, salt and pepper and chopped parsley.

In a small bowl, combine the cornstarch, the mustard, and the cream. Season with salt and pepper and pour this over and around the fish fillets. It will not completely cover them.

Sprinkle bread crumbs evenly over the dish, dot with butter and bake in preheated 450°F. oven for about 15 minutes or until the fish flakes easily. If the fillets are rather thick and you have doubts about the centers being quite done, cover with a piece of foil and bake 5 minutes more. Serve golden brown and sizzling with additional lemon wedges.

FILETS DE POISSON À LA FLORENTINE

Fish Fillets à la Florentine

"À la Florentine" means cooked with spinach. Spinach and fish have an affinity for each other. In this recipe I have added a few anchovies for extra flavor, but they can be omitted if you prefer.

The spinach in this case is served *en branche*, the French term for spinach meaning not chopped or puréed but with the coarse stems removed. Fresh spinach is best, of course.

FOR 4 PEOPLE:
  2 *pounds fresh spinach*
  Salt
  1 *small can flat anchovies (optional)*
  6 *tablespoons butter*
  Pepper
  1 *1-pound box frozen flounder fillets*
  1 *cup sour cream*
  ¼ *cup bread crumbs*
  4 *tablespoons grated Parmesan*

Cook the spinach in only the water that clings to the leaves after you have washed it. You need a large pot but it will cook down in no time. Season it lightly with salt and don't overcook it, it should still have a fresh green color. Drain it in a colander.

Rinse the anchovies in a little cold water to remove the excess salt. Chop them. Melt the butter in the spinach pot, add the chopped anchovies and the drained spinach and toss a few minutes over high heat. Taste and add more salt and pepper if necessary. Arrange the spinach in a well-buttered baking dish and arrange the fish fillets over that.

Season the fillets with salt and pepper and also season the sour cream in a small bowl. Pour the sour cream over the fish. Mix the bread crumbs with the grated cheese and sprinkle this in a ring along the sides of the dish. The cream is going to brown so well, you don't want to hide it, but the crumbs and cheese add a crunch which is delicious.

Bake in preheated 400°F. oven for about 25 minutes or until the fish is easily pierced with a skewer or pointed knife. Serve immediately.

PAUPIETTES DE SOLE

Sole Fillet Rolls

Here is a delicious way to stuff sole or flounder fillets. In fact, these rolls are so light and easy to eat that you had better make plenty. The dry white wine is essential in this recipe; it can be domestic or imported, but be sure it is dry. A sweet wine will not do at all!

FOR 4 PEOPLE:
   2 pounds sole or flounder fillets
   8 ounces fresh or frozen mushrooms
   4 tablespoons butter
   2 tablespoons very finely minced onion
   2 tablespoons very finely minced parsley
   4 slices day-old bread
   1 whole egg plus 2 yolks
   Pinch thyme
   Bay leaf
   Salt and pepper
   ¾ cup dry white wine
   1 cup light cream
   Juice ½ lemon

Thaw the fillets if necessary and cut them into fairly even pieces approximately 4 by 2 inches. Clean or thaw the mushrooms and chop them quite finely, then cook them in 2 tablespoons butter along with the onion and parsley. The mixture should just begin to get brown. Dip the bread very briefly in water and squeeze out as much as you can; place it in a bowl. Add to it the mushroom mixture, 1 egg, a little pinch of thyme, the bay leaf, and season well with salt and pepper to make a savory stuffing.

Place a little of this stuffing on each little strip of fish and roll up as you would a jelly roll. Fasten with toothpicks or a few twists of white cotton thread. Generously grease a baking dish with the rest of the butter and place the rolls upright in it. Pour in the wine and just enough water to come about halfway up the little rolls. Cover the dish with a buttered piece of white paper or aluminum foil and pop it in the oven at 400°F. (preheated) for about 20 minutes. The fish is done when it flakes easily. Carefully remove the fillets with a spatula to a serving dish which can stand the heat of the broiler. Cover to keep them warm while you quickly make the sauce.

Pour the juices from the fish pan into a small saucepan and cook over high heat until reduced to just a few spoonfuls. Remove from the fire. Beat 2 egg yolks with the cream, season with salt and pepper and stir into the slightly cooled juices. Reheat over hot water or a very low fire just until slightly thickened. It should just coat the spoon. Taste and correct seasoning if necessary and add lemon juice. Pour over the fish and place under the broiler just a few minutes until flecked with brown. This last is not absolutely necessary but it ensures that the dish is piping hot and the brown flecks look appetizing.

PAIN DE POISSON

Fish Loaf

Fish loaf can be absolutely delicious, definitel·ʳ gourmet fare, particularly if you take a few pains with the sauce.

The best fish to use for this dish is fresh salmon. If you can get it, this is a good way to stretch this rather expensive fish so that 1 pound of it will serve four. Any other kind of fresh or frozen fish will make a good loaf, though, and you can even make it with canned salmon as a budget stretcher. The finest-tasting loaf is made with fresh or frozen raw fish.

FOR 4 PEOPLE:
1 cup thick white sauce made with:
¼ cup butter
¼ cup flour
1 cup milk
Salt and pepper

*1 pound fresh or frozen fish, flounder, salmon, sole, ocean
perch, etc.*
3 slices day-old bread
*3 or 4 tablespoons dry white wine or sherry mixed with
equal amount of water*
1 whole egg plus 1 yolk
4 tablespoons finely chopped parsley
2 tablespoons finely chopped onion
Salt and pepper
Lemon juice
Butter

For the sauce:
12 oysters
3 egg yolks
1 cup cream
Salt and pepper
2 teaspoons chopped parsley

Start by making the white sauce, as it should have time to cool. Melt ¼ cup butter in a small pan, add the flour and cook until frothy. Gradually stir in the milk and cook until very thick. Season with salt and pepper, cover with wax paper or plastic film so that no skin will form and set aside. Remove any skin and bones from the fish with a very sharp knife, and chop the raw fish very finely. Put it in a large bowl and add to it the bread, dipped in water and white wine or sherry and squeezed dry. Mix well with a fork then beat in the white sauce, 1 whole egg plus 1 yolk, the parsley and onion, chopped very, very finely, and salt and pepper. When all is well mixed, grease generously an oblong baking dish and shape the fish into a loaf in it. Sprinkle lightly with lemon juice, dot the top with a little butter and bake in preheated oven at 375°F. for 45 minutes. Place another pan filled with hot water in the oven so it will give a moist heat.

To make the sauce: place the oysters in a small pan together with their liquor and heat to simmering. As soon as the oysters are nice and plump, take them out with a slotted spoon. Beat the 3 egg yolks with the cream, and add to the slightly cooled oyster juices. Season generously with salt and plenty of freshly ground black pepper. Cook over a very low heat or over hot water until slightly thickened. Do not let it boil, the eggs will curdle. Return the oysters to the sauce with a couple of spoonfuls of chopped parsley. Serve the fish loaf directly from the baking dish and pass the sauce separately.

RAÏTO

Fish Sauce with Nuts

Cooking in the South of France is as bright and sunny as the climate. Colorful tomatoes, eggplant, green peppers, golden olive oil, saffron bright as the sun, olives and garlic, garlic everywhere. In fact, if you don't like garlic, you can be quite miserable in Southern France. Everything and everybody is slightly redolent of it!

The following recipe is usually prepared with salt cod, which is not easily obtainable in all parts of the country. Although some people are very fond of it I find it too reminiscent of cod-liver oil, so I don't use it often. Instead of cod you may use frozen cooked breaded fish fillets or fish sticks. But the sauce is something else again. Tomatoes, white wine, simmered with sweet herbs, and at the last moment the surprise addition of walnuts. The fish served with it is first fried and then added to the sauce and kept warm a little while so that the flavor of the sauce can permeate it. Truly a great dish.

FOR ENOUGH SAUCE FOR 4 LARGE
SERVINGS OF FRIED FISH:

   2 cups fish stock or water and bottled clam juice
   4 tablespoons olive oil
   2 tablespoons flour
   2 large onions, minced
   *4 large tomatoes, peeled and seeded, or 1 1-pound can
      tomatoes, drained*
   2 cups dry white wine
   1 clove
   4 large cloves garlic, minced
   Pinch thyme, sweet basil and/or rosemary
   Bay leaf
   Salt and pepper
   12 walnuts
   1 tablespoon capers
   Chopped olives

If you are using fresh fish, you can make stock with the trimmings, heads, water and an onion, celery and carrot. If you are using frozen fish substitute 1 cup of water and 1 cup bottled clam juice.

Heat the olive oil in a nice heavy pot. Add the flour and cook until it is a nice golden brown. Add the onions and stir until they are transparent. Add the tomatoes, 2 cups of dry white wine, 2 cups of fish stock, the clove, garlic and herbs. A little pinch of this, a little pinch of that, don't go overboard. Bring to a boil and leave to simmer. Season with a little salt and pepper, taking into account that this is going to cook down a lot. Cook until reduced by half. Stir once in a while. This will take about an hour.

Fifteen minutes or so before serving add to the sauce large pieces of walnuts, the capers and some chopped olives. Place the pieces of fried fish in the sauce and leave in a warm place, without further cooking, so the fish and sauce blend their flavors.

SALADE DU VENDREDI SAINT

Herring Salad

This salad has always been served on Good Friday in my family, but it is so good that we had it at other times too! It is a wonderful mixture of white beans, apples and herring mixed with mayonnaise and served cold. This is a main dish salad; served with brown bread it makes a complete meal in a dish. Though unusual here, it is quite common in Dutch countries.

The first herrings of the season are the best and highly prized in Holland and Belgium. They are not as highly salted as later on; the eggs, spread on toast and sprinkled with lemon juice, make a wonderful democratic caviar. Any of the "rollmops" or pickled herring fillets available at the supermarket will do just fine for the salad.

FOR 4 PEOPLE:
>   1 1-pound can red beets
>   Vinegar
>   ½ pound dried navy beans
>   Salt
>   1 or 2 apples
>   ½ cup mayonnaise
>   1 celery heart
>   1 8-ounce jar herring fillets, drained
>   Pepper

Drain the beets, drench with vinegar and allow them to stand for several hours. Cook the white beans in water with very little salt until they are just tender, approximately 45 minutes to 1 hour. Drain them well and set aside to cool. Peel and core the apples, cut them in small pieces the size of the beans, place them in a large salad bowl and immediately add mayonnaise to them so they will not brown. Chop finely the whitest stalks of a small celery and add. Cut the herring fillets in very small pieces and add. If you have bought the rolled fillets with onion inside, you could chop a little of it also. Mix in the cooled beans with enough mayonnaise to bind the whole. At serving time add the drained beets. If you wish you can arrange them in a pretty pattern on top of the salad. Season lightly with salt and pepper. Serve with hot crusty French bread.

TRUITES AUX AMANDES

Trout Amandine

The finest Truite aux Amandes I ever ate was in a small restaurant in Versailles. We had tramped through the magnificent chateau and gardens most of the day and were tired and starving. From the outside, it looked like just another small café and we walked in thinking of a good but simple meal which would not wreck our budget. The inside was charming, cool and rather dark with a delightful smell of fine foods. By then we knew the budget was irretrievably forgotten but we were too hungry to care. We were served wonderful trout, firm and freshly caught, accompanied by a superb white wine. Strangely enough, when some weeks later we felt like splurging and tried to find the restaurant again, it had disappeared and no one seemed to have ever heard of it. It can't have been a mirage. . . .

FOR 4 PEOPLE:

4 large trout, about 3 pounds
A little flour
3 tablespoons cooking oil
¼ pound (1 stick) butter
Salt and pepper
½ cup slivered, blanched almonds
4 tablespoons dry white wine
½ cup thick heavy cream
Lemon wedges

Wipe the trout carefully on paper towels and roll them in a little flour. Shake off the excess. This is not to coat the fish, but to ensure that it is perfectly dry. Heat the oil in a heavy pan large enough to hold 2 trout, then add half the butter to it. As soon as the butter is melted add the fish. When one side is golden, turn them over carefully with a large spatula and cook the other side. Take your time, count 10 to 15 minutes per side. Season with salt and pepper as you go, and the trout will brown prettily. Add more butter as necessary. Keep these warm in oven and cook remaining fish.

While trout are kept warm in oven, add the almonds to the butter left in the pan and toss and shake them over the fire so they will brown evenly. Watch it, they burn very easily. Add more butter if the pan seems dry. When they are golden, spoon them evenly over the fish.

Pour just a little wine in the pan and stir and scrape until wine and butter are well mixed with any juices at the bottom of the pan. Then add the cream and let it get hot without boiling. Add a little salt and pepper, pour over the trout and serve immediately. Pass wedges of lemon separately.

MATELOTE

Eels in Red Wine

This is a traditional preparation for eels, and despite their unfortunate resemblance to snakes, eels make very good eating. If you get one, ask a stout-hearted member of the family to skin it for you. Tell him to slit the skin just below the gills and peel it off like a tight kid glove. Once the eel is cut into 2 or 3 inch pieces, you will forget completely that it looks like anything but fish.

If you cannot get an eel or you prefer other fish, you can use any good firm fish for this recipe, and utilize this delicious red wine sauce.

FOR 4 PEOPLE:
> ¼ pound (1 stick) butter
> 12 very small onions
> Salt and pepper
> 10 or 12 good-size pieces of eel or firm fish (2 to 3 inches each)
> 1 bottle dry light red wine
> Bouquet garni made with bay leaf, thyme, parsley
> 4 tablespoons flour

Melt about 2 tablespoons of butter in a large pot and gently cook the onions until they are golden on all sides. Dust them lightly with salt and pepper and remove them when brown. Gently cook the fish in the same butter, adding a little more if necessary. Return the onions to the pot and pour in just enough red wine to cover the fish. Add the bouquet garni and a good seasoning of salt and pepper. Simmer very gently until the fish is done, anywhere from 10 to 25 minutes, depending on the kind of fish. If it flakes easily from the bone, it is ready.

In a cup or small bowl, mix equal amounts of flour and butter. Work both well together with the back of a spoon. Now drop teaspoonfuls of this paste into the simmering fish liquid, shaking the pan gently as it melts. This will thicken the sauce, so add just a little at a time and shake and cook a few minutes before adding more. The sauce should be glossy and just thick enough to coat the fish nicely. Shaking the pan instead of stirring will prevent the fish from being broken to pieces. Serve with boiled potatoes or crisp French bread. This dish will reheat well providing you handle things gently, and do not to break up the pieces of fish.

ANGUILLES AU VERT

Eels in Green Sauce

Fresh-water eels are a great favorite in certain parts of Belgium. I remember a restaurant, ideally situated near a lake, which served nothing but eels and steak. The eels were either fried and served with tartar sauce or served chilled in green sauce.

As eels are not very easy to get, you can make this delicious dish with other kinds of fish, especially mackerel and large shrimp.

FOR 4 PEOPLE:

> 2 or 3 eels, prepared as for Matelote OR
>   8 or 10 pieces of firm fish
> 4 tablespoons butter
> Salt and pepper
> 1 small clove garlic, minced
> ½ cup finely chopped parsley, green onion tops and
>   spinach, mixed
> 1 tablespoon cheril (diced)
> 1 pinch sage and/or thyme
> 2 cups dry white wine
> 4 egg yolks
> Juice 1 or 2 lemons

Skin the eels and cut them in pieces as for the Matelote, or cut the fish in small serving pieces. Wash fish in cold water and dry the pieces on paper towels.

Melt the butter in a nice heavy pot, season the fish with salt and pepper and brown it gently in the hot butter. As soon as it is slightly golden on all sides, remove it with a slotted spoon. Add the garlic, the mixture of parsley, green onion tops and spinach and the herbs to the butter and cook just until limp, a few minutes. Pour in the wine, season with a little more salt and pepper, and as soon as the mixture comes to a simmer, add the fish. Cook for about 10 minutes or until fish or eel separates easily from the bones. Remove the fish again with a slotted spoon and place it in a serving dish.

Beat the egg yolks with the juice of 1 lemon. Add a little of the hot wine sauce to them, stir and return all to the pot, stirring vigorously. If you are no expert at making custards, do this off the fire and let the sauce cool a little. Reheat gently over a very low fire or over hot water, stirring all the time, until the mixture thickens. Do not let it boil or it will curdle. Taste and add a little more lemon juice if you think it needs it. It should be quite sharp and tangy. Pour over the fish and mix gently and thoroughly. Chill well before serving.

BOILED CRABS

I received this recipe from a charming Italian gentleman with whom I traded recipes for several hours a day once. We met in a hospital waiting room and whiled away rather anxious hours talking about food. I shall always be grateful to him, because through his words I escaped the dreary, antiseptic hospital world for a few hours a day and was back to my own kitchen.

Here is his recipe for boiled crabs, but it is equally good for shrimp:

FOR ABOUT 2 DOZEN CRABS:
5 parts salt
1 part black pepper
1 part paprika
1 part dry mustard
1 part celery salt
Few drops hot pepper sauce

Mix all the dry ingredients together; they can be stored in a jar if you boil crabs often. Use about 2 tablespoons to each quart of water to boil crabs. Cook the crabs quickly in boiling water. As soon

as they are done, take them out and let them cool a little. Break the
shells open and pour on the meaty part the following dressing:

> *6 tablespoons olive oil*
> *2 tablespoons lemon juice*
> *1 clove garlic, finely minced*
> *2 tablespoons finely chopped parsley*

Use as much dressing as necessary to moisten the crabs and add
a few tablespoons of the liquid the crabs boiled. in. Allow to stand
in a cool place for at least an hour.

Whether you then decide to pick all the meat out yourself and
serve a delicious and dainty crab salad over lettuce leaves, or whether
you let each pick his own crab is entirely up to you. While the second
way is messier, it is certainly a lot of fun and tastes even better!

If you cannot get fresh crabs, try pouring the dressing on lump
crab meat, canned or frozen, and leaving it to marinate a few hours
in the refrigerator.

LANGOUSTE À L'ORIENTALE

Rock Lobster Orientale

"À l'orientale" in French cuisine means served over rice, generally with tomatoes, sometimes with saffron. This casserole dish is a
nice one when you are planning on having guests and have little
preparation time.

As casseroles go, it is generally well accepted by men. Most men
have a deep suspicion of casseroles; they like to see what they are
eating I believe. In this casserole, the shellfish is well in evidence on
top of the dish, tempting to anyone. You can use the little frozen South
African lobster tails, or scallops or even large shrimp for this dish
and there is no reason why you can't use a mixture of all three if you
feel like it.

FOR 4 PEOPLE:

4 tablespoons butter
1 large onion, chopped
1 1-pound can whole tomatoes, drained
1 clove garlic, minced
Pinch thyme
Bay leaf
1½ cups raw rice
1½ cups water
Salt and pepper
1½ to 2 pounds (approximately) raw shellfish: rock lobster,
    shrimp or scallops (if frozen fish, thaw first)

For the sauce:
1 cup tomato sauce
4 tablespoons sherry
1 teaspoon Worcestershire sauce
1 cup heavy cream

Use a casserole or dish that can be used on top of the stove as well as in the oven. Heat the butter and cook the chopped onion for a few minutes until barely golden. Add the tomatoes, garlic, a pinch of thyme and a bay leaf and simmer for 10 minutes. Remove the bay leaf and add the rice with 1½ cups of water, salt and pepper. Cook, covered, on top of the stove for another 10 minutes or until the rice is swollen but not cooked, and the mixture is still very mushy.

Split rock lobster tails in two lengthwise; this takes a sharp, heavy knife and a good blow on the handle of the knife. Leave in the lobster shell. However, peel the shrimp if you are using them. De-vein them if you like. Arrange the shellfish on top of the casserole and dot with a little butter. Place, uncovered, in a preheated 375°F. oven and cook for about 20 to 25 minutes or until the rice and the fish are quite done. If you prepare the casserole in advance except for the baking, you may have to add a little water if the mixture seems too dry.

Make the sauce by starting with 1 cup of good thick tomato sauce, your own or a good canned brand. Heat it with the sherry and the Worcestershire sauce and add the cream at the last moment. Let it get hot and pass it separately.

CREVETTES À L'AMÉRICAINE

Shrimp à l'Américaine

This recipe is actually intended for lobster. Homard à l'Américaine or Armoricaine is featured on the menus of most famous French restaurants. Some say the first name is correct and that the dish was invented for some visiting American. Others insist the second version is right, Armorique being the old name of Brittany, which is famous for its lobsters. To which the first reply that the Bretons always eat their lobster cold with mayonnaise. In any case, this is a marvelous preparation. Unfortunately lobster is not an everyday dish for most of us, and even for special occasions is rather hard on the budget. However, shrimp fixed this way make a really glorious dish, fit for a king. Jumbo shrimp are ideal, but the smaller ones will taste as good. They will just take a little longer to shell.

FOR 4 PEOPLE:

6 to 8 really large shrimp per person or about 3 pounds in all. In order of preference: 1) Fresh with the heads on, if possible; 2) Frozen in the shell; 3) Frozen, peeled

4 tablespoons olive oil
¼ cup brandy
1 cup white wine
1 rib celery
1 onion
Salt and pepper
4 large tomatoes
½ clove garlic, finely minced
Lemon juice
4 tablespoons butter
Chopped fresh parsley

Rinse briefly the unpeeled shrimp in cold water to remove any sand. Drain well, leave the heads and/or the shells on. Heat the oil in a large heavy pot, add the shrimp and stir them quickly over high heat until the shrimp turn bright pink. Remove from the fire, immediately pour in the brandy and touch a match to the pot. Have a lighted match in one hand while you pour in the brandy with the other.

Let the shrimp cool a little and then shell them. Set them aside and return all the shells and heads (if any) to the pot. Pour the wine over these, add just enough water to cover them, a stick of celery, an onion, a little salt and pepper and bring to a simmer. Leave to cook for about 45 minutes to an hour, crushing the shells down once in a while with a heavy spoon or potato masher in order to extract all their flavor. Strain the whole thing and if necessary cook the juice down some more, until you have 1 cup.

While the shells are simmering, peel the tomatoes, cut them in two and squeeze them gently to press out the seeds. Chop them finely.

In a smaller pot, place the tomatoes, the garlic, the broth from the shrimp shells and cook until the tomatoes have practically melted. Add the shrimp and cook very gently for a few more minutes, until they are tender. Taste and season sharply with a little salt if necessary, a few drops of lemon juice and plenty of freshly ground black pepper. Add the butter, in small pieces, boil fiercely for a few seconds to melt and blend it in; serve, sprinkled with fresh parsley.

Serve simply with little triangles of bread fried a deep gold in enough oil to cover the bottom of a skillet. Add a pat of butter for flavor. Rice goes very well too.

CREVETTES À LA CHINOISE

Chinese Shrimp

Would a Chinese recognize these shrimp? Probably not, but there is soy sauce in the preparation. Don't be fooled by the utter simplicity of this recipe. It is very quick to make but tastes as if you had spent hours preparing it. A very good dish to prepare for spur-of-the-moment invitations. Serve with freshly boiled rice.

FOR 4 PEOPLE:
   2 pounds fresh or 2 1-pound boxes frozen shrimp
   3 tablespoons oil
   2 tablespoons (approximately) soy sauce
   Salt and pepper
   1 clove garlic, finely minced
   1 bunch scallions (6 to 8)
   1 tablespoon sugar
   1 teaspoon cornstarch
   ½ cup dry white wine

Wash and peel the shrimp. Heat the oil in a large skillet, add the shrimp and toss them over high heat until they turn pink. Season well with soy sauce, very little salt (the soy sauce is very salty), pepper and the finely minced garlic.

Wash the green onions, trim off their roots and chop them in ½-inch pieces, including as much of the green as you can, provided it is crisp and fresh. Mix the sugar and the cornstarch together and stir in the wine, in a small cup or bowl. Add the onions to the shrimp, heat briefly and pour in the wine mixture. Stir until thickened and bubbly. Correct seasoning to taste. *Voilà!* Ready to serve over freshly cooked rice. The onions should be still rather firm for the best flavor.

CREVETTES À LA MEUNIÈRE

Shrimp Meunière

Meunière means the miller's wife in French. It is applied to a way of preparing fish by lightly dusting it with flour and sautéing it in butter until golden. The flour serves more to dry the fish thoroughly than to coat it. It just ensures it will not stick to the pan and will come out evenly brown.

Whether the name means that the miller's wife would naturally use flour on her fish, or whether the fish looks like the miller's wife because it is covered with flour, I have never been able to determine. This recipe, which is a slight variation on the usual meunière recipe, is a simple and very good way to fix some fairly large shrimp.

FOR 4 PEOPLE:
   1½ to 2 pounds fairly large shrimp
   ¼ cup flour
   4 tablespoons butter
   2 green onions, finely chopped
   4 tablespoons chopped parsley
   1 clove garlic, minced
   Salt and pepper
   ½ cup dry white wine

Peel and de-vein the shrimp and place on paper towels to dry them. Put the flour in a paper bag, add the shrimp a few at a time, and shake to coat lightly with flour. They should have the thinnest possible coating of flour.

Heat the butter in a large skillet. As soon as it stops singing (sizzling), add the shrimp. Sprinkle with the chopped onions, parsley and garlic and keep tossing them over high heat until the shrimp have turned pink on all sides. Season with plenty of pepper and not too much salt. Turn the heat to low, add the wine and stir and scrape until the wine has dissolved any brown bits at the bottom of the pan. Simmer a few minutes to finish cooking the shrimp. Delicious simply as is with French bread or with rice or French fries.

NOUILLES OSTENDAISES

Ostend Noodles

Ostendaise in Belgium is applied to any dish that contains shrimp, for which the port of Ostend is famous. This recipe is for a casserole of noodles with a rich cheese sauce and plenty of shrimp. The combination is marvelous, particularly if you put lots of cheese on top and let it turn to a golden, sizzling layer.

If you make this dish with fresh homemade noodles, you can serve it to your most discriminating friends. The recipe for noodles is given separately.

FOR 4 PEOPLE:
> 4 cups freshly cooked noodles°
> Salt
> 2 tablespoons butter
> Black pepper
> 2 cups cooked peeled shrimp plus a little shrimp cooking
>   liquid
> 2 cups cheese sauce as follows:
> 4 tablespoons butter
> 4 tablespoons flour
> 1½ cups milk
> ¼ pound grated cheese (Cheddar or Gruyère mixed with
>   1 or 2 tablespoons Parmesan)

Cook the noodles in plenty of boiling salted water until just tender. Drain and toss them with 2 tablespoons butter and a little black pepper.

Make the cheese sauce by melting the butter in a small saucepan, adding the flour and cooking until frothy. Gradually stir in the milk and cook until thickened. Add the cheese (reserving 4 or 5 tablespoons for later). Stir until it is melted. Then add a couple of tablespoonfuls of shrimp liquid to make a velvety sauce. Season to taste with salt and pepper, remembering that the cheese has already added salt.

Place a layer of noodles in a casserole dish, a layer of shrimp, some of the sauce, and repeat until all is used up, finishing with the sauce. Sprinkle with plenty of grated cheese and bake until golden at 400°F. about 20 minutes.

HUÎTRES GRATINÉES AU PARMESAN

Oysters Parmesan

Hilaire Belloc said, somewhat condescendingly I fear, "Colonials like their oysters hot. . . ." It is true that in France and Belgium oysters are seldom cooked, and I attribute this to their high price. Personally I love cooked oysters. Here is a delightfully simple way to start a special meal. If you are very busy, you should use the shucked oysters and bake them in a dish. If you have the time, though, bake the oysters in their shells, more elegant and tastier too. This recipe serves 4 very generously. You could halve it (or serve 8) if you plan a filling dish to follow.

FOR 4 OR 8 PEOPLE:
   4 dozen oysters
   ½ cup dry white wine
   ¼ pound (1 stick) butter
   6 tablespoons grated Parmesan
   1 cup (approximately) bread crumbs
   4 tablespoons finely minced parsley
   Pepper

If you are using oysters in the shell, reserve 2 dozen of the nicest, deepest shells; scrub and dry them. It is much easier to serve 2 oysters in each shell! Six shells fit very nicely in rock salt on an ordinary pie pan.

Poach the oysters in their own juice and the ½ cup of white wine as follows: put them all in a deep skillet with the wine and simmer. As soon as the oysters are nice and plump, remove them with a slotted spoon and let the juices boil down. When you have just a thin layer of thick juice covering the bottom of the pan, stir in half the butter, let it melt and pour over the oysters. Mix well and then place in individual baking dishes or place 2 oysters and a little juice in each shell.

Mix in a small bowl the grated Parmesan, the bread crumbs and the parsley. Sprinkle this mixture evenly over the oysters and pepper them generously with freshly ground black pepper. Dot with the remaining butter. Refrigerate.

At serving time, bake in preheated oven at 400°F. for about 10 minutes or until the whole dish sizzles. Serve very hot.

HUÎTRES À L'ESCARGOT

Oysters in Snail Butter

Mussels are practically a national dish in Belgium. Many small restaurants build a reputation serving nothing but this delicious shellfish along with enormous bowls of French fries.

Sometimes cooked mussels are reheated in the same butter sauce that is used for snails. Mussels in snail butter were my favorite delicacy, one I would cheerfully walk ten miles for, which is a good idea in any case, to work off the extra calories. Alas, when I came to Louisiana, no mussels! Oysters, though, were plentiful and much cheaper than in Belgium, so this dish came into being one day when I was particularly homesick. I find these oysters in snail sauce better than snails even, and everyone who has ever eaten them, tends to agree with me. Also, this was the very first recipe of mine to be printed, so it's naturally one of my favorites. Halve the recipe for hors d'oeuvre.

FOR 4 PEOPLE:
    4 dozen oysters
    1 cup finely chopped parsley
    4 large cloves garlic, minced very finely
    ½ pound (2 sticks) butter
    Salt and pepper

If you are using oysters in the shell, reserve 2 dozen of the nicest, deepest shells, scrub and dry them. If you are using oysters in a jar or can, proceed.

Place the shucked oysters with their liquid in a large skillet and heat until bubbling. As soon as the oysters look nice and plump, just a few minutes, lift them out with a slotted spoon and place them in a bowl. Leave the liquid in the pan and cook it down to almost nothing. There should just be a couple of tablespoons of rich thick, brownish juice. Let this cool.

Chop enough parsley quite finely to make 1 cup. Mince the garlic very, very finely. I know that garlic presses have been invented and that you can buy garlic purée but really, in this case, finely minced garlic tastes best.

Cream the butter (no margarine please) with the parsley and garlic and beat in the oyster juices, not forgetting the juice which has accumulated at the bottom of the oyster bowl. Season with very little salt and plenty of black pepper. Taste and add a little more black pepper!

If you are using the shells, place 2 oysters in each with a good dab of the butter. Or mix the butter with the oysters in a bowl. At serving time have the oven very hot: 450°F. Arrange the oyster shells in pie pans filled with rock salt or in a baking dish. Pop in the oven and heat until sizzling but no longer. It should get piping hot but not have a chance to cook. Serve immediately with plenty of French bread to mop up every last bit of sauce.

If you prefer, these oysters can be heated in a chafing dish and served fondue style with cubes of French bread.

Any time you can get mussels, use them instead of the oysters. They could be left over from Moules Marinières or simply cooked in the shell in ½ cup dry white wine until they are open and plump. Then proceed as above. (See next recipe for cooking mussels in general.)

MOULES OU HUÎTRES À LA POULETTE

Mussels or Oysters Poulette

In Belgium, they serve a dish of mussels à la Poulette, which would turn a saint into a glutton! You are brought a huge pot, full of mussels cooked in their shells and bathing in a fragrant, creamy sauce flecked with lots of parsley. If you cannot get mussels, you can make it with oysters, out of their shells, and get an even finer dish. Whether you decide it's a soup or not, is up to you. It is certainly a satisfying main dish simply served with hot crusty French bread. See insert at end of recipe.

FOR 4 PEOPLE:

> 4 dozen shucked oysters in all or about
> 2 dozen mussels per person, depending on their size
> 4 tablespoons butter
> 4 tablespoons each chopped parsley, celery with leaves and onions or shallots
> Salt and pepper
> 1 cup white wine
> 4 egg yolks
> 1 cup heavy cream
> 4 more tablespoons chopped parsley

Scrub the mussels and leave them in the shell or shuck oysters.

Melt the butter in a large pot, add 4 tablespoons each chopped parsley, celery and onions to it, dust with a little salt and pepper and cook until wilted but not brown. Pour in the wine and as soon as it comes to a simmer, add the mussels or oysters. With mussels, let them cook in the steam of the wine until open and plump, over a rather high fire. Remove them to another pot with a slotted spoon and keep warm. With oysters: cook them in the wine until just plumped, keeping the fire low and the liquid just at a simmer so they do not get tough. Leave in the liquid and proceed.

Beat the egg yolks with the cream in a small bowl. Season generously with salt and pepper. Pour a little of the hot liquid from oysters or mussels into the cream, return all to the pot and heat very gently. Do not let it boil. Add the 4 more tablespoons of chopped parsley, plenty of freshly ground black pepper. Pour this over the hot mussels and serve immediately. The oysters can be served in bowls.

If you stop this recipe before adding the cream and egg yolk, you get Moules Marinières.

BROCHETTES DE COQUILLES ST. JACQUES

Scallops en Brochettes

Thyme and rosemary combine with scallops and jumbo shrimp to give this dish a wonderful flavor. For the sauce, the sharp flavor of anchovies will complement the mildness of fresh cream and a good dash of paprika will give the whole a lovely pink color.

Unless you live in the East you will almost certainly have to use frozen scallops. In France, where I bought them fresh, scallops have a delicious red part, called the coral, which is highly esteemed. I suppose it must not freeze well but I miss it, although the frozen scallops are delicious.

FOR 4 PEOPLE:
> *1 1-pound package frozen scallops* OR
>   *at least 1 dozen sea scallops* OR
>   *2 to 3 dozen bay scallops*
> *12 jumbo shrimp*
> *Salt and pepper*
> *1 teaspoon thyme, crushed*
> *1 teaspoon rosemary, crushed*
> *A little flour*
> *2 tablespoons oil*
> *2 tablespoons butter*

> For the sauce:
> *1 flat can anchovy fillets*
> *12 ripe olives*
> *1 cup heavy cream*
> *Salt, if needed*
> *2 teaspoons (approximately) paprika*
> *Pepper*

When using frozen scallops, defrost them. Peel and de-vein the shrimp. Take small skewers, preferably wooden ones, and alternate on them shrimp and scallops. Season with salt and pepper and roll them in crushed thyme and rosemary. A teaspoon of each should be sufficient for the whole dish. Dust the brochettes with a little flour and shake off any excess.

Take a skillet which will go in the oven without damage. Heat the oil in it and then add the butter. When all is sizzling, add the brochettes and cook them gently until golden on all sides. Pop the skillet into the oven preheated to 400°F. and leave it for 5 minutes or so, to make sure the fish is cooked all the way through. You could do the first step well ahead of time and reheat the dish in the oven at the last moment, but you should then heat it in the oven a little longer.

The sauce is delicious and so simple, you may want to use it with other seafood or fish dishes sometime. Drain the anchovies and soak them in cold water for a few minutes to remove excess salt. Drain and chop or mash them very finely. Chop the olives also.

Have the cream well chilled and whip it until it is beginning to thicken, not quite as stiff as for desserts. Fold in the anchovies and olives, taste and add salt if necessary. Stir in the paprika, about 2 teaspoons, and just a good dusting of black pepper. It will keep several hours or overnight in the refrigerator, so you may want to make it ahead of time.

Serve the brochettes piping hot with the chilled sauce separately. An unusual combination, but it works superbly!

COQUILLES ST. JACQUES À LA PARISIENNE

Scallops à la Parisienne

Scallops, with their taste reminiscent of lobster, deserve good treatment. They are fine just fried, but a little care and the addition of mushrooms and cream really brings out their finest possibilities. "À la Parisienne" means with mushrooms. The nice little white cultivated mushrooms are called Champignons de Paris for the very good reason that they grow in cellars all over the Paris region.

You can buy scallop shells in many variety stores. They make fine individual baking dishes.

FOR 4 PEOPLE:
    Stock:
    1 small onion
    1 stalk celery
    1 bay leaf
    1 slice lemon
    2 cups water
    Pinch salt and pepper

    ½ cup dry white wine
    1 pound frozen scallops, thawed
    1 6-ounce package mushrooms frozen in butter OR
        6 to 8 fresh mushrooms plus butter to cook them in
    4 tablespoons butter
    3 tablespoons flour
    2 egg yolks
    1 cup cream
    Salt and pepper, if needed
    A little lemon juice

Make a little court bouillon (or stock to cook the shellfish): place the onion, celery and bay leaf with a slice of lemon in a 2 quart pot, add 2 cups of water and a good pinch of salt and pepper. Bring to a boil and simmer for 10 minutes. Add the white wine and the thawed scallops. Simmer for 5 to 10 minutes depending on the size of the scallops. They are done when creamy colored all the way through. Don't overcook them. As soon as they are done, drain them and reserve the liquid carefully. Return it to the pot and cook it down to 1 cup.

Cook the frozen mushrooms according to package directions without letting them get too brown. If you can get fresh mushrooms, wipe them and cook them in a little butter. Set aside.

Make a cream sauce by melting the butter then adding the flour to it and cooking until frothy. Gradually add the scallop liquid, stirring until smooth and bubbly. Beat the egg yolks with the cream, remove the sauce from heat, and beat in the cream-egg mixture. Add the mushrooms and scallops, mix well, taste, and correct seasoning if necessary. A little lemon juice will perk up the taste. Now all is ready for the final reheating, which you can put off until the next day, if you should be so minded!

Simply spoon the scallops and their sauce into a large, rather flat baking dish or individual dishes or shells. Pop under the preheated broiler until heated through and flecked with brown. Serve with a flourish! If you want to be quite fancy, pipe or spoon a border of mashed potatoes around the dish or shells. They brown delightfully and taste delicious with the sauce.

CUISSES DE GRENOUILLE À LA PROVENÇALE

Frog Legs Provençale

In spite of all the publicity given to the fact that Frenchmen eat frogs, this isn't very common. Frog legs are quite a delicacy and many a Frenchman would envy the ease with which they can be picked up in American supermarkets.

"À la Provençale" means garlic! Lots of it mixed with parsley, toned down a little with bread crumbs and browned in the oven. Tomatoes are often served this way. Wait until you taste what it does for frog legs!

FOR 4 PEOPLE:
4 to 6 frog legs (approximately) per person
A little flour
4 tablespoons olive or cooking oil
Salt and pepper
2 cloves garlic, chopped very finely
½ cup minced parsley
1 cup fresh bread crumbs, made from day-old bread
4 tablespoons butter

Thaw the frog legs, if frozen, wipe them and roll them in a little flour. Heat the olive or cooking oil in a large skillet and gently fry the frog legs, seasoning them with salt and pepper as you go. Do this gently, taking your time. Frog meat is very like chicken and very tender. Remove the legs to a dish to keep warm in the oven.

Pour off any oil remaining in the pan. Mix the chopped garlic with the parsley and the bread crumbs. Melt the butter in the skillet, stir and scrape any juices remaining after you poured off the oil, toss in the bread crumbs-garlic mixture and mix well. Sprinkle this over the frog legs and pop them under the preheated broiler just long enough to get everything sizzling hot. Serve with a good white wine or "rosé de Provence."

CUISSES DE GRENOUILLES AUX CHAMPIGNONS

Frog Legs with Mushrooms

This is a rather different recipe for frog legs which you should especially enjoy if the idea of cooking with beer intrigues you. Large French fried onion rings made with beer-flavored batter go well with it, and I've included the recipe here.

FOR 4 PEOPLE:
  2 dozen (approximately) frog legs, fresh or frozen
  Salt and pepper
  1 can (10 or 12 ounces) beer
  Flour
  ¼ cup olive or cooking oil
  2 tablespoons butter
  ½ pound fresh or frozen mushrooms, chopped
  4 tablespoons chopped parsley
  4 tablespoons chopped scallions or onions
  1 clove garlic, finely minced

Clean or thaw the frog legs, place them in a deep dish and season them well with salt and pepper. Pour the beer over them and leave to marinate for 2 hours in a cool place. Drain the frog legs and roll them in flour, shaking off any excess. Heat the oil in a skillet and fry the legs until golden. Take your time and don't get things too hot or fry too many at a time. Keep warm.

Melt the butter in a small pan, add the chopped mushrooms, the parsley, the scallions, and garlic. Cook gently until the mushrooms are done. Sprinkle over the frog legs and serve with the following onion rings and with wedges of lemon.

Make a batter with:

1 egg
1 tablespoon oil
4 tablespoons flour
2 or 3 tablespoons beer

The batter should be fairly thin, just coating a spoon. Cut a couple of onions in ¼ inch slices and separate them into rings. Use only the larger nicer rings and keep the center and ends to chop in another dish. Roll the rings first in flour then dip in the batter. Fry until golden and crisp in a deep fryer or a skillet with at least ½ an inch of oil. Enjoy with large glasses of cold beer, of course.

6. POULTRY

AMERICAN HOUSEWIVES DON'T REALIZE how blessed they are when it comes to poultry. First of all chicken and turkey are very reasonably priced in this country. Even such delicacies as Rock Cornish game hens are not really outrageous when you want something special. Secondly, you practically know exactly what you are getting. If you want a young tender chicken to fry, all you have to look for is a label specifying "Fryer" and pick the weight you want. In France, however, when you go to the market or poultry shop you must first of all hope for the best. Then try to remember all your mother taught you about buying a chicken.

French chickens come to market half-plucked. This allows the buyer to determine the breed, assuming you know that much about chickens. You poke and feel each bird and look suspicious and displeased on general principle. No self-respecting French housewife would buy a chicken simply on the poultryman's word.

If all goes well or you are an expert, you will eventually serve what may well be the finest, tastiest chicken in the world, which considering the price, is only what it should be. American poultry may (or may not) taste quite as fine but you are assured of tenderness and the price makes it a family or everyday dish.

If you have not been very happy with your roast chickens or turkeys, read carefully the recipe for Poulet Rôti aux Champignons. Whether you are roasting a large turkey or the tiniest Cornish hen, the same general principle applies: start with high heat, diminish it as the bird browns, baste often and don't overcook. Roast poultry is considered an epicure's delight in France but it has to be done just right. I hope the following recipes inspire you!

POULET RÔTI AUX CHAMPIGNONS

Roast Chicken with Mushrooms

There is a French saying, *"On devient cuisinier mais on naît rôtisseur,"* or, one may become a cook but one is born a roaster! This may not be quite true but there is no doubt that roasting is an art.

Roasting is not baking although both are done in the oven. In roasting, meats are cooked relatively quickly, the outside seared to a golden brown quickly imprisoning the juices. When you cut into it, the meat is tender and the juices fragrant. Chicken cooked this way, and its gravy enriched with cream and mushrooms, can delight the most exacting gourmet. The timing is very important and I will try to give you all the tricks I know to judge the exact moment the chicken is ready to be removed from the oven. If you don't meet with absolute perfection the first time, remember that practice makes perfect!

FOR 4 PEOPLE:
>   *1 chicken, 3 pounds, (approximately)* OR
>   *2 smaller ones for really large servings*
> *Salt and pepper*
> *Thyme*
> *Chicken liver, if you have, plus 2 tablespoons butter*
> *¼ pound (1 stick) butter*
> *1 onion*
> *1 bay leaf*
> *½ pound fresh mushrooms*
> *1 cup heavy cream*

French cooks are so particular about roasting that they will indignantly reject any chicken whose skin is nicked! You need not get mad, just select one with a nice complexion and no blemishes.

Wipe the chicken and rub the cavity with a little salt and pepper and a small pinch of thyme. Place it in a rather shallow roasting dish or flat pan which you have generously buttered. Fold the wings under so the chicken will sit straight. Tie the legs together also or slip them under the skin of the vent if it has not been cut. If you received the liver with the chicken, place it in the cavity before tying the legs, along with 2 tablespoons of butter.

Dot the chicken with softened butter, placing a nice lump on each drumstick and one on the breast. Salt and pepper over all. In the pan, you place the whole onion, a bay leaf and a pinch of thyme. These will serve to flavor the drippings deliciously as the chicken cooks.

Heat the oven to 475°F. I know, this is HOT! Place the chicken in it and cook for about 15 minutes, basting often with the drippings and a little more butter. By now the chicken should already be a deep rich brown and sizzling like mad, though not evenly done!

On no account pierce the skin with a fork; if bubbles form under the skin, spoon a little butter over them so they will not crack. It is very important to keep the juices in the meat where they belong. Although the browning will not be even, do not turn or move the chicken. Place a small piece of aluminum foil loosely on the chicken, just large enough to cover the tops of the drumsticks and the breast. Turn the oven down to 375°F. and continue cooking, basting occasionally until the chicken is done. To judge doneness: a 3-pound chicken will take approximately 50 minutes. Look at the juices inside the cavity: suck a little of them with a baster or with a spoon, they should be clear with no trace of pink. The liver should be a uniform grayish color and firm. If you are sure of this, then, but only then, prick the thickest part of the thigh with a fork. It should pierce very easily and the juice that flows should be quite clear also. You can now remove the chicken to a serving dish and keep it warm while you finish the sauce.

While the chicken is cooking, you will have cleaned and sliced the mushrooms. Brown them gently in a little butter with a good seasoning of salt and pepper. When the chicken is done, add the mushrooms to the juices in the roasting pan. Pour in the cream and heat, stirring and scraping, on top of the stove. It must not boil, just barely simmer. Remove the onion and the bay leaf, taste and correct seasoning, if necessary, and pass gravy separately.

POULET DIRECTOIRE

*Roast Chicken with Cream and Tarragon
Sauce*

Once you have mastered the art of roasting a chicken, you can vary it infinitely by serving it with different sauces. For instance, instead of the mushrooms mentioned in the previous recipe, use tarragon inside the chicken and an additional pinch in the cream. This is the delicious Poulet à l'Estragon. You can add with glorious results a little brandy to the chicken juices before adding the cream, or sherry or white wine. The plain roast chicken served with French fries and a watercress garnish is a favorite French family Sunday dinner.

Here is another and delicious variation: a sauce with a little wine, fresh tomatoes, tarragon and cream. Really quite sensational!

FOR 4 PEOPLE:
   1 chicken, about 3 pounds
   ½ cup dry white wine
   1 tablespoon tarragon
   2 large fresh tomatoes
   1 cup heavy cream
   Salt and pepper

When the chicken is perfectly done and juicy as described previously for Roast Chicken with Mushrooms, remove it to a serving dish and keep it warm.

Pour the half cup of wine into the juices remaining in the pan and heat on top of the stove, stirring and scraping to melt any delicious browned bits sticking to the pan. Add the tarragon and leave to simmer until the wine has almost completely evaporated, while you prepare the tomatoes.

You should use fresh tomatoes for this dish, their firmness is needed. Peel them, cut them in two, squeeze out the seeds and chop them not too finely. Add them to the cooked-down wine and tarragon and just let them get hot. Pour in the cream and add a good seasoning of salt and fresh black pepper. Let it just get hot, not boiling, and serve separately.

POULET À LA DIABLE

Chicken *à la diable* means chicken in a hurry more than deviled chicken in French. This is a fine dish for a Sunday when you are feeling lazy.

FOR 4 PEOPLE:
4 tablespoons butter
1 fryer, about 3 pounds, cut as for frying
Salt and pepper
Tarragon and/or thyme
1½ cups finely chopped onion
Juice 2 or 3 lemons (about ¼ cup)

Melt the butter in a large skillet and when it sizzles add the pieces of chicken, skin side down, crowding them a little together if need be.

Season well with salt and pepper and a light sprinkling of tarragon and/or thyme. When the pieces are well browned, do NOT turn them. Simply pour over them an even layer of rather finely chopped onion. Sprinkle lemon juice over all and plenty of black pepper, not too much salt. Cover the skillet and leave to cook for about 10 minutes. The chicken is done when no pink juice flows when you prick the thickest pieces with a fork. Don't overcook it. Cooked this fast, the chicken will be tender and juicy, and the onions will not be completely cooked but will blend with the lemon juice for a wonderfully spicy taste.

POULET GRILLÉ FARCI AU CITRON

Lemon-stuffed Broiled Chicken

Here is a dish that makes you feel as fresh and light as spring itself! This delicious combination of chicken, lemon and herbs is the perfect thing for a day you want to celebrate without too much trouble.

Take a nice fresh fryer or broiler, split it so it will cook quickly, and fill the cavity with a delicious mixture of herbs and lemon.

FOR 4 PEOPLE:

> 1 *chicken, fryer or broiler, about 3 pounds*
> *Salt and pepper*
> 6 *tablespoons butter*
> 2 *lemons*
> 2 *cups soft bread crumbs, made from day-old bread*
> 2 *tablespoons chopped parsley*
> 1 *teaspoon dried tarragon*
> 2 *tablespoons chopped green onions* OR
>   *chopped onions and chives*

Wipe the chicken carefully and split it in two: use a good sturdy knife, insert the point at the tip of the breast and press down firmly with both hands. Quite easy really!

Rub both pieces well with salt and pepper and about 1 tablespoon of butter. Place rather low under the preheated broiler and cook, basting frequently with a little butter and lemon juice, until it turns a beautiful golden color. About 15 minutes should do it.

While this is going on, tear enough day-old bread to make 2 cups of crumbs. Toss them with the herbs and onion, salt and pepper, 2 tablespoons lemon juice and about ½ teaspoon grated lemon rind. Drizzle 2 tablespoons melted butter over them and mix. Remove the chicken from the broiler and turn it. Pack each cavity with half the bread-crumb mixture. Cover loosely with aluminum foil and return to the broiler, at the lowest level, for another 20 minutes or so. During the last 5 minutes remove the foil so the bread crumbs can brown and crisp. Baste occasionally with the drippings and/or more butter and lemon juice. The chicken is done when the thickest part of the thigh is easily pierced with a fork and no pink juices run out.

If it is more convenient, you can do the second part of the cooking in a rather hot oven, 400°F. You will not need to cover the chicken with foil; it will brown beautifully.

POULET FLAMBÉ À LA CRÈME ET FINES HERBES

Flambéd Chicken with Cream and Herbs

Chicken cooked this way is a "special occasion" dish. Not for a crowd, no, for a small dinner party, a special anniversary or birthday, perhaps just for two.

FOR 4 PEOPLE:
    2 very small chickens, about 1½ pounds each, OR
    chicken breasts, 2 small halves per person
    4 tablespoons (½ stick) butter
    Salt and pepper
    Mixed herbs: Use a mixture of any or all the following,
    counting 1 tablespoon in all dried herbs or 4 tablespoons
    fresh; tarragon, basil, thyme, sage, parsley, chives
    or onions
    1 cup heavy cream
    4 tablespoons brandy or cognac

For complete witchery at the table you will need the following: a chafing dish or handsome casserole for the chicken, a small pan or bowl to hold the cream gravy and a miniature pan or ladle to hold the brandy.

Split the chickens into 2 or 4 pieces, depending on their size and your liking. Heat the butter in a large shallow pot and when it sizzles brown the pieces of chicken with simply a little salt and pepper. Let them get that beautiful golden brown that butter gives. Sprinkle on the mixture of herbs, cover the pot and cook over low heat for about 20 to 25 minutes. Watch closely so that nothing burns but only add water if absolutely necessary and then just a few drops. When the chicken is done, it should have just a little very dark strongly flavored gravy at the bottom of the pot. You can cook the chicken to this point ahead of time if you like. Just reheat and proceed:

Take out the pieces of chicken and place them in the casserole or chafing dish. Keep them warm. Stir the cream into the chicken juices and heat, mixing well to blend all. Do not boil, just get very hot. Pour into a small pan or bowl which can come to the table.

Warm the brandy gently for a few seconds in a small pan or ladle over a candle or long match. Touch the flame to it and pour flaming over the chicken pieces. Let it burn down, then pour the cream sauce over the chicken and mix a little. Serve immediately.

For a less festive occasion, you can omit the brandy and come up with a delicious chicken in cream sauce. The flaming brandy, however, is practically guaranteed to bring out the best not only in the chicken but also in the husband!

POULET SAUTÉ DES GRANDS DUCS

Sautéd Chicken Grand Dukes

I call this recipe "des Grands Ducs" because of the sauce. A night on the town in French is called a *"tournée des grands ducs,"* no doubt because at the turn of the century Paris had quite a few grand dukes who were very gay blades. This chicken is as full of spirits as any grand duke around three in the morning. So whatever the special occasion, have fun.

FOR 4 PEOPLE:
> 1 (3-pound) fryer chicken plus 2 breasts
> Salt and pepper
> ¼ pound (1 stick) butter
> Pinch thyme
> ½ cup dark port wine
> ¼ cup brandy
> ¼ cup Scotch whisky
> 3 egg yolks
> 1½ cups heavy cream
> 2 tablespoons Grand Marnier or Cointreau OR
>   ½ teaspoon (scant) very finely grated orange peel

One chicken will not give you much by way of seconds, so buy 2 extra breasts or 2 chickens and save half of one for another time. Cut the chicken in large pieces as for frying. Salt and pepper all the pieces generously and brown them well on both sides in butter. Do a few pieces at a time, adding more butter as you go. If you have a large skillet that can go into the oven, use it.

When all the pieces are golden, sprinkle a pinch of thyme over them and arrange them all in the skillet or a baking dish. Pop it in the oven at 375°F. to finish cooking. It should take about 35 minutes until the chicken is tender. Check once in a while and baste with the juices.

When the chicken is done, remove it to a serving dish and keep warm. Pour the port wine, brandy and whisky in the pan and stir and scrape over low heat until the pan is clean. Pour this fragrant mixture into a small pan and leave it to cook at a simmer for about 10 minutes or until slightly reduced. The aroma is terrific; don't just stand there inhaling, you may get too gay before the guests arrive!

Beat the egg yolks with a little of the cream in a small bowl. Add the rest of the cream to the sauce, stirring well, and let it heat without boiling. Pour a little of the hot sauce over the egg yolks, stir and return all to the pot, stirring madly. Heat again gently, stirring, but do not let it boil or it will curdle. Taste and add more salt, if necessary. Isn't it marvelous? And it's going to get better!

Just before serving drizzle about 2 tablespoons of Grand Marnier over the chicken pieces. You can use Cointreau instead but the Grand Marnier is even better because it is not as sweet as Cointreau. If you have neither, add a scant ½ teaspoon very finely grated orange peel to the sauce; a subtle orange taste is what we are after. Pour the sauce over the chicken pieces and serve.

This is so good you should not detract from the flavor with any vegetables but potatoes, perhaps. Or eat it like the French with plenty of crusty bread. À votre santé and have a good time!

POULET VALLÉE D'AUGE

Chicken with Madeira and Cream

The Vallée d'Auge is in the Department of Calvados and this department gives its name to a wonderful apple brandy made there. Calvados is the ingredient that gives this dish its characteristic flavor, but since it is hard to find in this country and is expensive when you do find it, you can use applejack or a little brandy combined with apple cider. Whenever you are lucky enough to get pheasant, this recipe is eminently suited to it.

FOR 4 PEOPLE:

4 tablespoons butter, or a little more!
1 cup chopped onions
1 large chicken, capon if possible, 3 to 4 pounds
Salt and pepper
Pinch thyme
½ pound fresh mushrooms (optional)
1 cup Madeira or dark port wine
¼ cup Calvados (apple brandy) OR
   ½ cup apple juice or cider and 4 tablespoons brandy
2 cups heavy cream
A little lemon juice, if needed

Heat the butter in a deep heavy pot and cook the chopped onions until a pale gold color. Cut the chicken as you would a fryer. Remove the onions with a slotted spoon and gently brown the pieces of chicken on all sides. Do a few pieces at a time; season them well with salt and pepper and a little dusting of thyme as you go. Add more butter if necessary if the chicken does not render enough of its own fat.

Return the onions to the pot along with the mushrooms, cleaned and quartered. Season again lightly and toss together in the butter so the mushrooms can absorb some of it. Pour in the Madeira and the apple juice or cider if you are using it. Cover the pot and leave to cook until the chicken is quite tender. This should take about 45 minutes to an hour; don't overcook it, the meat should not be falling off the bones. You should not have to add any liquid. All you want is just enough thick, fragrant juice to bathe the bottom of the pot. If there is too much, leave the lid off; too little, add a little water or wine. All this can be done well in advance if you wish.

At serving time, remove the pieces of chicken to a hot serving platter. Add the Calvados or brandy to the juices in the pan, heat and stir to mix well. Pour in the cream, stirring as you go, and taste and rectify seasoning if necessary. You may want to add just a few drops of lemon juice, particularly if you used apple juice, which is rather sweet. Don't add so much that it is recognizable, though, the taste of lemon must not predominate; just liven the flavor a little, if it needs it. Don't let the sauce boil.

Pour the sauce over the chicken and serve immediately. If you do not care to mop up the sauce with pieces of bread, serve plain boiled potatoes.

CHAUD-FROID DE POULET

Hot-Cold Chicken in Cream Aspic

This dish is said to have acquired its peculiar name of "hot-cold" in the following fashion: A cook had prepared a beautiful dish of hot chicken in a cream sauce for a very important personage, Napoleon if I remember correctly. The personage was delayed so much that the cook assumed he was not coming and put the chicken away. He was roused several hours later out of a sound sleep and told to serve immediately! The cold chicken was such a success that the cook was sent up to receive the congratulations of the assembled company. When asked for the name of this creation, the poor cook, completely flustered, replied, "It is a chaud-froid, Monseigneur!" and the name stuck!

This is a wonderful dish for a buffet supper. You make it the day before the party and although it takes a little time, it is not difficult. The finished dish is so appealing that it will be a conversation piece. For a really large gathering, you can double the recipe and decorate individual servings. For smaller parties, you can either carve the chicken at the table or, but this is a little more difficult, carve it first, put it back together with toothpicks and then encase it in its sauce. It will fall into serving pieces at the mere touch of a fork that way, and simplify service. Although the truffle is optional, it not only flavors the sauce wonderfully, the contrast of black truffle and creamy white sauce is irresistible!

FOR 6 SERVINGS:

> *1 large chicken, capon if possible, about 4 pounds—*
> *not a hen—for boiling*
> *2 cans consommé*
> *1 carrot, cut up*
> *1 onion*
> *1 stick celery*
> *Thyme*
> *Bay leaf*
> *Pinch tarragon*
> *1 black truffle (optional)*
> *Salt and pepper*
> *2 envelopes plain gelatin*
> *1 cup good dry white wine or champagne*
> *4 egg yolks*
> *1 cup heavy cream*
> *2 tablespoons brandy or sherry*

Start by cooking the chicken (at least a day ahead) in this flavorful broth: Take a pot large enough to accommodate the chicken. Put in it the consommé, the carrot, onion and celery, a seasoning of thyme, a bay leaf and a pinch of tarragon. If you are using a truffle, peel it and add the peelings and the juice from the can too. Add enough water just about to cover the chicken but don't put the chicken in yet. Season the liquid lightly with salt and pepper and simmer for 45 minutes to an hour. Now add the chicken, rubbed with salt and pepper inside and out, with its wings neatly folded under and its legs tied.

Cover and simmer the chicken until tender, being careful not to overcook. This means just simmering for approximately an hour. Turn the chicken once or twice carefully, not adding more water, keeping the pot covered. As soon as the chicken is done, remove it from the broth and take off all the skin. This is very easy to do while the chicken is hot. Refrigerate separately the strained broth and the chicken, covered with several layers of plastic film.

When the broth is well chilled, carefully remove all the fat from the top. Heat it, strain it though several layers of cheesecloth, or fine cloth, like an old dish towel and measure 2 cups. Soften the gelatin in a little cold water and add it and the wine to the broth. Heat, stirring, until the gelatin is completely dissolved and the mixture simmering. Beat the egg yolks with the cream, pour a little of the hot broth over them, return to the pan and cook, stirring very well, until slightly thickened. Don't let it boil, or it will curdle. Taste and correct seasoning if necessary, stir in the brandy or sherry. Allow sauce to cool and then chill until it is the consistency of egg whites.

As soon as you put the jellied sauce to cool, deal with the chicken: if it is to be left whole, simply place it in the freezer for about 10 minutes, to get very cold. Or cut it in serving pieces if it is to be served that way. For the seemingly whole chicken, carve it this way: cut the joint between thigh and body, leaving the drumstick attached to the thigh; cut off the breasts, close to the bone as possible, and the wishbone. Put the chicken back together, holding the pieces in place with a few toothpicks. Place on its serving dish and chill in the freezer. If the serving dish will not fit in your freezer, you should transfer the chilled bird to it before proceeding with recipe. It is difficult to transfer later.

Now gently spoon a thin layer of sauce onto the very cold chicken. It will set almost immediately. Scrape up any sauce which falls to the dish. Warm the sauce slightly over hot water when it becomes too thick. As soon as the first layer is set, pour on a second and even a third layer, if necessary, covering all the chicken evenly and carefully. The sauce will set as a shiny creamy glaze. Before the last coat of sauce sets completely, you should add the final decoration.

The prettiest and best-tasting decoration is very thin slices of truffle. Out of the largest of these, cut little diamond shapes, crescents, circles, as you wish. (A thimble cuts circles and crescents very well.) Chop finely all the truffle trimmings. Arrange cutouts and chopped truffle in a pretty design. Other designs can be made with pimiento, thinly cut green pepper, parsley, sieved hard-boiled egg yolks, etc. If the dish has to wait more than a few hours before being served, wrap it well with plastic wrap.

Truly elegant served with a variety of salads made with young spring vegetables, such as baby carrots, green beans, cauliflowerets. Marinate in French dressing and arrange so that the colors contrast prettily. Parsley or, even better, watercress will add the final touch.

COQ AU VIN

Chicken in Red Wine

In France this dish is served by itself in all its glory, simply surrounded by little slices of fried bread. In Belgium, a dish of plain boiled potatoes goes along with it. There is no absolute law against your adding another vegetable if you feel you must, but a green salad and crisp French bread would be enough. The wine is rather important: the more full-bodied, the better the dish. A Burgundy or Beaujolais, domestic or imported, will give wonderful results. Be sure to have another bottle to serve with the meal for full enjoyment.

FOR 4 HEARTY EATERS:
   ½ pound thick-sliced or slab bacon
   2 fryers, about 2 pounds each
   ½ pound (approximately) butter OR
       ¼ pound butter and ½ cup oil
   10 to 12 very small white onions
   1 pound fresh or frozen mushrooms
   Salt and pepper
   ½ cup brandy
   Bouquet garni: 1 sprig parsley, thyme and bay leaf
       tied together
   1 bottle (approximately) red wine
   4 tablespoons flour
   6 slices day-old bread

(Note: The large amount of butter is mostly for the fried bread. You can, if you prefer, fry the bread in oil and butter mixed. If you serve potatoes instead, you only need about 4 tablespoons of butter for the chicken.)

Start by cutting the bacon into small cubes, ½ inch or so if you are using slab bacon, or ½-inch strips for the thick-sliced kind. Cut the chickens as for frying; this is plenty of chicken, so although we shall cook the whole lot for flavor, we shall only serve the best pieces. You can nibble on the leftover wings and necks for lunch later during the week.

Take a large heavy pot with a good lid. Heat about 2 tablespoons of butter in it and fry the bacon pieces until golden but not completely crisp. Transfer them with a slotted spoon to a bowl and brown the onions in the same fat. If you can't get the tiny onions, use larger ones cut-up. Remove the onions to the same bowl and brown the mushrooms slightly. Clean the fresh ones by simply removing the bottom of the stalk and wiping or rinsing them with cold water very briefly. The frozen ones can go right into the pot. Remove the mushrooms and add them to the onions and bacon.

Now brown the chicken pieces. Add a little more butter if you have to, but the bacon probably gave off enough fat. Season the chicken with a little salt and pepper as it browns. Now *flambez* the chicken. To do this, warm a very small pan or ladle over the fire. Don't get it too hot, you should be able to touch your finger to it quickly without burning yourself. Pour the brandy in it and slosh it around for a second or two, then touch a match to it. Pour flaming over the chicken. If you are an expert at this sort of thing, you can pour the brandy right over the chicken and then light it.

Let the flames die, add the bouquet garni, bacon, onions and mushrooms to the pot, pour on enough wine to almost, not quite, cover the meat. Season with not too much salt because of the bacon, pepper and the bouquet garni. Bring to a boil and leave to simmer, very, very gently, for about an hour. Shake the pan from time to time to mix things a little. After that time, thicken the sauce:

Mix 4 tablespoons of flour with an equal amount of butter, drop teaspoons of this mixture into the simmering liquid, stirring a little. Do this a little at a time, just until the sauce reaches a velvety consistency. It should not get thick or gooey, just silky or syrupy. Cook for at least 10 minutes after you have added the flour. The chicken is quite ready when the thickest pieces can be pierced easily with a fork. By now the whole house is filled with a heady aroma.

Make the fried bread croutons by trimming the slices of bread of their crust. Cut each slice in two. If you want to go all out, you can cut out the bread in fancy shapes with a cooky cutter.

If you are using oil, heat it first, just enough to cover the bottom of the skillet, about ½ cup. Then add 4 tablespoons butter. When it sizzles, fry the pieces of bread until golden on both sides, and add more butter or oil as needed.

Serve the chicken in a deep dish, surrounded by the croutons. The beauty of this dish is that it tastes even better when reheated! You can therefore cook it a day ahead of time with total impunity. If you are pressed for time at the last moment, you can make the fried bread early in the day and reheat in the oven at 375°F. for about 10 minutes. Just be sure it is crisp and hot.

If you start the meal with something light, like a fancy salad, and you follow the chicken with a good cheese to complement the wine that's left, you will have a memorable meal.

FRICASSÉE DE POULET AU VIN BLANC

Chicken Stewed in White Wine

Chicken stew is a delicious way to serve chicken to a crowd. It can be prepared well in advance and reheated with a minimum of watching. Plenty of fluffy rice, a salad and ice cream and cake for dessert make a superb meal to serve a great many friends.

This is a really glamorous chicken stew: white wine and mushrooms enhance the flavor, tarragon and cream add the finishing touches. This dish is wonderful also served in pie shells; little individual ones are perfect. Bake them empty and fill them with hot chicken just before serving.

FOR 6 TO 8 PEOPLE:

2 fryers, about 2½ to 3½ pounds each
¼ pound (1 stick) butter
Salt and pepper
1 small onion, finely chopped
1 pound fresh or frozen mushrooms, sliced
2 tablespoons flour
1 bottle dry white wine
1 tablespoon dried tarragon
1 cup heavy cream

Cut the chickens for frying. Heat the butter in a large pot and brown the pieces of chicken until golden on all sides. Do just a few pieces at a time and season them with salt and pepper as you go. Remove the pieces of chicken, and add the onion and the cleaned, sliced mushrooms to the butter that remains in the pot. Cook these until they are beginning to turn golden. Sprinkle 2 tablespoons of flour over them, stir well to mix and let the flour get golden also. Return the chicken to the pot and pour in the wine. Season generously with pepper, a little salt and the tarragon. Cook, covered, until the chicken is quite tender, about 1 hour. Don't overcook it, particularly if you intend reheating it; the chicken should be tender but the pieces recognizable.

If the sauce seems too thin, thicken it with a little flour mixed to a thin paste with a little water or wine. Stir in and simmer for at least 10 minutes.

Just before serving, add the heavy cream, stirring well. The sauce should not boil after the cream is added.

POULE AU CURRY

Simmered Hen in Curry Sauce

Henry IV of France is well remembered by his countrymen for his desire to see a chicken in every pot. This version of it may have surprised him, but I am sure he would have found it delicious.

As I have mentioned before, the French are not very fond of extremely hot sauces, because they do not go with wine and a French meal without wine is unthinkable! So the resemblance between this curry sauce and an Indian one is that of a pampered Persian kitten to a Bengal tiger! Curry used with a lavish hand is pungent and fiery hot. Used sparingly it has an aroma and flavor which blends wonderfully with the mild taste of chicken. With this dish serve rice cooked in the chicken bouillon for additional flavor. You will need:

FOR 4 PEOPLE (OR EVEN 6):
1 hen (fowl), 3½ to 4 pounds or more
1 onion, quartered
1 carrot, cut in large pieces
2 or 3 stalks celery, cut in large pieces
Salt and pepper
Pinch thyme
Bay leaf
2 cups raw rice
4 tablespoons butter or chicken fat
4 tablespoons flour
1 tablespoon (approximately) curry powder
Lemon juice
2 egg yolks
Chopped parsley

Put the whole hen to cook in a large pot with the coarsely cut onion, carrot, celery and water to cover. Salt moderately, add a little pepper, a pinch of thyme and a bay leaf. Cover, bring to a simmer and cook for about 2 hours. The time will depend on the age of the hen; it should be tender but not falling to pieces.

When the hen is beginning to get tender but is not quite done, begin cooking rice. Measure 4 cups of broth from the simmering chicken into another pan, bring to a boil with just a little salt. Pour in 2 cups of rice and simmer, tightly covered and over a very low fire, until the rice is tender. This will take about 25 minutes. Don't stir; this makes the rice stick to the bottom of the pot.

If there is really not enough liquid left around the hen, add a little water to it. It need not be covered anymore, the steam will finish cooking it. When the hen is done, transfer carefully to a serving dish, taking care not to break it, and keep it warm. Covering it with a piece of foil and placing the dish over the pilot light may be enough; it stays hot quite a long time.

Make the sauce by melting 4 tablespoons of butter or, better still, chicken fat skimmed off the broth, in a small pan. Stir in 4 tablespoons flour and cook until frothy but not brown. Gradually stir in with a wire whisk about 2 cups of chicken broth from the hen, or enough to make a creamy smooth sauce. Let it bubble a few minutes and season it to taste with salt and pepper and curry powder. Add just a little curry at first, a teaspoon or so, and gradually increase it to what you judge perfect. Add a good dash of lemon juice.

Remove the sauce from the fire. Pour a little over the well-beaten egg yolks and return all to the pot, stirring vigorously. The sauce will be the most appetizing golden color. Do not reheat it; it must not boil after the eggs are added. Pour a little over the chicken, sprinkle parsley over it and serve, with the rest of the sauce in a separate dish.

Two cups of raw rice will give you a plentiful amount of cooked rice, but this is so good with the sauce that you may eat it all. Any left over can be mixed with the rest of the sauce and a few chicken pieces and reheated like a casserole in the oven. Makes a splendid lunch with a salad!

WATERZOOIE DE POULET GANTOISE

Ghent Chicken Soup

This is technically a soup but a soup you eat with a knife and fork in addition to a spoon! As the Belgians say, *"Il y a à boire et à manger,"* or "there is to eat and there is to drink," so don't plan to serve it as soup but as a main dish.

This recipe includes all the rich things Belgians love: young and tender chicken, butter, cream, mushrooms, all simmered lovingly with young vegetables and then thickened with eggs. The resulting thick chicken soup is served in bowls over plain boiled potatoes. You eat the chicken, drink the cream soup and generally end up eating too much! But what are a few calories between friends, and you can always diet tomorrow. The chicken in this recipe is cooked very quickly. At just the right time, it will be quite tender and yet juicy and firm. Cook it just a little too long and you will have to cook it much longer before it gets tender again. It will then be more like stewed chicken and not nearly as flavorful. So keep an eye on the pot!

FOR 4 PEOPLE:
> 1 *medium carrot*
> 1 *stalk celery with a few leaves*
> 1 *large leek* OR
> > 4 *green onions with some of the green*
> 4 *tablespoons butter*
> Salt
> 2 *very small tender fryers,* 1½ *pounds each if possible*
> Pepper
> Pinch thyme
> ½ *pound fresh or frozen mushrooms*
> 1 *tablespoon liquid beef extract*
> 4 *egg yolks*
> 1 *cup heavy cream*
> A *little lemon juice*
> 4 *tablespoons chopped parsley*
> 4 to 6 *boiled potatoes*

The addition of the liquid beef extract is not absolutely necessary. The traditional recipes generally don't use it but it was one of

Maria's inventions and it made the sauce incredibly rich and dark. It should be the best, rather thick extract, sold in little jars.

Chop very finely all the vegetables except the mushrooms. You can grate the carrot on the large holes of the grater if you like, it is quicker. Melt the butter in a large pot and let the vegetables simmer in it with a little salt without browning. Cover the pot and turn the fire very low.

Cut the chickens as for frying but separate the breasts from the bones. Set aside the wing tips, necks and giblets and use them another time for soup.

Add the chicken to the vegetables, season with salt and pepper and a little pinch of thyme. Cook slowly, covered, for about 10 minutes or until the chicken begins to turn golden in a few spots. Add the cleaned and sliced mushrooms, stir to mix them in, then pour in just enough water to come about three-quarters of the way up the meat. It should not cover it completely. Stir in the beef extract and bring to a simmer. Cook covered for about 10 to 15 minutes or until the chicken does not ooze any reddish juices when pricked with a fork. Don't let it boil fast, remember, and don't overcook it.

In a large bowl or soup tureen, beat the 4 egg yolks with the cream. Pour a little of the hot chicken juices on them with a ladle, stirring briskly, then pour in the rest of the chicken and broth. It will thicken a little immediately. Stir in a little lemon juice and sprinkle with chopped parsley.

Have ready a dish of boiled potatoes cut into rather small pieces. Let each guest help himself to potatoes and ladle the "soup" over them. You should not have to worry about any leftovers!

PÂTÉ DE POULET

Chicken Pâté

Here is another pâté which could make your reputation as a cook. Served in small slices at the beginning of a meal, it is as elegant as the Pâté Maison served in famous French restaurants. A meal of cold cuts and salad including this pâté is immediately out of the ordinary.

About the only absolute requirements for making pâtés are a meat grinder and a couple of good sharp knives. From there on, if you can make meat loaf, you can turn out pâtés like a professional chef! Poultry can gain the greatest status when complemented with truffles.

In this one a small can of truffle peelings and pieces definitely adds the true gourmet touch.

FOR ONE LARGE PÂTÉ (3 TO 4 POUNDS):
   1 large chicken, or capon, weighing about 4 pounds
   Salt and pepper
   1 small can truffle pieces and peelings
   Small glass brandy, cognac or sherry (about ¼ cup)
   Small bunch parsley
   1 carrot
   1 onion
   Bay leaf
   1 stalk celery
   1½ pounds ground pork or pork and veal mixed
   Thyme
   Nutmeg
   A little butter or lard to grease dish

You start by boning the chicken. This is not as hard as it sounds if you have a good sharp knife. Cut it first as for frying then remove the bones from each piece and pull off the skin.

Set aside the two breasts. Cut these into long strips, place them in a soup plate, season with a little salt and pepper, add the truffles and their liquid and pour on the brandy or sherry. Leave them to absorb these heady flavors while you prepare the rest of the pâté.

Take all the skin and bones you trimmed off the chicken, put these in a pot with the parsley, carrot, onion, bay leaf and celery. Season with salt and pepper lightly, cover with water and leave to simmer until you obtain about 1 cup of very strong chicken broth.

Put all the rest of the chicken meat through the finest blade of the grinder twice. Place it in a large bowl and mix it with the ground pork or pork and veal. Season generously with salt and pepper, a little pinch of thyme and a grating of nutmeg. Add also the brandy or sherry which bathed the breasts and the truffle pieces.

Stir in about ½ cup chicken broth to make the mixture good and moist. Grease or butter generously a round, 2 or 2½ quart glass or earthenware baking dish. Pat about half the meat mixture in the bottom of it, arrange the breast strips over that, and cover the rest of the meat, patting it firmly in place. Pour on a few tablespoons of the reserved broth with a little more brandy. Cover the dish tightly with a lid or aluminum foil. Place it in a larger dish containing about

1 inch of water and bake for about 2½ hours; start in preheated 300°F. oven for about 45 minutes, then turn the oven down to 275°F. for the rest of the cooking time. Replenish the water with boiling water from time to time.

When the pâté is done, take it out, place a plate over it and a weight over that. Leave it to cool weighed down, the texture will be closer and firmer. If you possibly can, let the pâté rest for a day or so in the refrigerator before slicing it. The flavors mellow marvelously, but you may have trouble keeping it for any length of time after the family discovers what a wonderful snack a slice of pâté makes with French bread!

PÂTÉ DE POULET AUX CHAMPIGNONS

Chicken Pâté with Mushrooms

This is a rather unusual concoction, half pâté half soufflé, a poultryman's delight! Eggs and chicken combine with lots of mushrooms, tarragon and chives to form a kind of pâté, delicious hot or cold.

Fresh mushrooms will definitely give the best results in this dish; if you can't get any, use frozen ones, which are also excellent. As a last resort you could use canned mushrooms with the addition of a few dried ones.

FOR 4 TO 6 PEOPLE:
   4 chicken breasts, raw, or cooked leftover chicken
   1 pound fresh or frozen mushrooms
   4 tablespoons butter
   1 shallot or green onion
   Salt and pepper
   4 fresh eggs
   6 slices day-old bread
   1 tablespoon finely chopped chives
   1 tablespoon dried tarragon
   4 hard-boiled eggs

Trim the chicken breasts of any bones and skin. I prefer to use raw ones for this dish but if you should have some cooked leftover chicken you can use it for all or part of this amount. Cut the chicken in thin strips, about ½ inch thick at the most.

Clean the fresh mushrooms and slice them thinly. Melt the butter in a skillet. Add the finely chopped shallot or onion to it, cook until transparent. Then add the mushrooms, season with salt and pepper and leave to cook over a low fire until the mushrooms are rather golden and smell heavenly.

Break the four raw eggs into a large bowl. Trim the crusts off the bread and tear it into very small pieces. Gradually add these to the eggs, beating well with a fork until the mixture looks like soft scrambled eggs. Season with salt and pepper, add the finely chopped chives and the tarragon, crumbled between your fingers.

Take a loaf pan, 9½ x 5½ x 2½ inches is about right. Line it with foil if you intend serving this dish cold; it makes it much easier to get it out in one piece. Leave enough foil extending over the sides to be able to fold it over like a lid. Grease generously with butter.

Pour about half the egg mixture on the bottom of the dish. Arrange on this half the mushrooms, then a layer of chicken, the hard-boiled eggs cut in four lengthwise, the rest of the mushrooms and finish with the rest of the raw eggs and bread mixture. Cover tightly with foil, well buttered on the side that touches the eggs. Place the pan into a larger one containing 1 inch of water and bake at 375°F. in preheated oven for about 1 hour. A knife inserted in the middle should come out clean.

Serve hot immediately or let it cool in the pan before unmolding it to serve cold. Slice with a very sharp knife. A really wonderful blend of flavors.

POULET FARCI EN GELÉE

Jellied Stuffed Chicken

This is a really glamorous dish, fit to be the *pièce de résistance* at the smartest buffet. It can be prepared well in advance, leaving you free for all those last minute arrangements.

This dish is a combination evolved from the very particular way our old cook Maria taught me how to bone chickens. The traditional Poulet en Gelée is usually simply a cold roast chicken with its bones in, served lightly covered and surrounded by a delicious topaz-covered jelly. Roast chicken with its golden skin, the drumsticks covered with those little paper frills, looks as inviting as any dish I know. The only drawback for large parties is that it has to be carved at the last moment and eaten with knife and fork.

There is another French specialty, usually served at buffet suppers, the Galantine de Poulet. In this case the chicken is completely boned, stuffed and rolled like a sausage, although a very glamorous sausage. This is very delicious, easy to eat with just a fork but not nearly as appetizing to look at as the roast chicken! So in this dish we combine the best of one with the best of the other and come up with the perfect conversation piece, lovely to look at and delicious to eat.

The work is spread out over two days, not that you will spend every minute of both just preparing the chicken! As the chicken tastes and behaves even better if it has a night's rest before the party, on the day itself you will be able to forget all about it until the last moment. Do take into account, however, that it is likely to take up almost a whole shelf of the refrigerator!

FOR 8 TO 10 SERVINGS:

Stuffed chicken:
1 large frying chicken, about 3½ pounds
½ cup brandy OR
  1 cup sherry
1 can whole truffles (optional)
2 to 3 tablespoons butter
1 8-ounce box chicken livers, thawed
Salt and pepper
Dried tarragon
1 shallot or scallion
1 pound cooked ham
2 slices day-old white bread
1 egg
1 small jar whole pimientos

Jelly:
1 envelope unflavored gelatin
¼ cup cold water
1 can beef consommé
*2 tablespoons brandy or ¼ cup sherry, remaining from
  above preparation*
Pinch tarragon
Salt

Garnish:
1 *hard-boiled egg*
Pimiento
Fresh parsley
Green pepper
Lettuce
Radish

Two days before the party:

Start by boning the chicken. Starting at the vent, carefully cut the meat from the bones, working from the inside of the chicken. Cut as close to the bone as you can and turn the chicken inside out as you work. Remove the thigh bone by detaching it from the drumstick at the joint and making a slit on the inside. Try not to cut the skin but don't worry too much if you make a little nick in it once in a while. Leave the bones in the drumsticks and the wings. You will find that the ribs and the breastbone are very easy to remove, you can practically detach the meat from them with your hand. The whole process will not take you much more than 15 or 20 minutes the first time you do it, probably a lot less next time. And what a feeling of accomplishment!

Sprinkle a little sherry or brandy over the chicken and tuck the truffles (left whole so far) into it. Cover and refrigerate while you prepare the stuffing.

Heat 1 tablespoon of butter in a small skillet and quickly toss the chicken livers in it. They should turn gray and be firm but still pink inside. Season with salt and pepper, a pinch of tarragon, and the finely chopped shallot or scallion. Pour on a couple of tablespoonfuls of sherry or brandy and leave to cool.

Grind the ham finely, twice preferably, then the chicken livers. Mix in a large bowl. Add the slices of bread, trimmed of their crusts and moistened with a little more brandy or sherry, the egg and another pinch of tarragon. Don't forget to stir in the juices from the chicken livers. Taste and add salt and pepper if necessary. It should be quite highly seasoned.

Remove the truffles from their hiding place inside the chicken. Peel them not too thinly, cut them in two or four, so that you have enough pieces to go the whole length of the chicken later. Chop peelings and trimmings finely and add every bit to the stuffing. Add the juice and the brandy from the chicken to the stuffing also.

Prepare a good sturdy needle, an embroidery or darning needle is fine, with a good length of strong white thread. Fine crochet cotton or dental floss is perfect. Sew up the neck opening of the chicken and any small tears in the skin. Leave a long piece of thread hanging loose so you can find it easily after the chicken is cooked.

Place the boned chicken on its back, the breast meat on top. Gently arrange the meat with your fingers so that you have an even layer all around. Pat a layer of the stuffing into the chicken. Arrange in the center of this a row of truffle pieces as close together as you can and a row of pimiento strips on each side of the truffles. This will be approximately in the center of the slices later and will look exceedingly pretty. Cover with more stuffing, patting it in rather tightly; it does not swell much in cooking. Sew up the tail end and pat and press it to give it as much as possible its original shape. Tie the legs together and the wings close to the body.

Butter a dish large enough to hold the chicken, place the chicken in it and dot it with a little more butter. Season lightly with salt and pepper. Roast the chicken, uncovered, in preheated oven at 350°F. for 1½ hours. Baste occasionally and use a small sheet of foil to cover the breast and the drumsticks if they seem to get too brown. The whole chicken should be appetizingly golden. When it is done, let it cool in the dish; refrigerate until the next day.

The day before the party:

To make the jelly, dissolve the gelatin by softening it in ¼ cup cold water, adding the undiluted consommé and about ¼ cup of sherry or 2 tablespoons brandy. Add a pinch of tarragon, taste and add a little salt if necessary. Heat, stirring, until the gelatin is completely dissolved. Let stand 15 or 20 minutes to extract all the goodness from the tarragon, then strain and cool.

You are now ready to decorate the chicken. Remove all strings and thread from the chicken. Just give a sharp tug and the thread will pull out easily; hold the skin down with your fingers if it seems to pull off with the thread. Wipe the chicken all over with paper towels gently but thoroughly to remove as much of the grease as possible.

Now if you want the greatest possible ease in serving you can slice the chicken before encasing it in jelly. If the party is not too large, however, it is easier to slice it right at the table. If you decide to pre-carve it, cut the slices not too thin, about ¼ inch at least, cutting off the drumsticks and the wings neatly first. Press all the slices back together and refasten the wings and drumsticks with toothpicks. Cut the drumsticks off at a slant, so that they can almost rest in place against the chicken; they will stay in place much better that way.

Arrange the chicken on what will be its serving dish. Pop it in the freezer if possible or the coldest part of the refrigerator until it is thoroughly chilled. This will take about 15 minutes in the freezer, but longer in the refrigerator.

Have the jelly the consistency of unbeaten egg whites. This means placing it over cracked ice or hot water, if it is too thin or too thick! Have both ready. Take the chicken out and spoon a little jelly over it evenly with a large spoon. The jelly will set almost immediately as it touches the cold meat. When the chicken is covered with a thin coat of jelly, return it to the refrigerator so it can set completely.

Prepare the trimming: cut out fancy little shapes out of thin slices of egg white, pimiento. Use a sharp knife, and a thimble makes a good cutter for little rounds or crescents. Little strips of egg white can make pretty daisies with egg yolk centers. Select pretty parsley leaves, thin strips of green pepper for leaves and stalks. For certain occasions you can cut hearts out of pimiento. Get as fancy as you like.

Take the chicken out of the refrigerator again, dip each little piece of garnish in jelly and stick it in place. When all is arranged and set, pour on a second layer of jelly. Any leftover jelly can now be poured into a flat dish.

When all the jelly is perfectly set, scrape off any that dripped onto the serving dish. You can now cut out little triangles of jelly from that in the flat dish and arrange them all around the chicken. More simply, you can chop all the leftover jelly and arrange that around the chicken, both are pretty. You can now refrigerate and forget all about the chicken until party time; you will want to peek at it and gloat over the results, though. It can safely be covered loosely with plastic wrap, it won't stick. At party time, you can garnish the dish with a few little bunches of fresh parsley, radish or lettuce leaves. It will be the star of the show! If the chicken was sliced, remove the toothpicks! Macédoine de Légumes is a perfect salad to serve with this dish, and is included in the vegetable section.

A last note: if you have a silver tray or platter, the chicken will look beautiful on it. Cover the bottom of the tray with two or three layers of plastic film; it will protect the tray from scratches and prevent the chicken from getting a slight metallic taste.

CANARD AUX OIGNONS

Duck with Onions

This recipe is especially good for the domesticated ducks. The duck is first stuffed with onions and sage and then roasted with more onions around it. A really excellent combination!

For a little different flavor you can use a little beer or English pale ale to moisten the stuffing; it gives a faint but extremely pleasant flavor which goes particularly well with the onions. If beer is definitely not your drink, you can substitute chicken bouillon.

FOR 4 PEOPLE:
2 large and 10 small onions
Salt
6 to 8 slices day-old bread
1 teaspoon powdered sage
Pepper
4 tablespoons butter
Duck liver
1 egg yolk
¼ cup beer or chicken bouillon
1 good-size duckling, dressed, about 4 to 5 pounds

Peel all the onions and boil the two large ones in salted water for about 10 minutes. They won't be cooked entirely through! Set aside the small onions until later.

Have the bread good and dry. With American packaging, you should leave the slices out of the bag for a few hours or overnight. Break the bread into small pieces with your fingers, removing most of the crust as you go. You need about 3 to 4 cups, depending on the size of the duck. Chop the parboiled onions finely and place them in a large bowl with the bread. Sprinkle with about ½ teaspoon powdered sage and season with salt and pepper.

Melt the butter in a small skillet and add the duck liver to it. Let it cook until firm but still pink inside. Chop it and add it with the butter to the bread mixture. Toss well so all the bread gets a chance to absorb some butter. Moisten with the egg yolk beaten in the beer or bouillon. It should not be soggy, just barely damp. Taste and add more salt and pepper if necessary and perhaps a touch more sage. It should have a definite sage aroma.

Rub the duck inside and out with a little salt and pepper. Stuff the cavity with the bread mixture, packing it not too tightly. Sew up the opening with a strong needle and thread or use skewers and string.

Place the duck in a baking dish large enough to hold it, leaving room for all those little onions, but don't put these in yet. Place the duck in the preheated oven at 350°F. without any additional fat. Prick the skin once in a while with a fork as it begins to cook and you will soon have plenty of fat in the dish. At that time, add the little onions dusted with salt and pepper and a little sage all around the duck.

Baste the duck occasionally and turn the little onions once in a while so they brown evenly. The cooking time should be about 2 to 2½ hours if the duck is really very fat. At that time, remove the duck to a serving dish. It should be quite tender when tested with a fork. Keep it warm for a few minutes.

Skim off as much fat as you can with one of those bulb basters or a spoon. Pour a few tablespoonfuls of water or beer into the pan and heat on top of the stove to loosen and melt all the delicious browned bits. Spoon out the little onions and arrange them around the duck. Pour the gravy into a sauceboat and serve immediately.

CANARD À L'ORANGE

Duck in Orange Sauce

Canard à l'Orange is one of the triumphs of French cooking. Wild ducks benefit particularly from the flavor of the oranges and other good things which go in this recipe. These ducks sometimes feed on something which gives them a very faint but disagreeable fishy taste. The tang of oranges and a prior dousing with brandy takes care of that! So even if you are not exactly wild about wild ducks, I assure you this is different.

Usually, for Canard à l'Orange, the ducks are roasted in the oven. This is fine provided you are absolutely positive they are little more than ducklings and exquisitely tender. If I have the slightest doubts when using wild ducks, I prefer to cook them on top of the range. This process ensures that the ducks will be always tender, deliciously orange-flavored and, last but not least, I can prepare them ahead of time and be out of the kitchen when the guests arrive.

FOR 4 TO 6 PEOPLE, DEPENDING ON
THE SIZE OF THE DUCKS:

> 2 *wild ducks (or more!)* OR
>   *1 4- to 5-pound duckling*
> *Salt and pepper*
> *Pinch thyme*
> *2 small oranges*
> *2 large onions*
> *4 tablespoons (½ stick) butter*
> *¼ cup brandy (preferably cognac) or Scotch*
> *1½ cups fresh or reconstituted frozen orange juice*
>   *to which add juice 2 lemons*
> *4 fresh oranges for garnish*
> *1 teaspoon cornstarch, if needed*

Optional but makes a big difference:
2 or 3 tablespoons Grand Marnier or Cointreau

Clean the ducks well and do not forget to remove the small oil sack at the base of the tail if your hunter has not already done so. Wipe the ducks dry with paper towels. Rub the cavities with salt and pepper and a pinch of thyme and place in each duck one small unpeeled orange cut in two and half an onion. Tie the legs together and the wings close to the body.

Melt the butter in a large heavy pot and brown the ducks well on all sides. Do them one at a time if you have to and season them well with salt and pepper as you go. When all are well browned, remove the pot from the fire, pour in the brandy and *flambez* them. The pot will heat the brandy immediately so have a match ready and lit in your hand as you pour. Keep your head back and touch the flame to the ducks. Keep tilting the pot this way and that until the flames die down.

Return the pot to the fire, add the other onion, left whole, and about one-third of the orange-lemon juice mixture. You don't want actually to boil the ducks in orange juice, but rather to braise them in it. Hence, keep the fire low, the pan only partially covered so steam can escape, and watch.

As the juices cook down to a syrupy brown sauce, add the rest of the orange juice, a little at a time, just enough each time to prevent burning. Remove the lid entirely if there seems to be too much juice accumulating. There should be enough to bathe generously the bottom of the pot but no more. It should cook down to a deep, rich, succulent dark brown. Depending on the size and the age of the ducks they will be done in 45 minutes to 1½ hours. They should be tender but not falling apart. A domestic duck can roast in the oven for 2 to 2½ hours at 375°F., basted often with orange juice.

While they are cooking, peel the oranges reserved for garnish. Use a sharp knife and peel them to the quick, no white pith or membrane remaining. Slice them neatly. Take a few pieces of peel, remove the white pith completely and cut them in the thinnest possible slivers. Place these in a small pan with water to cover, and cook them gently until they are tender and the water evaporated. You need about 2 tablespoons of these fragrant little pieces.

At serving time: remove the ducks from the pan and cut them into pieces. The French slice the breasts into thin little strips called *aiguillettes*; the mark of the perfect carver (and carving knife!) is to get eight slices from each side. Arrange all this on a warm dish, surround with the sliced oranges and keep warm a few minutes while you make the sauce.

Remove the onion from the pot, add the little strips of orange peel, and stir in the Grand Marnier. Bring to a simmer and pour over the duck. If you have watched the cooking carefully, the sauce should be dark and shiny, almost syrupy. If it is too thin, you may add a teaspoon of cornstarch mixed to a thin paste with a little orange juice. Add this BEFORE the Grand Marnier and let it boil up for a minute or two. Then add the Grand Marnier and pour over the meat.

If it is more convenient, you can prepare everything a day ahead of time, even to carving the ducks. Gently reheat the pieces in the sauce but don't let them boil in it—their texture and flavor would not be the same. Pour in the Grand Marnier at the last minute before serving. You may add a little more orange juice if the sauce seems too thick.

CANARD AUX PRUNEAUX

Wild Duck with Prunes

This is an unusual but marvelous recipe for young tender wild ducks. They are served with plump juicy prunes in a sauce well spiked with cognac or brandy.

The way you prepare this dish depends a lot on how much of a gourmet you are and the kind of friends you have. To be absolutely perfect, a good deal of the preparation should be done at the last moment. If you have a couple of good friends who enjoy coming into the kitchen and helping a little, preparing this dish becomes great fun. Plan the apéritif and appetizers so that you can have them in the kitchen while you work magic. True gourmets enjoy the anticipation as much as the meal!

If you can't stand the thought of anyone in your kitchen while you work, prepare things ahead and reheat. But you lose a certain elusive little something by way of flavor.

FOR 4 PEOPLE:
> 12 *large prunes*
> ½ *pound duck livers or ½-pound box frozen*
>   *chicken livers, thawed*
> 2 *to 4 small, young wild ducks, depending on size*
>   *(of ducks and/or guests!)*
> 1 *lemon*
> *Salt and pepper*
> *Pinch thyme*
> 2 *slices bacon per duck*
> 1 *stick plus 2 tablespoons butter*
> 2 *eschalots or 1 onion*
> ½ *cup brandy, preferably cognac*
> 6 *to 8 pieces crisp dry toast*

Soak the prunes overnight in cold water to cover. The next day cook them gently in the same water without sugar, until tender and plump. Set them aside and cook the juice down to about ½ cup.

Ask whoever is cleaning the ducks to be sure to reserve the livers. If unfortunately you can't get any, cry a little and thaw a box of chicken livers.

Wipe the ducks with paper towels, rub them all over with the cut lemon, then salt and pepper them generously and rub them with a pinch of thyme. Wrap each duck in bacon and place them on a shallow baking dish. Pop this into a very hot oven (500°F.) just long enough to get them sizzling and brown. This will be from 7 to 17 minutes depending on their size. At that time they will still be quite rare inside. Take them out, remove the bacon and with a very sharp knife make a slit along the breast bone and neatly remove the breasts and wings. Slip the knife between the meat and the bone; the whole thing comes off quite easily. Set breasts and wings aside on a dish, cover tightly with foil and keep warm. The turned-off oven is a good place; they will finish cooking gently in their own heat. If you are doing things ahead of time, just refrigerate them. They will finish cooking when you reheat them gently at serving time.

While the ducks are in the oven, melt 2 tablespoons butter in a small skillet, add the chopped shallots or small onion, and cook until transparent. Add the livers, season with salt and pepper, and cook until the livers are firm but not cooked through. They should still be pink inside.

Now take the duck carcasses and, using your fingers and a sharp knife, remove all the rest of the meat from the bones. A French chef would now pound the meat, the livers, and shallots in a mortar and press the juices from the bones in a duck press. If you don't own such exotic implements as a mortar and pestle and a duck press, squeeze out as much juice as you can from the bones with a potato masher or such and put the meat, livers, etc., through a meat grinder or in a blender. A blender gives a fine smooth purée in seconds.

While this is going on, let the prunes warm in their reduced juice. Place the prunes with the breasts to keep warm. Pour the prune juice in the roasting pan, heat, stirring and scraping any browned juices, and pour into a small saucepan. Add the brandy, the meat purée and juices, and heat very gently, stirring all the time. Add 1 stick of butter cut in small pieces and stir and mix briskly until completely melted and blended with the juices. Do not boil, and barely simmer. Taste and hand the pepper mill to the man nearest to you. Let him finish the seasoning; men are notably uninhibited with pepper!

Have someone make crisp dry toast while you are finishing the sauce. Serve the duck breasts with the toast, the sauce poured over them and the prunes as a garnish. Listen to the sigh of satisfaction of the true gourmet after the first bite.

CANARD À LA BRUGEOISE

Duck Bruges Fashion

Bruges is a charming little Belgian town famed for its lace and its canals. The inhabitants call it the Venice of the north. A friend from Bruges gave me this delicious duck recipe, hence the name. In her family, there is quite a tradition in the preparation of this duck. The head of the family—and I do mean the man!—personally goes to the kitchen to carve the duck and season it for its last stage into the oven. As this recipe requires a lavish hand with chopped raw onions and black pepper, it is probably better to let a man do it. Women are often timid about pepper and such, which is probably why men are such great chefs.

FOR 4 PEOPLE:
>   2 *wild ducks with livers*
>   *Salt and black pepper*
>   *4 to 6 ounces (1 to 1½ sticks) butter*
>   *1 cup finely chopped onions*
>   *½ cup freshly squeezed lemon juice*

Clean and wipe the ducks, making sure the little oil sack at the base of the tail has been removed. Rub them inside and out with salt and pepper, place a piece of butter the size of a walnut inside each and the liver if you have it. Tie the legs and wings neatly. Place the ducks in a roasting pan just large enough for them to fit comfortably. Dot them generously with butter and roast them uncovered at 450°F. in preheated oven until they are well browned all over, about 20 minutes or so, depending on the size of the ducks. At this time they will be just rare.

Call in the man of the house and let him carve the ducks. With a really sharp knife he may be able to slice the breasts into thin slices with ease. These are the finest pieces of the duck; keep them separate. Butter very generously a shallow attractive baking dish. Arrange in it a layer of the less esteemed duck pieces, that is, the legs and wings. Over this goes a layer of chopped onions, about ½ cup and half the lemon juice. Season very generously with freshly ground black pepper and just a little salt. Now arrange on top the best remaining breast pieces and cover them with the rest of the onions and lemon juice. Add a little black pepper and a dash of salt.

Pour the juices from the carving dish back into the roasting pan, add a couple of tablespoonfuls (or more) of butter and heat, stirring and scraping on top of the stove until the butter has melted. Pour this over the ducks. Return the dish to a hot oven, 400°F., just until the whole thing is sizzling hot, about 10 minutes. Don't overcook it. The ducks will be deliciously tender, the lemon, onions and pepper will blend into a tangy, spicy sauce. The onions will not be quite cooked, they will simply have lost their acridity.

This is a dish to gladden the heart of any hunter. He may like it so much that he will want to do the whole thing by himself. At the very least, he should keep you well supplied with plucked and cleaned ducks!

TURKEY CASSEROLE À LA MARIA

As far as I know, Maria, who still lives in Belgium, has never met a frozen, boned turkey roast in her life. Moreover she would probably regard it with deep suspicions! Yet I have found these roasts to be very good, especially with a little preparation.

Maria used to prepare a veal roast for special occasions over which guests would become poetic! Imagine a combination of tender veal, deep golden cheese sauce, pink ham, fragrant browned mushrooms, all served together and yet separate in their different flavors. Well, instead of the veal, I substitute boned turkey roll and the results are as good.

This is not exactly instant cooking. The preparation takes a little time and care. However, this is one of those dishes which require no last minute preparation and which can be done well in advance. With potatoes and a good green salad, you will have a meal fit for a king.

FOR 4 PEOPLE:
   1 boned, frozen turkey roll
   4 ¼-inch-thick slices good boiled ham

   For the cheese sauce:
   8 ounces sharp Cheddar cheese
   2 tablespoons butter
   2 tablespoons flour
   1 cup milk
   Salt and pepper

4 egg yolks
1 pound fresh or frozen mushrooms
4 tablespoons butter
1 shallot or small onion
Salt and pepper
1 tablespoon liquid beef extract
2 tablespoons brandy (optional)

Prepare the turkey roast as indicated on the label. Let it cool. You will need 8 nice, not too thin slices, about ½ inch thick. The rest can serve for another meal.

To make the cheese sauce: grate the cheese first. Melt the butter in a small saucepan. Add the flour to it and cook until frothy but not brown. Stir in the milk gradually, return to the fire and cook until thickened and bubbly. Add the cheese, stir over very low heat until melted. Taste and season with little salt, if any, and plenty of black pepper. When the mixture has cooled a little, beat in the 4 egg yolks, cover with a film of plastic wrap or wax paper and let it cool completely.

Clean the mushrooms, slice them very thinly. Melt the 4 tablespoons butter in a skillet, add a finely chopped shallot or onion and cook until transparent. Add the mushrooms, season them well with salt and pepper and leave them to cook until they have absorbed most of the butter. Let them cool also.

Butter generously an oblong baking dish. If you have one on the order of a rather shallow loaf pan, use it. Take a slice of turkey, place a thick layer of cooled cheese sauce on it, about ½-inch thick, a half slice of ham over that and stand it upright or almost upright in the baking dish. Repeat with the rest of the turkey slices. Very gently spoon in a layer of mushrooms between the slices of ham and the next turkey slice. Divide them evenly so all get their share. Cover the dish with aluminum foil. You may now refrigerate it until the next day if you wish.

About 45 minutes before serving heat the dish, still covered, in a preheated 375°F. oven. It is ready when bubbly and hot. Remove the foil during the last 5 minutes or so to let it brown a little. Serve with the turkey gravy, prepared as directed on the turkey roast package but into which you have stirred 1 tablespoon beef extract and brandy for extra flavor. Even the most anti-casserole husband (and most of them are) should not have any complaints!

DINDONNEAU AU CHAMPAGNE

Young Turkey Roasted with Champagne

A *dindon* is a French Tom Turkey, a *dinde* his wife and their offspring goes by the name of *dindonneau*. Of the three the *dindonneau* is the most highly prized, next comes the *dinde*. As to the *dindon*, he is never identified as such when he comes to the table! By some minor miracle, the flock of *dindons* you admired at the farm have all turned into hens when the time comes to buy them!

This is no economy dish suitable for 24 people! However, it will delight a small gourmet gathering. The turkey should be small and tender, one of the "fryer" turkeys weighing 4 or 5 pounds. It shall be simply roasted with pure butter and basted with champagne. A little cream in the gravy and *voilà!* a dish to serve your most discriminating friends. In France, chestnuts, either in purée or cooked whole in a little butter, are served with the bird. A dish of sweet potatoes in butter and cream makes an excellent substitute. Applesauce, well seasoned with brown sugar and baked in the oven for about an hour with generous dots of butter, goes perfectly also.

FOR 4 TO 6 PEOPLE:
> *1 small (4 to 5 pounds) broiler-fryer turkey, with liver,*
>   *neck and giblets*
> *Salt and pepper*
> *Pinch thyme*
> *¼ pound (one stick) butter (not margarine)*
> *1 onion*
> *1 bay leaf*
> *1 cup champagne*
> *1 cup heavy cream*

Go over the turkey with a pair of tweezers and make absolutely certain no pin feathers remain. Wipe the turkey well inside and out with paper towels. Rub the cavity with salt and pepper and a pinch of thyme. Place the liver in it and about 2 tablespoons butter; tie the legs together and fold the wings back and under. Rub the turkey all over with a little softened butter and dust it lightly with a little more salt and pepper and thyme. Place the onion, left whole, and the bay leaf in a large baking dish and enthrone the turkey in it, on a rack if possible. Place the neck and giblets in the dish also.

Place the bird in a preheated 400°F. oven and cook at that temperature until it is a beautiful pale golden brown. Baste it once in a while with butter. Then turn the oven down to 325°F., and cover the bird very loosely with a sheet of foil just large enough to protect the breast and the drumsticks. Add a few tablespoonfuls of champagne to the drippings in the pan. Continue cooking, basting once in a while, counting a scant 20 minutes per pound. Since this turkey is not stuffed, it cooks faster. Keep adding the champagne just a little at a time every time you baste. The bird is done when a fork pierces the thickest part of the thigh easily and no pink shows in the juices. The juices in the cavity should show no trace of pink and be quite clear, flecked with brown.

Remove the turkey to a serving dish and keep it warm while you finish the sauce. Remove the neck, onion, etc., from the pan. Pour in any remaining champagne and heat on top of the stove, stirring and scraping to loosen any drippings at the bottom of the pan. Stir and heat until these juices are almost syrupy. Add the cream, taste and correct seasoning if necessary. Heat but do not boil. Serve separately.

DINDE FARCIE À LA MARIA

Stuffed Turkey Maria's Way!

I think this turkey recipe, which I prepare for really large family gatherings at Thanksgiving and Christmas, is my favorite. Old Maria, who taught me to cook, worked for an American family in Brussels before coming to us, and this recipe combines the very best of French and American cooking.

French stuffing has usually a finely ground pork meat base. The flavor is made delicious by the addition of such delicacies as truffles, brandy, liver pâté, etc. but the pork meat tends to be rather compact and heavy. But add these French touches to a basic American bread dressing and the result is something light and flavorful beyond belief. I have on occasion used cornbread, which is completely unknown in France, with excellent results. So count 1 pound of turkey per person plus 1 or 2 pounds just to be sure, and 1 cup of dressing per pound of turkey. And start getting ready!

FOR 10 PEOPLE:

   10 cups day-old bread torn into little pieces
   About 1 pound (4 sticks) butter
   ½ cup finely chopped onion
   1 cup finely chopped celery and leaves
   ½ cup chopped parsley
   ½ pound French pâté de foie with truffles OR
       ½ pound good liver sausage
   1 8-ounce box chicken livers
   1 10- to 12-pound turkey, with liver
   Salt and pepper
   ¼ cup brandy, preferably cognac
   1 small can truffles or truffle peelings and pieces
   1 whole onion
   Bay leaf
   Thyme
   Flour (optional)

If you are planning to make stuffed turkey for a Christmas cele-
bration, remember that you will be very busy with other things also
and need to plan ahead. One should NOT stuff turkeys, particularly
frozen ones, well in advance of their cooking time. Therefore, two
days before, chop all the vegetables, prepare the bread crumbs and
put them in plastic bags and refrigerate. The day before, prepare the
stuffing and insert the truffles in the turkey. On THE day, you will
only have to fill the bird and cook it.

If you are using whole truffles, their aroma will permeate the
whole bird if you use them this way: peel them, saving the peelings
and juice to use in the stuffing. Slice them about as thick as a nickel.
Very gently, using a long thin knife, insert them under the skin of
the bird, working your way through the neck and vent openings and
being extra careful not to break the skin. As the bird cooks, the truffles
will show as black dots, delightful to the eye of the initiated.

Crumble the bread and place it in a large bowl. (This is a good
job for children.) Melt 1 stick of butter in a skillet, add to it the
chopped onion, celery and parsley, and cook until the onion is transparent. Add the liver pâté or sausage and break it up with a fork.
Pour this over the bread and toss to mix well. In the same skillet,
melt about 4 tablespoons butter, add the chicken livers and the turkey
liver, and season with a little salt and pepper. Cook them until firm

but still pink inside. Pour the brandy over them, and immediately set it aflame with a match. Do this off the fire. When the flames die down, remove the livers and chop them. Add to the dressing along with the brandy. Now add the chopped truffles or truffle peelings, taste and season with more salt and pepper if necessary. The mixture should be moist but not soggy. If it seems too dry, you can add a little more brandy but don't go overboard. The dressing can now be refrigerated, well covered, with the turkey.

Rub the cavity of the turkey with a little salt and pepper. Fill both the body cavity and the neck cavity with the stuffing, packing it lightly or it will try to escape during the cooking. Sew up the openings or skewer them and tie with string. I find that for sewing up poultry nothing beats dental floss. One gentle tug and it slips right out after cooking. Leave a long piece to find it easily after cooking.

Rub the turkey all over with softened butter. Place it on a rack in a shallow roasting pan. Season it lightly with salt and pepper and place a whole onion, a bay leaf and a pinch of thyme in the pan to flavor the drippings. Place the turkey in a fairly hot oven, 400°F., and cook it at that temperature until it begins to get brown. This seals in the juices. Don't add water and don't poke the poor bird with a fork. Cover the bird lightly with a small tent of aluminum foil and turn the fire down first to 350°F. then to 300°F. for the last half hour of cooking. The time should be about 20 minutes per pound for a bird this size. Test for doneness by piercing the thigh with a fork. If it is tender and the juices are clear with no trace of pink, the bird is done. Don't overcook it, it will dry out. Keep basting as it cooks, the skin will be crisp and evenly golden that way.

Remove the turkey to a serving platter, cover with a sheet of foil and leave it to stand for about 10 minutes to make carving easier. Make the gravy simply by adding a little water to the juices in the pan and letting them boil up, stirring and scraping any browned bits. If you must have thickened gravy, you can add a little flour to the fat in the pan before adding the water. Some find the lustrous brown juices tastier without flour.

DINDE TRUFFÉE, FINE CHAMPAGNE

Brandied Turkey with Truffles

Turkey and truffles seem just made to go together. The French often stuff turkey with an all meat dressing which can be sliced and served hot or cold, a good idea if you are planning a large gathering for a buffet supper. The stuffing varies: the most delicious but also very expensive is pure goose liver. Not pâté, mind you, just a succulent pink whole *foie gras* from Strasbourg. This delicacy is simply studded with black truffles, seasoned with salt and lots of butter and cooked right inside the turkey. It emerges pale pink and soft as fresh creamery butter, so soft, in fact, that it has to be spooned out. This is food for the gods.

You can, however, make a more reasonably priced version of this dish, starting with chicken livers and the addition of truffles and perhaps a can of *mousse de foie gras*.

TO STUFF A SMALL 4- TO 5-POUND TURKEY:
(This stuffing being very rich, this is
sufficient for up to 8 people)
> ½ *pound (2 sticks) butter*
> *1 pound chicken livers*
> *Salt and pepper*
> *1 pound ground pork*
> *8 ounces French liver pâté or pâté de foie gras*
> *1 small can truffles*
> ¼ *cup brandy (fine champagne), preferably cognac*
> *1 cup fine white bread crumbs*
> *Pinch thyme*
> *Bay leaf*

Melt 4 tablespoons butter in a skillet and gently cook the chicken livers until they are firm. They should still be a deep pink inside. Season with a little salt and pepper. Cool them a little and put them through the finest blade of the meat grinder. Mix this purée with the pork meat and put it through the grinder again; the mixture should be exceedingly fine. Add to the mixture the butter used to cook the livers, the pâté (you can substitute the finest domestic liver sausage you can get if you can't find goose liver pâté) the truffles, reserving about 6 nice truffle slices. Add the brandy and just enough bread crumbs to bind the mixture, which should not be too thick and capable of holding its shape. Season with a little salt and pepper and a little pinch of thyme.

Insert the reserved truffle slices under the skin of the turkey. Use a long pointed knife and work them in place just under the skin, working from the vent and neck openings. Don't tear the skin.

Stuff the turkey with the meat mixture and sew up the openings. If possible, leave the turkey in the refrigerator about 2 or 3 hours before cooking it to give the truffles a chance to spread their aroma through the meat. Truffles are all aroma, and have amazingly little taste by themselves.

Roast the turkey as usual (see recipe for Maria's stuffed turkey) but omit the onion in the roasting pan unless you are absolutely crazy about it. There is such fine flavor, and the onion tends to be a little overpowering. Drop a bay leaf in the pan. Baste the bird often with butter as it cooks, starting with a 400°F. preheated oven and decreasing the heat as time goes by. Count about 30 minutes per pound for this turkey, though, because of the pork in the stuffing. Serve hot or cold, this is really fine eating!

DINDE FARCIE AUX NOIX DU BRÉSIL

Turkey Stuffed with Brazil Nuts

If you have a large family, there are probably one or two or more members who don't care for dressing of any kind. Others may be counting calories and all this makes it rather difficult when planning meals. I solved the problem one year by roasting the turkey without any dressing. This made it cook faster and it was quite low in calories for the counters. For those who felt like splurging, I cooked the dressing separately. In this case I cooked just a small amount of it, about 4 cups. Remember though, if you wish to stuff the bird, count 1 cup of dressing per pound.

This recipe includes Brazil nuts, and not only does the delicate flavor of the nuts blend deliciously with the turkey but their crunchiness is an unexpected yet delightful touch. If you cover the nuts with water and boil them for about 15 minutes, they will crack easily and will come out practically whole. Then slice them not too fine.

FOR ABOUT 4 CUPS DRESSING:
> *4 tablespoons butter and oil or margarine*
> *Turkey liver*
> *1 large onion or 2 or 3 scallions*
> *2 or 3 shallots*
> *2 or 3 small tender stalks celery*
> *Salt and pepper*
> *5 cups day-old bread, torn into small pieces*
> *12 to 15 Brazil nuts*
> *4 tablespoons chopped parsley*
> *2 tablespoons brandy (optional)*
> *A little broth*

To make broth:

Turkey neck and giblets	*Salt and pepper*
1 onion	*Pinch thyme*
1 carrot	*1 bay leaf*
1 stalk celery	

You will probably be making a little broth with the turkey neck and giblets for gravy. You know the usual procedure: put them in enough cold water to cover, along with an onion, carrot and celery stalk. Season lightly with salt and pepper, a little pinch of thyme, and a bay leaf. Simmer until the meat is falling to pieces, the giblets tender and the broth well flavored and strong. You'll have about 2 cups.

If you are using margarine, be sure that it is the kind that does not burn in the pan. Otherwise use butter or butter and oil. Chop all the vegetables finely. Brown first the liver, then the vegetables lightly in the butter. Chop the liver finely, seasoning it well with salt and pepper.

Place the bread, torn into small pieces, and the chopped nuts in a large bowl. Add the buttered vegetables, the parsley and liver. Toss well and season with salt and pepper. Sprinkle on the brandy and just enough broth to moisten the mixture slightly. The bread should cling together when you press it in your hand but don't make it a gooey mess.

Butter generously a baking dish and spoon the mixture in it lightly. Bake during the last hour of cooking the turkey, drizzling a little of the turkey drippings over it when you baste the bird. If you prefer, you can, of course, stuff the bird with this dressing. See Stuffed

Turkey Maria's Way for more information about cooking the bird itself.

ROCK CORNISH GAME HENS FINE CHAMPAGNE

Once in a while you like to share a good meal with a couple of congenial friends. This is it! You take these little game hens, stuff them with as fine a pâté as you can afford and roast them in their own juices. Delectable! If you know where to get a few fresh grape leaves, use them to wrap the little birds; they will add to the flavor.

If you can get French pâté de foie gras with truffles the dish will attain an incomparable excellence, but there are many excellent much cheaper pâtés, both imported and otherwise. So let your purse decide . . . a little good liver sausage will do wonders if you have champagne tastes on a beer budget.

About liver sausage: The Germans are masters at making this concoction, so shop around and see if you can find one made by a German firm. It should be rather pale colored.

A French earthenware dish known as a *cocotte* is ideal for cooking Rock Cornish hens. However, any casserole with a good lid that can withstand the heat from the top of the stove and the oven will do. Just be sure it is not too large: the birds should be placed closely together, bathed in the fragrance of many good things.

FOR 4 PEOPLE:

3 or 4 Cornish game hens, 12 ounces each
Salt and pepper
A little thyme
½ pound fine liver pâté
4 tablespoons butter
4 to 6 slices Canadian bacon
3 or 4 grape leaves (optional)
2 ounces brandy (fine champagne), preferably cognac
4 slices bread.
Extra butter for frying the bread

Wipe the hens well and rub their cavities with salt and pepper and a little thyme.

Place about 2 tablespoons of pâté inside each bird and the liver.

Fold the wings back and under to hold them in place and sew or fasten with toothpicks the neck and vent openings. Melt 4 tablespoons butter in a pan with a good lid, just large enough to hold the birds. Fry the Canadian bacon in it. While it is frying, wrap the birds in the vine leaves, and secure them with a few twists of white thread. When the bacon is done, remove it. Then gently brown the birds on all sides, and season with salt and pepper. Allow the hens to become a pretty golden color.

Remove the pan from the fire, pour the brandy into the pot and immediately set a match to it. As soon as the blue flames die down, return the bacon to the pot, cover it, and let the hens finish cooking over a very low fire. Leave it covered and peek in only once in a while so that the fragrances of the pâté and brandy seep into the meat rather than over the house. Or, you can pop the dish into the oven and let it finish cooking in there. Either way, the birds become tender in about 30 to 35 minutes on top of the stove, and in 40 to 45 minutes in a 375°F. oven. The oven method requires little or no watching if the dish is well covered.

While the birds are cooking, trim the bread of all crusts and cut each slice in two or four pieces. Fry this bread in plenty of hot butter, a few pieces at a time. Watch it carefully since it burns when you least expect it. Arrange these croutons on a hot serving dish.

When the birds are done, remove threads and toothpicks and vine leaves. Split the birds in two and spread some of the pâté from each on the croutons. Arrange the birds, cut into serving pieces, over the croutons. Pour on the juices from the pan and serve immediately. This is the kind of dish which rates a good bottle of wine, red preferably, and is enjoyed all by itself!

The butter you used to fry the bread can be saved for the next occasion, if you store it in a tightly covered little jar in the refrigerator.

ROCK CORNISH GAME HENS DUCHESSE

This is a really elegant dish for a gala little evening among friends. Start with something really fine, such as a small can of imported French pâté or a little caviar. Danish caviar is quite inexpensive and really good served on hot buttered toast with lemon and pepper. Then serve the Rock Cornish hens roasted on their own little cushions of Duchesse potatoes to catch all the delicious juices, surrounded by the tiniest green peas you can find. Follow this with a good salad and cheese and fruit for dessert. Thus, you have only the main dish to cook! A good way to acquire a reputation as a superb cook with little trouble.

Game hens are really quite plump, so I have counted only one half per person. If you suspect that your guests are hearty eaters, you might add an extra one for seconds. The same with the mashed potatoes: I suspect that the servings indicated on the envelopes of instant mashed potatoes are for midgets! Even if you have a "thing" against instant mashed potatoes, you will find them good in this preparation. Some brands are better than others, so experiment a little. Some of the flakes in plastic pouches are practically indistinguishable from the fresh.

FOR 4 PEOPLE:
> 8 servings instant mashed potatoes (dry)
> ¼ pound (1 stick) butter
> Salt and pepper
> Thyme
> 2 or 3 Rock Cornish game hens, with livers
> Grape leaves, if possible
> 4 slices bacon
> 4 tablespoons brandy
> 1 cup heavy cream
> 1 1-pound can tiny green peas

Make up a recipe of Pommes de Terre (Potatoes) Duchesse, counting 8 servings, according to directions in Vegetable Chapter.

Grease generously a large cooky sheet. Form the Duchesse potatoes into 6 or 8 oval-shaped cushions, making a depression in the center with the back of a spoon. Brush with a little melted butter and bake at 375°F. for about 20 minutes or until well browned. Remove to a serving dish with a large flat spatula. These potatoes can be prepared well ahead of time and baked at the last moment.

Wipe the little hens with paper towels and rub them inside and out with salt and pepper and a little thyme. Place the liver and about 1 tablespoon of butter in each cavity. Tie the legs together and fold the wings back and under. If you have been able to get vine leaves, wrap each bird first in vine leaves then with a strip of bacon and secure the whole thing with thread or fine string.

Heat about 4 tablespoons butter in a nice heavy pot, brown the

little birds on all sides, then cover and finish cooking gently for about
30 to 35 minutes. When they are tender, take them out and unwrap
them, return to the pot for a few minutes so they can brown a little.
The bacon and vine leaves have done their subtle flavoring job, so
discard them.

All this can be done ahead if you wish. At serving time, reheat
the birds until really hot. Remove from the pan and with a sharp,
sturdy knife, cut each hen in two. Place one half on each hot potato
cushion, already on the serving dish. Pour the brandy into the juices
left in the pot and boil for a few seconds, stirring well. Stir in the
cream and heat. Taste and correct seasoning if necessary. Pour a little
over each hen. Surround with the little peas heated with a little butter.
Garnish with parsley.

SALMIS DE FAISANT OU CANARD

Pheasant or Duck in Salmis

This is a preparation often made with game birds such as pheasant or ducks. Cornish game hens are excellent this way. The bird is
first very briefly roasted, sealing in all the juices; the best of the meat
is then carved and a delicious sauce made from the bones, skin, etc.
Add to this truffles or mushrooms, reheat the meat in it and you have
a sumptuous preparation. This dish is good for entertaining also, since
one can prepare it in advance and keep the food warm in a chafing
dish.

FOR 4 PEOPLE:
   2 small pheasant or ducks or game hens,
      about 1½ pounds each
   Salt and pepper
   Thyme
   About ¼ pound (1 stick) butter
   1 onion
   1 carrot
   1½ cups white wine
   1½ cups bouillon
   ½ pound mushrooms OR
      1 small can truffles
   4 tablespoons brandy
   Fried bread, for garnish (optional)

Wipe the birds with paper towels, rub them with salt and pepper and a pinch of thyme inside and out. Smear them generously with butter. Place them in a baking dish, on a rack if possible, and into a hot oven, 450°F., for 10 minutes. Turn the oven down to 350°F. and cook them another 15 minutes, basting often. The birds should be sizzling and brown, but rare on the inside so they will not get tough with further cooking later on.

Take the birds out of the oven, let them stand for about 15 minutes and then carve them into nice serving pieces, removing all the skin and as many of the bones as you can in the process. Cover and refrigerate the pieces.

Slice the onion and the carrot very thinly and cook them in a little butter until the onion is transparent. Add all the bones, skin and any such pieces as the neck and giblets, a little salt and pepper and all the drippings from the roasting pan. Add enough liquid to cover, probably about 3 cups in all, half white wine, half liquid beef extract (or bouillon made from a cube). A pinch of thyme will add aroma. Cover the broth and let it simmer gently, until it has reduced by about half. It should become a rich fragrant thin gravy. Strain it, pressing hard to extract every last bit of goodness from those bones. Add to this sauce the mushrooms, cleaned and sliced and cooked in a little butter or the sliced truffles right out of the can.

Just before serving: arrange the pieces of pheasant in a large skillet or chafing dish. Dot with butter, pour in the brandy and heat just a few seconds. Remove from the fire and touch a match to the dish. If you are trying to impress someone and are using a chafing dish, just lift the dish off the flame and tilt it toward it, the brandy will flame up immediately! Pour the sauce over the meat and heat very gently until all is heated through. Do not boil or the roast meat will toughen. Serve immediately. If you wish to garnish this dish with little croutons of fried bread, prepare them before the final heating and keep them warm. The crunchiness of the bread is out of this world with the sauce!

7. MEATS

CARBONNADES À LA FLAMANDE

The French love their wine; the Belgians love it too but perhaps not as much as their beer. There are villages in Belgium where beer is cheaper than drinking water! There are hundreds of breweries, I would guess, some very well known, sending their beer all over the country, others producing strictly for local consumption. Many of these beers are unknown even a few miles away but sometimes a delightful surprise to tourists. Some are light fragrant beers, pale blond like the Flemish children's hair, slightly bitter with the taste of hops; others are dark with a creamy froth, almost sweet in taste.

Beer is used in many dishes, in thick Belgian pancakes for instance as a leavening agent, and it makes a wonderful batter for fritters. But most often it goes in the carbonnades, the Belgian answer to Boeuf Bourguignon. Well prepared, this stew is absolutely delicious. The Belgians make it with thick slices of beef, counting one per person. You can ask the butcher to cut some for you, from stewing beef such as chuck. Or you can buy a chuck roast and cut it yourself. And if you simply pick up a package of cubed beef stew meat on the counter, only the shape will differ, not the taste.

FOR 4 PEOPLE:

4 tablespoons bacon drippings or lard
1½ pounds beef stew or chuck in ¾-inch slices
4 large onions, chopped coarsely
Salt and pepper
Pinch thyme
1 can (10 or 12 ounces) beer
Bay leaf
1 teaspoon flour
2 tablespoons French Dijon mustard

Heat the bacon fat in a large heavy pot and when it begins to smoke, brown the meat in it. Do this over high heat and quickly, making sure the meat gets really brown on the outside. The inside should remain very rare. Remove the meat, add the onions and brown them also. You can tell good carbonnades by their color before tasting them. They should be a rich almost chocolate brown. Once you add the liquid, they won't brown anymore, so don't rush.

Return the meat to the onions, season it well with salt and pepper and a generous pinch of thyme. Pour just enough beer to come about halfway up the meat and drop in a bay leaf. Cover the pot and simmer very gently for about 1½ hours or until the meat is tender. The onions will have practically melted by then to make a rich sauce. Stir gently once in a while during cooking and don't let it dry. Add a little more beer if necessary.

When the meat is done, mix a rounded teaspoon of flour with a little water in a cup. Add the mustard and mix well. Stir this into the gravy and cook for another 10 minutes or so. If the sauce seems a little thick, add a little beer. It must cook for 10 minutes after the flour is added so there will be no flour taste. It can of course cook longer if dinner is delayed.

Serve with plain boiled potatoes—no Belgian meal is complete without them—and carrots or peas and carrots mixed.

CROQUETTES DE BOEUF HACHÉ

Chopped-meat Croquettes

Properly speaking these are not real croquettes, in the sense that you don't start with a thick sauce base. They are great to remember, though, on a day when you have nothing but a little hamburger in the house and friends drop in to lunch. It happened to me once and these croquettes were so good that since then I have made them often. They are also a great budget stretcher.

You can serve these little patties plain or with something spicy, such as tartar sauce, mustard or pickles and French fries. At other times you can make a very good meal with mashed potatoes and tomato or mushroom sauce. In this recipe I use the Italian-style seasoned bread crumbs, which contain grated cheese. If you are using plain bread crumbs, try adding a pinch of your favorite herb and plenty of salt and pepper.

FOR 4 PEOPLE:

½ pound ground chuck or hamburger
3 tablespoons minced parsley
2 eschalots or green onions, finely minced
1 small clove garlic, finely minced
4 eggs
½ cup (about) seasoned bread crumbs
Salt and pepper
Oil for frying

Place the meat in a fairly large bowl, add the parsley, eschalots and garlic and beat in the eggs. Add enough bread crumbs to make a mixture resembling fluffy mashed potatoes. It should not be runny but still quite moist. Season generously with salt and pepper.

Heat just enough oil to cover the bottom of a skillet. Drop the mixture into it by tablespoonfuls. Turn as they brown on one side and let the other side get golden also. Don't try to fry too many at a time. Serve piping hot.

You can make a quick tartar sauce by adding a well-mashed hard-boiled egg and chopped pickles to mayonnaise. A little onion too adds flavor.

BOEUF BOURGUIGNON

I would choose a good stew over an indifferent steak any day, and, Boeuf Bourguignon is probably the grandest of all stews. Choose a good, full-bodied red wine and get two bottles of it—one for the stew, and one to drink with it, and finish with a wonderful cheese. Fix something really light as a first course. Finish with fresh fruit after the cheese. You will be relaxed (there is no last minute preparation), and will feel particularly beautiful and witty with such contented guests.

FOR 6 PEOPLE:
> 2½ pounds good, rather lean, heavy beef,
>   cut in stewing pieces
> 1 slice bacon ½-inch thick
> 12 very small onions or larger ones cut up
> Salt and pepper
> 2 tablespoons flour
> 1 bottle red wine
> Pinch thyme
> 1 bay leaf
> 4 sprigs parsley and/or 1 parsley root
> 1 small clove garlic, finely minced
> ½ pound fresh mushrooms
> 1 tablespoon tomato paste

Choose good heavy beef, a very deep red and lightly marbled with fat. Cut it, or have it cut, in cubes, about 1 to 1½ inches.

If you can, buy the bacon in one thick ½-inch slice and cut this into small cubes. Take your nicest, heaviest pot, put the bacon in it and let it brown and render some of its fat, until just golden all over. Remove with a slotted spoon and add the onions. Brown them in the bacon fat, remove them, and let them wait with the bacon while you brown the beef.

Brown the meat thoroughly, for its juice gives stews their color and flavor. Toss the meat with a spoon or fork over high heat, seasoning it well with salt and pepper. Let the juices get quite dark at the bottom of the pot as you do this.

Return the onions and bacon to the pot and sprinkle the flour over all. Mix with a spoon so the flour can absorb some of the fat. Give it a chance to brown slightly, and then pour in enough wine barely to cover the meat. Add a good pinch of thyme, the bay leaf, the parsley and parsley root, and the crushed garlic. Cover the pot and simmer gently for about 1½ hours. Keep the fire very low and the pot well covered.

Clean the mushrooms, fresh ones if possible, and cut off the bottom of the stem. Don't peel them; it wastes the mushrooms. Slice them and add them to the stew. Their fragrance and taste will mix with the sauce. Stir in a tablespoonful of tomato paste. (The purpose of the tomato in this case is just to thicken slightly and give a rich color to the sauce so don't use too much; it should add a little body to the flavor but no tomato taste.)

Simmer for another half hour or so after you have added the mushrooms and tomato paste, taste and correct the seasoning if necessary. All is ready! Note: This is one of those wonderful dishes which taste even better reheated, so you can make it the day before.

FRICADELLES

Meat Balls

Our cook Maria used to make quite a production of these meat balls. First of all she used half veal, half pork and the meat had to be just so. She had a deep mistrust of the butcher's ready-ground meat, accusing him, to his face, of putting in it nothing but fat! As their feud was a longstanding one which I am sure they both enjoyed, he would always end up by letting her pick the piece of meat she wanted and grinding it for her. Supermarkets may be more convenient but not nearly as much fun.

FOR 4 TO 6 PEOPLE:
   3 slices day-old bread
   1 egg
   3 tablespoons chopped parsley
   1 onion, chopped
   1 stalk celery with leaves, chopped
   1 small clove garlic, chopped
   ¼ teaspoon grated lemon peel
   ½ pound ground veal
   ½ pound ground lean pork
   Salt and pepper
   Pinch thyme

For the gravy:
4 tablespoons butter or oil
3 tablespoons flour
3 cups water
2 beef bouillon cubes
2 tablespoons wine vinegar
Small piece lemon peel
Salt and pepper
4 tablespoons finely chopped sour pickles

Dip the bread in water and squeeze out immediately as much water as you can. Put it in a large bowl and beat in the egg thoroughly with a fork until there are no lumps of bread left. Add the parsley, celery, garlic, onion, the lemon peel, the meat, and season with salt and pepper and thyme. Mix well. It will be quite sticky at first, but if you persevere it will eventually form a large ball which does not stick. Shape this mixture into large meat balls, about the size of small oranges.

Take a pot large enough to hold the meat balls one layer deep. A Dutch oven works well. To make the gravy: heat the butter or oil in it and add the flour. Let it cook, stirring until a pretty pale gold. Stir in gradually 3 cups of water, crumble 2 bouillon cubes in it, and add 2 tablespoons of good vinegar. Let this come to a boil. It will not be thick, just velvety. Turn to a simmer and drop in the meat balls gently. Add a little strip of lemon peel, cover and simmer for about 45 minutes. Once in a while shake the pan a little but try to keep the fire so low that you don't have to stir. Stirring can break the meat balls, which are very light and delicate. Taste the gravy and add salt and pepper as needed. Just before serving add to the sauce about 4 tablespoons of finely chopped sour pickles.

This is the kind of family dish which makes husbands exclaim that you are a genius!

ROULADE DE BOEUF

Beef Roll

This Belgian dish is especially good made with a large round steak which you suspect is a less tender cut. It is pounded a little, seasoned with a meat tenderizer, and filled with scrambled eggs! The idea may startle you, but it is really delicious and pretty enough for company.

FOR 4 PEOPLE:

1 large thin round steak, about 1½ pounds
Pepper
Pinch tarragon
Meat tenderizer and/or salt
4 eggs
2 frankfurters
1 large dill pickle
A little butter
½ cup cream

Choose a large steak which holds well together, cut less than ½-inch thick. Rub the meat well with pepper and tarragon and meat tenderizer and/or salt.

Scramble 4 eggs, making them a little less creamy than usual— they must not be runny. Season them nicely with salt and pepper. Pound the meat until it becomes thin but be careful not to tear it. Then, spread the slightly cooled eggs evenly over the meat.

Take a couple of frankfurters or some of the little canned wieners. The important thing is that they should have a nice smoky flavor and no bright red skin to run off over the eggs. Arrange the frankfurters and long slices of dill pickle in the center of the meat and eggs combination. Roll up the meat as you would a thick jelly roll and tie it securely but not too tightly with string in several places. You now have a roll with meat on the outside, a layer of eggs and a pretty center of franks and pickles.

Place the roll in a well-buttered baking dish. Dot it with a little additional butter and roast it gently, in preheated oven at 350°F. for about an hour. It should become an appetizing brown but not dry out. Add a couple of tablespoons of water in the pan if necessary.

At serving time, remove the meat gently to a serving dish and take off the strings. Boil up the juices on top of the stove, adding a little water if necessary to melt any crusty brown bits at the bottom of the pan. Let the water evaporate until you just have a rather thick juice. Stir in the cream and let it heat but not boil. Taste just in case it needs a little more salt. Cut meat in rather thick slices with a very sharp knife. Pass sauce separately.

STEAK AU POIVRE

Pepper Steak

I once heard a great French cook declare that women are incapable of cooking a steak properly! It is due, he said, to women's natural reluctance to make a great deal of smoke in the kitchen. He did not add that the cleaning up is usually left to women, which may account for our reluctance! There is some truth in what he said, though, and a really well-cooked steak is "rare," if you will pardon the pun.

You have probably seen countless recipes telling you exactly how many minutes to cook steak on each side. Unfortunately, you rarely measure steak with a precision ruler and, moreover, the meat itself varies considerably. The amount of fat and bone changes the cooking time. I have found that the best way is just to watch it carefully.

This recipe is marvelous if you are as fond as I am of the taste of black pepper. I mean the taste, not just the spiciness of it. The classic French recipe uses cognac in the sauce, but I have found it delicious with brandy and even whisky or bourbon for a change.

FOR 4 PEOPLE:
> Approximately 2 pounds steak, or as much as your budget
> allows or your appetite dictates. Choose porterhouse,
> T-Bone or beef rib cut ¾-inch thick
> Whole black pepper
> Salt
> ¼ cup cognac or brandy
> ¼ pound (1 stick) butter

Choose your steaks carefully; it must be heavy beef for best flavor, the meat finely marbled with creamy fat and a deep red. Three or four hours before cooking the meat, sprinkle it liberally with crushed black pepper. It should not be really ground, just broken in little lumps. Do not salt the meat. Just let it sit and absorb the aroma of the pepper.

Take a very heavy frying pan, just large enough to hold the steaks, and heat it, without any fat, until a drop of water will bounce off it. Put in your steak. It will sizzle like mad and smoke. But just watch and do *not* touch the steak, until you see a slight "beading" of the juices on top. If you like your steak rare, turn it at once. If you like it medium or well done, wait until this dew becomes quite heavy. Turn it and salt after turning. Watch the other side for the same "dew" and then remove the steak.

Pour off any excess fat from the pan but not the meat juices. Add the cognac or brandy and stir and scrape to melt all the caramelized bits. Do this over low heat, you don't want to "flame" the liquor. Add the butter and stir until melted and well mixed with the pan juices. Pour over the steaks and serve with pride.

TOURNEDOS BÉARNAISE

Steaks with Béarnaise Sauce

Tournedos is the name of a really pampered, luxury steak. Like most good things, they are not very large, certainly not by American standards. But every last mouthful is as tender and delicious as the first. The finest tournedos are thick slices of prime fillet of beef or rib-eye steaks, trimmed of all fat, cut nicely and evenly round.

French butchers have a way with their meat. They cut it and trim it in such a way that you have a piece of meat of the same tenderness all the way through. Some pieces, being very lean, are wrapped in a thin layer of beef or pork fat, hardly thicker than a piece of strong paper. This cooks down to nothing but keeps the meat juicy as it cooks. Tournedos cut from the fillet are usually wrapped this way. Bacon has no place with such a fine steak—its smoky flavor, delicious as it may be in other dishes, tends to detract from the pure, good beef taste of a tournedos.

FOR 4 PEOPLE:
*Béarnaise sauce**
4 thick slices peeled tomato
A little butter
4 really large mushrooms
Salt and pepper
4 1-inch thick steaks cut from fillet of beef or rib eye

Choose your steaks carefully. If you have them cut from fillet, see if the butcher will give you a thin sheet of fat or will even wrap them all around with it himself. If not, cut thin strips of fat as wide as the meat is thick, wrap one around each steak and tie with string. This is excellent for fillet, which is quite lean, although hardly necessary for rib eye, which is usually well marbled with fat.

Before starting on the steaks, prepare the garnish. Make a good béarnaise sauce and keep it warm. Peel the tomatoes and cut four thick slices. Heat these gently in a pan with a little butter, they should just get warm.

Choose four really very large mushroom caps, fresh or the imported French canned ones, which are excellent. Cook or heat the mushrooms in a little butter, seasoning them lightly with salt and pepper.

Fillet being such fine meat deserves more gentle treatment than rib eye. Cook it in a skillet with a little butter over a lower heat than rib eye. To judge the doneness, see the recipe for Pepper Steak, the same fine beading of juices on top of the meat will guide you.

When the steaks are ready, top each with a slice of tomato, a mushroom cap over that and fill the caps with béarnaise sauce. Pass more béarnaise separately. I can't think of anything nicer to serve with these steaks than simply golden French fries and watercress seasoned with a little oil and lemon juice. This is gourmet eating at its most luxurious.

TOURNEDOS DAUPHINOISE

Steaks with Mushrooms and Cream

The wonderful thing about steak is that after enjoying it, you seldom feel stuffed and sleepy as with other rich foods. On a hot summer day, particularly, after some strenuous activity there are few things men enjoy more than a good steak.

Sometime try serving an entirely French meal. Start with radishes perhaps, simply scrubbed and eaten whole with salt and a little butter and crusty French bread. Or a tomato salad made with ripe and firm tomatoes, peeled and sliced and simply seasoned with oil, vinegar, salt and pepper and lots of finely chopped onion and parsley. Then serve these delicious steaks and, finally, fruit and cheese for dessert. Uncomplicated, unstuffy, but perfect in its simplicity.

FOR 4 PEOPLE:

8 ounces fresh or frozen mushrooms
About 3 tablespoons butter
Salt and pepper
4 slices fillet of beef, 1-inch thick
¼ cup red port wine
½ cup heavy cream

Clean the mushrooms, if fresh, and cook them until golden in a little butter and a good seasoning of salt and pepper.

Melt about 2 more tablespoons of butter in the skillet and cook the steaks. Fillet deserves tender treatment, so cook them rather gently, watching for the fine beading explained for Pepper Steak, and season with salt and pepper as you turn them. When done, keep them warm for a minute while you make the sauce.

Pour the wine, a fragrant ruby port, into the pan and scrape and stir to melt all the sticky juices where the flavor is. Add the mushrooms with their juices and pour in the cream. Heat but do not boil. Pour over the steaks and serve immediately.

TOURNEDOS À L'ESTRAGON

Steaks with Tarragon

Tarragon means summer to me and on a cold winter day, I can open a jar of the dried kind and forget the cold and rain. We always had a small bush of it growing in our garden in Brussels. It is quite pretty, and we would often crush a few leaves in our fingers, just to inhale the delightful fragrance.

We used it all summer long, in salads, on tomatoes, a sprig of it inside a roasting chicken to flavor it delicately. Tarragon grown from seed is Russian tarragon and has no taste, but you can grow real French tarragon if you buy tarragon plants from a reputable nursery.

In this recipe, tarragon is combined with Madeira wine to perfume delicate tender fillets of beef steaks. The sauce will be plentiful so try serving these steaks with glamorized mashed potatoes, such as Pommes de Terre Duchesse.* And if your guests go French and mop up a last bit of sauce with a little piece of crusty tender French bread, condone it and do the same! This sauce is worth it, you couldn't bear to leave a smidgen.

FOR 4 PEOPLE:

4 tablespoons butter
4 slices fillet of beef about ¾-inch thick
2 tablespoons liquid beef extract
½ cup (scant) water
1 tablespoon dried tarragon
¼ cup Madeira wine
1 teaspoon flour mixed with
  2 teaspoons butter
½ cup heavy cream
Salt and pepper

Heat 2 tablespoons of butter in a heavy skillet and gently cook the little tournedos, watching for the beading as described for Pepper Steak. Cook them rarer than you want them, because they will go on cooking in their own heat while you make the sauce. Remove them from the pan and keep warm. Add two more tablespoonfuls of butter to the pan and 2 tablespoonfuls of good beef extract. Stir until the butter melts and pour in a scant ½ cup of water. Boil quickly and add 1 tablespoon of dried tarragon. Season with salt and pepper. Stir and cook over quite high heat until the water has evaporated almost entirely and you have a thick fragrant juice. Pour in the wine and stir well while it simmers gently. Then add the teaspoon of flour mixed with butter to thicken the sauce very slightly, stir well and cook a few minutes. The sauce should be glossy and just coat a spoon. If it is too thick, add a little more wine. Pour in the cream, stir well and let it get hot. Pour over the steaks and serve immediately.

ENTRECÔTE À LA MOELLE

Rib Eye Steaks with Marrow

This is a robust dish, good steak, beautifully cooked, bathed by a sauce made of full-bodied red wine into which we simmer marrow and spices!

This is no dish for calorie counters! Marrow is definitely fat but such a fine, delicate fat, more flavorful than butter even, which blends with the steaks for supreme perfection. Choose the meat carefully. It should be thinly veined with fat, like marble. The marbling inside the meat means the animal has been incurably lazy from birth and never wondered where its next meal was coming from. Not a misspent life either, when you consider its glorious end in this dish!

If you never see neat little packages of inch-thick marrow bones at your supermarket, ask the butcher to slice a nice thick one for you.

FOR 4 PEOPLE:

> 2 tablespoons butter
> 4 tablespoons chopped shallots or onions
> 1½ cups good dry red wine
> 4 tablespoons chopped parsley
> Pinch thyme
> Bay leaf
> 1 tablespoon sugar
> Salt and pepper
> ½ lemon
> 6 or 8 (1-inch-thick) slices marrow bone
> A little flour
> 4 steaks, rib eye or porterhouse or T-Bone,
>   cut ¾ to 1 inch thick

Take a small skillet, heat a tablespoonful of butter in it, and cook the chopped shallots or onions until transparent. Pour in the wine, add the parsley, thyme and bay leaf. Season with the sugar, sparingly with salt and pepper and drop in the ½ lemon. Bring to a simmer and cook until reduced by about half.

Take a sharp pointed knife, pass it between the marrow and the bone and push the marrow out. Roll these little slices gently in a little flour seasoned with salt and pepper and shake off any excess. This helps them keep in shape as they cook. Add these to the wine sauce and leave them to cook very gently while you do the steaks. Season with plenty of salt and lots of black pepper, but don't stir or the marrow will break up.

Cook the steaks simply in a dry skillet sprinkled with salt. See Pepper Steak for details on doneness. Place the steaks on a serving dish, take a slotted spoon and gently garnish each steak with a slice of marrow. Pour off any fat remaining in the skillet in which you cooked the steaks. Then, pour the rest of the marrow sauce into it, boil up fast to get all the goodness from the steak juices mixed with the sauce. Pour over and around the steaks and serve speedily on HOT plates. Marrow is delicious hot but it cools and congeals very quickly. Hot plates, the hotter the better, retard this disastrous moment.

BLANQUETTE DE VEAU

Veal Stew

To be at its best this dish requires real veal, not baby beef, not heavy calf, but tender, white as chicken real veal. This means you may have to look for it, but believe me it has a flavor all its own, completely different from beef, its parent.

Milk-fed veal demands gentle care in cooking. It dries out easily, but if you treat it properly, you'll be amply rewarded. In this recipe, the best cut to use is short ribs, because the bones, which are still very gelatinous, give the richest broth for the sauce. When you add to this delicate broth white wine, cream and egg yolks, wonders happen!

FOR 4 PEOPLE:
  4 tablespoons butter
  1 onion, chopped
  About 3 pounds veal stew meat, bone in
  Salt and pepper
  Pinch thyme
  Bay leaf
  Juice ½ lemon
  2 cups beef bouillon (from cubes)
  1 cup dry white wine
  1 very small carrot
  1 tablespoon (approximately) flour
  2 egg yolks
  1 cup heavy cream

The delicacy of this dish lies in the white meat, so this is one time we shall not brown the meat first. Simply melt the butter in a heavy pot, add the onion to it and cook until wilted and clear but not brown. Add the meat and toss it in the butter for a few minutes but don't let it get the least bit brown. Season it lightly with salt and pepper (the bouillon will add a lot of salt), a good pinch of thyme and a bay leaf. I think it very important to season meats for stews with herbs, etc., at the beginning of the cooking time. Many cooks simply add the seasoning along with the liquid, but this first seasoning before liquid is added penetrates more deeply into the meat and makes for a tastier dish. Sprinkle a few drops of lemon juice over the meat, then add the bouillon and the white wine. Drop in the carrot, which will flavor the stew as it cooks.

Simmer, very gently and covered, until the meat is tender, approximately 1 to 1½ hours. At that time, the liquid in the pot will have reduced by about half. If there seems to be too much liquid, uncover the pot for a few minutes.

Mix 1 tablespoonful of flour with enough water to make a very thin paste, add this to the pot, stirring, and leave to cook for another 10 minutes or so. You now have a clear, fairly thin sauce. Remove the carrot and discard or eat it! Taste the sauce, it should have a really good taste and be almost too seasoned as the cream will thin it down a little. Correct accordingly. Beat the egg yolks with the cream. Remove the blanquette from the fire, add a little of the sauce to the egg yolks and cream, stir, and return all to the pot, stirring like mad. The sauce will thicken slightly immediately and will acquire a delightful creamy pale gold color. Taste and add a little more lemon juice if necessary. Do not reheat. Serve with rice.

For a special occasion, add mushrooms to the blanquette. It becomes even more delicious, if possible. If you are pressed for time, you can do everything but add the cream and egg yolks a day or so before. At that stage it freezes well also. Just add a little fresh white wine when you reheat it before adding the cream and eggs to give it that "just cooked" flavor!

CÔTES DE VEAU ZINGARA

Veal Chops in Rich Tomato Sauce

The recipe for this dish was created in 1808 by Viart, a famous French chef. He christened it "Saint-Garat" to honor a French singer named Garat. Such is fame that Garat's singing is forgotten but the veal chops are not, although their name has gradually been misspelled over the years to end as "Zingara," which gives it a slight gypsy tone.

The recipe also has changed over the years. The original calls for a great many ingredients. Some chefs use them all, others discriminate and cut them down to two or three. The basic ones are of course the veal chops and tomato sauce. Add the ingredients you wish from those listed and create your own Zingara!

FOR 4 PEOPLE:

    2 cups tomato sauce
    2 tablespoons beef extract
    ¼ cup Madeira or ruby port wine
    Any or all of the following ingredients, about
        1 cup in all: Thinly slivered ham, smoked tongue, sliced
        mushrooms, sliced truffle or truffle pieces and peelings
    6 tablespoons butter
    4 thick veal chops
    Salt and pepper
    Paprika

Make a good tomato sauce from scratch with tomato paste or use a good canned brand. Make it more flavorful with 2 tablespoons beef extract and the Madeira or port. Sliver the ham or tongue or both in little ¼ inch strips and add to the sauce. Add also sliced mushrooms cooked in butter and if you can afford it, a truffle, thinly sliced. Cheaper, and almost as good is one of those tiny cans of truffle pieces and peelings. Add 2 tablespoons of butter to the sauce, cover the pot and leave it to simmer barely, for about 1 hour. This will blend all the flavors into a perfect combination. You can do it ahead of time if you wish. Take care that it barely simmers—just very hot is the ideal point, since it can burn rather easily.

Get the whitest veal chops or steaks that you can find. Season them on both sides with salt and pepper and a good dusting of paprika. Cook them until well done and golden on both sides in about 4 tablespoons butter in a skillet. Take your time, veal likes gentle rather than fierce heat and must be well done. Allow 15 to 20 minutes. Place the chops on a dish, pour the sauce into the skillet the veal was in, stir and scrape any juices sticking to the bottom of the pan. Pour over the meat and serve. Deep-fried potato puffs go wonderfully with this dish.

JARRET DE VEAU

Veal Shank in Tomato-Wine Sauce

The mark of a good cook is to make tasty dishes from cheaper cuts of meat. In this case, you need veal shank or leg round. Count a large slice, about ¾ inch thick, per person. Each has a little marrow bone in the center which tastes delicious. This is a very good dish for a busy day, since it can cook practically without watching or can be made the day before and reheated. It goes well with rice or noodles.

FOR 4 PEOPLE:

3 tablespoons butter or cooking fat
4 slices veal shank
Salt and pepper
1 onion, chopped
3 large tomatoes, fresh or canned, chopped
2 cloves garlic, finely minced
Pinch thyme
Bay leaf
½ cup beef bouillon and ½ cup dry white wine OR
   1 cup beef bouillon
1 anchovy (optional)
Small strip lemon peel

Melt the butter or cooking fat in a nice heavy pot and brown the meat gently on both sides. Season it with salt and pepper. Add the onion and cook until it begins to color, then add the tomatoes, the garlic, the thyme and a bay leaf. Pour in the bouillon (made from a cube) and the white wine. Or you can use 1 cup of bouillon and omit the wine.

Simmer very gently until the meat is tender. This should take from 1 to 1½ hours. Cover the pot at the beginning and then take the lid off so the sauce can thicken when the meat is almost tender. This should be a good rich tomato sauce, just enough to smother the meat. When the meat is done, mash or chop the anchovy fillet very finely. Peel a strip of peel off a nice fat lemon. Remove the meat to a platter, drop the anchovy into the sauce and pinch the piece of peel so that the oil squirts out into the sauce, then drop it in. Boil furiously for a second or two, remove the lemon peel, and pour the sauce over the meat. The lemon and anchovy flavors make this sauce incredibly good. You will have fun seeing how your guests try to find out what makes it so different.

OISEAUX SANS TÊTE

Veal Birds

The French are very fond of eating different kinds of little birds. It may seem a shame, but they are delicious! They are quite expensive usually and rare. So housewives stuff veal steaks, tie them neatly and call them "headless birds." Not as good as a tender little quail, certainly, but a delicious dish if the stuffing is well made and rather economical.

Lemon and thyme go particularly well with veal. So does rosemary. A little pork meat will add enough fat to the rather lean veal. Add to this a sauce made with a little brandy and some cream and you have a superlative dish!

FOR 4 PEOPLE:

4 to 6 thin veal steaks, about 1½ pounds in all
Salt and pepper
2 slices day-old bread
¼ pound ground pork
1 tablespoon finely chopped chives or green onion
¼ teaspoon grated lemon peel
Thyme, rosemary or tarragon
1 egg yolk
4 tablespoons butter
1 shallot or small onion, chopped
4 tablespoons brandy, preferably cognac
1 cup heavy cream

Pound the steaks quite thin; if you have no mallet, the heavy handle of a large kitchen knife does well. Just don't cut yourself! Season well with salt and pepper.

Make the stuffing by dipping the bread briefly into cold water and squeezing out as much as you can. Place it into a bowl with the ground pork. Add the finely chopped chives or green onions, the tiny bit of grated lemon peel, and your favorite herb. Mix well and add the egg yolk. Season with salt and pepper. Share the stuffing between the steaks, placing it in the middle. Roll up the steaks, tucking the ends in to form neat little packages so that the stuffing won't fall out. Twist strong white thread around them to keep them in place.

Heat the butter in a heavy pot, place the little veal birds in it and let them brown on all sides. Add the chopped shallot or onion and let that get golden too. Pour in just, but only just, enough water to cover the bottom of the pot. Cover with a good-fitting lid and cook for about 45 minutes. Peek in once in a while and add a few drops of water if necessary. Don't let it get dry and burn.

When the meat is done, take the birds out of the pot and remove their threads. Pour in the brandy and heat for a second, scraping any juices sticking to the pot. Add the cream, stirring well, and let it get hot. Taste and correct seasoning if necessary. Pour over the birds and serve.

ROULADES DE VEAU

Veal Rolls with Ham and Swiss Cheese

Veal is a delicate meat which tastes wonderful mixed with such flavorful things as ham and cheese. This recipe includes just those plus thyme. But in this case, instead of using thyme as a just perceptible accent as in most dishes, we shall get the full flavor of it. This is quite unusual; you have to like thyme, of course, but if you do, you still may have no idea of the heady aroma it gives to this dish. If at all possible, get whole thyme, still attached to its little twigs. The next best is whole thyme leaves, which are easily obtainable. Powdered thyme won't do here.

FOR 4 PEOPLE:
 8 small veal steaks, cut thin (1½ pounds in all)
 4 slices boiled ham
 4 ounces Swiss cheese
 Thyme
 Salt and pepper
 4 tablespoons (approximately) butter
 ½ cup (scant) water

You need thin little veal steaks, at least two per person, for this recipe. You can buy larger ones and cut them, of course, or explain to the butcher what you need and he will cut them for you. Cut the slices of ham to fit the veal steaks, and cut the cheese in strips about the size and thickness of your little finger, less than ½ inch thick.

Place a slice of ham over each veal slice, a strip of cheese in the center and a little branch of thyme on the cheese. Roll up the veal and tie it with thread so you have neat little bundles.

Heat about 4 tablespoons butter in a skillet and fry the rolls until golden on all sides, seasoning with salt and pepper. When all are browned, add a scant ½ cup of water to the pan, just enough to cover the bottom. Cover the pan and allow to cook gently for about 15 minutes so the centers get well done. The cheese melts as you cut into the rolls, while the thyme releases its fragrance. After the first mouthful, you will find all is well with the world.

ROULADE DE VEAU AUX RAISINS

Rolled Veal Roast with Raisins

Few things make a housewife happier than to discover a dish glamorous enough for company and at the same time inexpensive enough not to strain the budget. This dish qualifies: veal rolled-roast or breast of veal is usually available at a reasonable price, particularly when you take into consideration that there is no waste. This roast is sometimes available frozen at an even cheaper price. If so, let it thaw completely and unroll it. If it is fresh, tell the butcher not to tie it.

FOR 4 TO 6 PEOPLE:
   4 slices bacon
   2½ to 3 pounds rolled veal roast, breast or shoulder
   Salt and pepper
   1 large onion, finely chopped
   1 cup raisins
   2 tablespoons Worcestershire sauce
   1 teaspoon flour (optional)

Take a pot large enough to hold the roast and fry the bacon in it until crisp. Leave the fat in the pot, remove the bacon, drain and crumble it.

Unroll the roast, season it with a little salt and pepper, sprinkle the bacon and the onion evenly over it. Now sprinkle half the raisins and drizzle about a tablespoonful of Worcestershire sauce over all. Roll up the roast and tie it securely with string. It won't be quite as neat as when the butcher does it but never mind; add a couple of twists lengthwise to make a neat package.

Reheat the bacon fat in the pot and brown the roast well on all sides in it. When it is a deep gold, add just enough water to cover the bottom of the pot, put the lid on and leave to cook over a very low fire for about 1½ hours or until the meat is quite tender. Peek in once in a while and add a little more water if necessary. Season lightly with salt and pepper. About 20 minutes before the roast is completely done, add the rest of the raisins to the sauce and a good dash (about 1 tablespoon) of Worcestershire sauce. The raisins will plump up and absorb a good bit of the sauce so be careful not to let it burn. Add enough water to make about a cupful of gravy, if necessary. Taste and season with more salt if it seems to need it. Veal makes a very rich gravy all by itself. If you browned the roast well at first, it will be full of flavor and a shiny brown. If you prefer your gravies thick, you can stir in a little flour, about a teaspoonful, mixed to a thin paste with water. Be sure it boils up and cooks 10 minutes before serving, though.

CHOESELS AU MADÈRE

The inhabitants of Brussels take a particular delight in the *zwanse*, which can be translated as "pulling your leg." Choesels au Madère figures in just such a joke. It is an absolutely marvelous concoction of long-simmered sweetbreads, little veal meat balls, good beef and sometimes sheep's feet. The whole is cooked for four hours with beer and Madeira wine, flavored with a little tomato and lots of mushrooms. It is eaten at the peak of perfection in little restaurants near the slaughterhouse. So what do the Brussels people tell friends who inquire as to what are *choesels?* They hem and haw and explain that you have to have a bull, not an ox to start with. . . . As you need quite a variety of meats to make this dish as good as it should be, don't try to make it for just two or three people. The meats are all relatively cheap, though, and you could serve quite a crowd on a budget. A last word of warning: order these meats from the butcher several days in advance; usually such things as kidneys and sweetbreads are only available certain days of the week.

FOR 8 TO 10 PEOPLE:

2 pounds sweetbreads
1 beef kidney or 2 veal kidneys
4 tablespoons lard or drippings
1 large oxtail, cut in pieces
1 large onion, coarsely chopped
1 carrot
1 rib celery
Salt and pepper
Thyme
Bay leaf
1 pound breast of lamb or lamb stew
1 pound veal shank or veal stew
Nutmeg
2 cans beer
1 6-ounce can tomato paste
2 slices day-old bread
½ pound ground veal and
    ½ pound ground pork, ground twice very finely
1 egg
4 tablespoons finely chopped parsley
2 tablespoons finely chopped onion
1 pound mushrooms
1 cup Madeira wine
2 tablespoons flour

Armed with this impressive list of ingredients, patience and time, here is how to proceed!

Start by soaking the sweetbreads in cold water for several hours. Change the water once or twice. Split the kidney and remove the tough parts inside, slice and cover with cold water also.

Heat about 4 tablespoons of lard or bacon drippings in a large pot and brown the pieces of oxtail in it. Chop coarsely 1 large onion, a carrot and a rib of celery. Add these to the oxtail, cut in pieces, seasoning with salt and pepper, a good pinch of thyme and a bay leaf. Cover and cook a few minutes until the vegetables begin to brown. Add just enough water to cover the meat and leave to simmer for about an hour. Leave the pot partially uncovered for some of the time so that there will be a rich fragrant stock at the end.

Cut the lamb and the veal into even small serving pieces. Add them to the oxtail along with the slices of kidney. Add some more seasoning of salt and pepper and thyme and just a whiff of nutmeg. Pour in enough beer to cover all the meats and simmer for about 30 minutes.

Now take the sweetbreads and plunge them in boiling water for 3 or 4 minutes. Drain and cool a little, then cut them in serving pieces also, removing any cartilage you may find. And off they go into the pot! Now you can stir in the tomato paste also. Cook all these meats for another 45 minutes or 1 hour so that everything is perfectly tender. Add more beer from time to time if the liquid goes down too much; keep tightly covered and just simmering, not boiling fast.

You now have to make the meat balls with the veal and pork. Dip 2 slices of bread briefly in cold water, squeeze out as much as you can. Mix with the ground veal and pork and 1 egg until completely blended. Season with salt and pepper, another whiff of nutmeg, a pinch of thyme and the finely chopped parsley and onion. Shape into very small meat balls the size of a walnut.

Clean the mushrooms and cut them in thick slices. Drop them and the meat balls into the stew. By now the juices will be succulent with the flavors of the many meats. Pour in the Madeira, reserving ¼ cup. Mix 2 tablespoons of flour into a thin paste with the reserved wine and pour in, stirring very gently, mixing it in rather, without breaking up the meats. Taste and correct the seasoning if necessary. About 20 minutes after the meat balls and mushrooms are added, the *choesels* are ready.

Involved as this is, you could very well spread the work over a couple of days, leaving the addition of the meat balls, mushrooms and Madeira for the day of the party. Be sure to refrigerate everything well. All you need to serve with this potent brew is plain boiled potatoes. Beer, or else a fine old Burgundy, is fine to drink with this.

PAIN DE VEAU

Veal Loaf

Here is a way to make that old standby meat loaf look and taste a lot more glamorous. If the budget is not too tight, try using ground veal mixed with a little ground ham. The results are almost like an expensive pâté! Make a large loaf; it is delicious cold with a salad or in sandwiches—more economical that way too!

FOR 1 LARGE MEAT LOAF:

2 *hard-boiled eggs, 1 raw egg*
1 *cup bread crumbs*
2 *tablespoons chopped parsley*
2 *tablespoons chopped onion*
1 *tablespoon tarragon*
2 *pounds ground veal* OR
　 1½ *pounds ground veal and* ½ *pound ground ham*
Salt and pepper
2 *large dill pickles*

Hard-boil two of the eggs and shell them. Put the bread crumbs in a large bowl with the chopped parsley, onion and tarragon and the raw egg. Mix well adding just a few drops of water to moisten all the bread crumbs thoroughly. Mix in the meat and keep kneading until it forms a nice smooth mixture. Season with little salt, if you are using the ham, and plenty of pepper.

Grease a baking dish generously; choose a rather flat one, and pat half the meat mixture into an oblong. Arrange the hard-boiled eggs cut in two lengthwise in a row in the center of the meat and place the dill pickles cut in strips alongside the eggs. Cover with the rest of the meat and pat into shape.

Bake in preheated oven at 350°F. for about 1 hour or until the loaf is golden all over. Let it cool a few minutes before serving in thick slices. A can of undiluted mushroom soup added to the drippings in the pan and heated on top of the stove makes a delicious gravy with this.

RIS DE VEAU À LA DARTOIS

Sweetbreads with Shrimp and Crawfish

One of the pleasant surprises of my life in the United States was the discovery that sweetbreads, when you can get them, are rather cheaper than meat. In France, where they are esteemed on a par with caviar and pâté de foie gras, their price is *très cher*.

I have a collection of recipes which have been handed down in my family for generations. Some are dated 1844, all written by hand in a beautiful, spidery script. Among them is this one, which combines sweetbreads with a sauce made of shrimp and crawfish. Crawfish abound in Louisiana; elsewhere you can substitute rock lobster pieces with equally good results.

FOR 4 TO 6 PEOPLE:
  2 *pounds sweetbreads*
  Salt
  1 *pound shrimp,* cooked and peeled*
  1 *cup crawfish tails or rock lobster pieces*
  ½ *cup shrimp broth or lobster juice or clam juice*
  ¼ *pound (1 stick) butter*
  2 *tablespoons flour*
  ½ *cup Madeira or ruby port wine*
  1 *cup light cream*
  Pepper
  2 *eggs*
  1 *cup fine bread crumbs*

Start by soaking the sweetbreads in cold water for several hours or overnight. Then plunge them in boiling salted water for 4 or 5 minutes to blanch and firm them. Drain and cool. Cut them in serving pieces, as neatly and evenly as you can, removing any cartilage or fat as you go.

Boil the shrimp with plenty of seasonings and the crawfish or lobster also. Reserve about ½ cup of shrimp broth and/or the lobster juice or clam juice. You don't need much but it makes a great difference. Make a sauce by melting 3 tablespoons butter in a small pan, adding 2 tablespoons flour and cooking it until frothy but not brown. Stir in the shrimp broth and the wine to make a velvety sauce which you season well with salt and pepper. Add the peeled shrimp and crawfish or lobster to it and leave to simmer very, very gently for the flavors to blend. Add the cream just before serving.

Beat the eggs in a soup plate. Dip the pieces of sweetbreads, well drained on paper towels, in the egg, then roll them in the bread crumbs to coat them well. Heat the rest of the butter in a large skillet and gently fry the pieces of sweetbreads in it. Do this gently, taking your time and keeping the fire rather low so they brown evenly. When the sweetbreads are golden, sprinkle them lightly with salt and arrange them in a circle on a large platter. Pour the fragrant sauce in the middle and serve. All I would serve with this is "croutons" of fried bread or hot and crusty French bread. Anything else would detract from the fine flavor.

RIS DE VEAU GRAND-MÈRE

Sweetbreads

Sweetbreads are absolutely delicious practically any way you fix them. This is a marvelous dish to serve a few gourmet friends by candlelight. A nice bottle of dry white wine, your prettiest tablecloth and a few flowers, and you will have a relaxed, delightful evening.

This dish takes very little last minute preparation. You can easily make it early in the day and warm it up while before-dinner drinks are being served. The last-minute addition of cream and egg yolks takes no time at all. Serve it with tiny green peas and little potatoes.

FOR 4 PEOPLE:

2 pounds (approximately) sweetbreads
Salt
4 tablespoons butter
2 small carrots
2 or 3 very tender stalks celery
3 or 4 very small onions
Pepper
Pinch thyme
½ pound mushrooms, fresh or frozen
2 egg yolks
½ cup heavy cream
Chopped parsley for garnish

Soak the sweetbreads in cold water several hours or overnight, changing the water once or twice. Plunge them in salted boiling water for a few minutes to firm them, drain and cool. Cut them in serving pieces, removing any cartilage you may find but leaving the membrane which covers them intact since it keeps them in shape.

Melt the butter in a heavy pot, just large enough to hold the sweetbreads comfortably. Add the carrots and celery cut into small ½-inch cubes and the onions. Leave these last whole if they are really very small, the size of a pecan. Cut them in two or four, if larger. Season with a little salt and pepper and a pinch of thyme. Cover and let cook very gently for a few minutes so the vegetables can absorb some of the butter. Add the sweetbreads and the mushrooms, cut in two or four depending on their size, and cook some more, adding a little more seasoning, until it all begins to sizzle and brown very lightly. Now pour in just enough water to bathe the bottom of the pot, cover tightly and cook for about 40 to 45 minutes. Add a little more water from time to time if the juices seem to dry out but don't let anything swim in juice; there should be only enough liquid to prevent anything from sticking to the bottom of the pot.

When all the vegetables are tender remove the pan from the fire. Beat the egg yolks with the cream and gently pour it into the dish, stirring as you go. Stir very gently so you don't break up vegetables and meat. The sweetbreads and vegetables should be coated with a thin layer of sauce. Taste and correct seasoning if necessary. Serve immediately. After the cream and eggs are added the dish must not be reheated, but it can be kept warm for a few minutes.

RIS DE VEAU À LA MAINTENON

Sweetbreads with Mushroom Purée

This is what the French call *un bon petit plat mijoté*, a lovingly simmered little dish, and they usually say it with half-closed eyes and lick their lips in happy anticipation! It does not require a great deal of work, particularly not at the last moment. Since it is a very rich dish, plan something light as a first course and for dessert. To be appreciated at their finest sweetbreads and creamed mushrooms do not require any other vegetable. In lieu of potatoes or rice, simply serve slices of bread toasted with butter in the oven, crisp and a delicious contrast to the creamy sauce. A good wine will make the meal memorable. Either a red of the Bordeaux type, or a light and fragrant white, goes well with sweetbreads.

FOR 4 PEOPLE:
>   2 *pounds (approximately) sweetbreads*
>   4 *slices bacon*
>   2 *tablespoons butter*
>   1 *carrot, thinly sliced*
>   1 *onion, thinly sliced*
>   Salt and pepper
>   Pinch thyme
>   Bay leaf

For the sauce:
1 pound fresh or frozen mushrooms
¼ pound (1 stick) butter
Salt and pepper
2 tablespoons flour
1 cup heavy cream

4 slices day-old bread
1 cup heavy cream

Prepare the sweetbreads as described for Ris de Veau Grand-mère.

Take a large skillet with a good lid. Fry the bacon until a little crisp, then pour off the fat and replace it with 2 tablespoons butter. Add to this the carrot and onion, then the sweetbreads. Season with not too much salt (because of the bacon), pepper, a pinch of thyme and a bay leaf. Cook gently until it all begins to brown and sizzle, then pour in just enough water to prevent sticking, cover and cook for about 45 minutes. Look in once in a while and add a little water only if there is danger of burning.

Make the mushroom sauce as follows: Clean the fresh mushrooms by removing the sandy part of the stalk and wipe them gently. Cook them until golden in 4 tablespoons of butter, seasoning with salt and pepper as they cook.

Make a very thick cream sauce by melting 2 tablespoons of butter in a small pan, adding 2 tablespoons flour and cooking until frothy. Gradually stir in 1 cup of heavy cream and cook, stirring all the time until bubbly and thickened. Season with salt and pepper also. If you have a blender, you can now buzz both mushrooms and sauce together to make the purée. If not, chop the mushrooms as finely as you can with a sharp, heavy knife and mix with the sauce. Taste and correct seasoning if necessary. This can be done well in advance if you wish, just be sure to cover the bowl with wax paper or plastic film so that no skin forms as it cools.

Trim the slices of bread of their crusts; you can cut them in fancy shapes if you like, butter both sides and place them on a cooky sheet. At serving time, pop them in a preheated 450°F. oven for about 5 to 7 minutes to turn golden and crisp. Keep warm.

Heat sweetbreads and mushroom purée separately. Arrange the mushrooms in a circle on a serving dish, and place the sweetbreads in the center. Keep warm in the turned-off oven. Pour the cup of heavy cream over the bacon and vegetables left in the skillet, heat and stir for a few minutes. Pour through a strainer over the sweet-breads, pressing with the back of a spoon so that all the flavor is extracted.

CARRÉ DE PORC EN GELÉE

Jellied Pork Roast

Here is an impressive dish for a large party: a nice pork roast, well trimmed of its fat, roasted to flavorful perfection, served cold with a savory piquant jelly. A perfect party dish which can be prepared a day or two before the party and decorated as beautifully as by any French chef.

Cold meats look much more appetizing encased in shimmering jelly. It really isn't very difficult to make, and you can use this trick for such things as cold ham or chicken also. You cover the meat with a coat of jelly, then add the decorations and, finally, another coat of jelly. The beauty of it is that your decorations will not dry out and you can spend as much time preparing this dish as you want, providing you are not rushed. At the last moment, fresh parsley and/or lettuce can be used to surround the dish in all its shimmering loveliness. So try this:

FOR 8 TO 10 PEOPLE:

3 or 4 pounds pork roast—boned roast is perfect—OR
boned fresh ham
Salt and pepper
Thyme
1 carrot
1 large onion
1 celery rib with leaves
1 clove garlic
Bay leaf

For the jelly:
1 envelope gelatin
3 tablespoons sherry
1 tablespoon frozen orange juice concentrate
1 10-ounce can undiluted consommé
Pimiento, green pepper, carrot slices, parsley, etc. for
garnish (optional)

Rub the roast well with salt and pepper and a good pinch of thyme. Place it in a well-oiled baking dish and arrange all the vegetables, coarsely chopped, around it, along with 1 bay leaf. Roast at 350°F. in preheated oven counting about 40 to 45 minutes per pound. Pork should always be very well done. While it cooks, pour a little water into the roasting pan occasionally to keep the vegetables from burning. I don't usually recommend adding water to a roast but in this case we want gentle cooking and lots of flavor without a thick crust. Baste occasionally as the spirit moves you.

When the meat is quite tender, remove it from the dish to cool. Trim it and scrape free of any fat. When quite cold, slice it cleanly and evenly with a very sharp knife. Arrange the slices, slightly overlapping, on a serving dish. Refrigerate while you make the jelly.

If you don't mind a little extra work for a lot of extra flavor you will use the juices from the roast to make the jelly. If you are in a hurry, simply soften the gelatin in a little cold water, and add it along with 3 tablespoons of sherry and 1 tablespoon of frozen orange juice (undiluted), to 1 can of beef consommé. Heat and stir until the gelatin is melted, taste and correct seasoning if necessary.

For those who would like to use the juices of the roast for the jelly proceed as follows: Scrape off as much as possible of the congealed fat on top of the juices in the roasting pan. Add ½ cup of water and heat on top of the stove, stirring and scraping any brown bits sticking to the pan. Bring to a simmer for a few minutes. Strain through a wire strainer to remove the bits of vegetables, then strain through several thicknesses of cheesecloth. Pour into a bowl and chill. Remove any last speck of fat from the surface. Measure into a small pan, discarding any sediment at the bottom of the bowl which would cloud the jelly. Add enough consommé to make about 1¼ cups, add sherry and undiluted orange juice and the gelatin softened in water. Heat to a simmer, stirring until the gelatin has completely melted. This gives a better-flavored, darker jelly than plain consommé.

Allow the jelly to thicken as much as unbeaten egg whites, or just before it sets. Place the dish of meat in the freezer or freezer compartment of the refrigerator for about 10 or 15 minutes. It must not freeze, just get very, very cold. Take it out and spoon a thin coat of jelly evenly over it all. The jelly will set almost immediately as it touches the cold meat. When you have a nice thin coat of jelly, return the meat to the freezer for a few minutes while you prepare the garnish of hard-boiled egg white, pimiento, green pepper, parsley leaves, sliced stuffed olives, pickles, anything you think will look pretty and taste good!

Apply the garnish to the first coat of jelly, dipping each piece in jelly before placing it on so it will stick. Wait a few minutes for it to set and pour on more jelly evenly over it all. You can let this coat set and add another one, if you have enough jelly left. Cover the whole dish with plastic film, it will not stick to jelly, and refrigerate it until party time. Add a garnish of fresh parsley, sliced tomatoes, watercress or lettuce at the last moment.

To have the jelly at exactly the right consistency, you may have to reheat it once or twice. Stir it over hot water to thin, stir it over a bowl of ice to thicken it. Not really difficult, is it?

CÔTES DE PORC CHARCUTIÈRE

Spicy Pork Chops

The *charcuteries* are the French delicatessens, more or less. They sell mostly pork in all its forms. It may seem strange but some French butchers don't sell anything but beef, veal and lamb. If you want pork chops, sausage or bacon, you have to go to the *charcuterie*.

These fragrant pork chops are one of the many dishes you can buy ready to warm up in a French *charcuterie*. You can make them yourself very easily and they can be made ahead of time and reheated, a good thing when you are busy. It freezes well too, particularly if you omit the pickles until you reheat.

FOR 4 PEOPLE:
>   *1 tablespoon vegetable oil or fat*
>   *4 large thick pork chops, about 1½ to 2 pounds*
>   *Salt and pepper*
>   *Pinch thyme*
>   *1 3-ounce can tomato paste*
>   *Tablespoon mustard*
>   *1 clove garlic, finely minced*
>   *2 to 3 tablespoons pickle juice*
>   *4 to 6 small sour pickles*

Heat about a tablespoon of fat or oil in a large skillet and brown the pork chops well on both sides. They will give off quite a bit of fat so you don't need much to start. Season them with salt and pepper and a pinch of thyme as they brown. Push the chops to one side when that is done and spoon out all but a couple of spoonfuls of fat. Add the tomato paste and stir it in the pan a minute or so until it loses its bright red color. Pour in enough water to bathe the bottom of the pan generously; stir in the mustard and the garlic. Add 2 or 3 table-spoons of pickle juice also to make the sauce really spicy. Arrange the pork chops in this sauce, cover tightly and leave to simmer over a very low fire for about 30 minutes or until the chops are thoroughly done and tender. Just before serving add 4 to 6 pickles thinly sliced or chopped. This goes well with rice or mashed potatoes.

CÔTES DE PORC AU CHOU ROUGE

Pork Chops with Red Cabbage

Red cabbage has an affinity for pork. In this dish the cabbage is cooked to a glistening, deep dark red, with the addition of a touch of vinegar and apples. The sweet-sour contrast goes perfectly with the pork chops.

Many cooks feel that cabbage improves by being reheated, so you can start the day before. This is hearty, stick to the ribs fare, perfect to serve with great glasses of beer to hungry men!

FOR 4 PEOPLE:

2 to 3 tablespoons fat or bacon drippings
4 to 8 pork chops, depending on size
Salt and pepper
1 medium head red cabbage
2 apples
1 onion, chopped
1 clove garlic, finely minced
Pinch thyme
2 tablespoons vinegar
2 tablespoons sugar

Take a deep heavy pot with a well-fitting lid. Heat a couple of tablespoonfuls of lard or bacon drippings in it and brown the pork chops on both sides, seasoning them well with salt and pepper as you go.

Shred the cabbage finely and peel and slice the apples. When the chops are brown, remove them and set them aside. Add the cabbage to the hot fat with just the water that clings to it after you have rinsed it in a colander. Salt lightly. Put the lid on and leave a few minutes; the cabbage will shrink very quickly. Add to it the sliced apples, the onion and garlic, a pinch of thyme and just a little salt and pepper. Pour in the vinegar and add the sugar. Cover tightly and leave to cook for at least an hour. Stir once in a while and add water only if it seems in danger of burning, and then very little.

After an hour the cabbage is technically done. If it suits your schedule, you can arrange the pork chops on top of it, cook another 30 minutes or so until they are tender and serve. But if you are the patient type, you will cook the cabbage for as long as another hour before adding the chops. Just keep watching so it does not burn. This prolonged cooking turns the cabbage into what I can only describe as cabbage jam! Dark, moist with its own succulent juices, shiny and fragrant. If convenient, you can refrigerate it and cook it for the second hour the next day or so. If the pot is heavy and the lid on tight, it does not require much watching and the results will be amply rewarding.

If any is left over, warm it up again. You will find it better than ever.

CÔTES DE PORC À L'ORANGE

Pork Chops in Orange Sauce

Pork and fruit, especially tart fruit, are made for each other. In this case, we use orange juice with the pork chops to cut any greasiness. Frozen orange juice works beautifully, because it can be used undiluted to get a strong orange flavor. The sauce cooks down to a thick caramel brown gravy, pungent with garlic and orange. This is simple to make, glamorous enough for company and, as an added bonus, usually well liked by children. With a great mountain of fluffy mashed potatoes and a green salad, you have a perfect main dish for a large family gathering. The recipe is for 4 people: multiply accordingly!

FOR 4 PEOPLE:

1 tablespoon fat or oil
4 large thick pork chops 1½ to 2 pounds
Salt and pepper
Thyme
½ (6 ounce) can undiluted frozen orange juice
1 or 2 tablespoons sugar
1 large clove garlic, minced
1 teaspoon flour or cornstarch, if needed
Thin slices peeled oranges for garnish (optional)

Heat a tablespoonful of fat or oil in a large skillet. Brown the pork chops well on both sides, seasoning them with salt and pepper and a little pinch of thyme as you go. When they are very well browned, spoon out all but about 3 tablespoons of fat. Pile the pork chops to one side of the pan. There should be some crusty brown bits at the bottom of the pan; pour in just a little water and stir and scrape them until melted. Now pour in the undiluted orange juice, 1 tablespoon sugar, garlic and an extra pinch of thyme. Stir to mix well and arrange the pork chops evenly in the sauce. Simmer, uncovered, for about 30 minutes, turning the chops in the sauce once in a while so that both sides can bathe in it and imbibe the flavor. The sauce gets very thick, so watch that it does not burn and add just a few drops of water once in a while as it cooks. Taste and add the rest of the sugar if you like things rather sweet or if the orange juice is particularly sour. When the chops are tender the sauce should just coat them with a glistening juice, appetizingly orangy-brown in color. If the sauce seems a little thin, you may mix a teaspoon of flour or cornstarch with water and stir it into the sauce.

Serve immediately. You can if you wish garnish the dish with thin slices of peeled oranges. Be sure to rub the salad bowl with a little garlic if you serve a green salad with this, it goes perfectly!

FOIE DE PORC AU FOUR

Liver and Potato Casserole

Pork liver is very popular in Belgium. In delicatessen shops you can buy it in thin slices, like any other cold cut. It is simply boiled in well-seasoned water and chilled. In this dish, which is a very old recipe, though, the liver is seasoned with bacon and onions, always a good combination, and baked slowly under a layer of sliced potatoes. Add a green salad and you have a good family meal which does not require any watching as it cooks.

FOR 4 PEOPLE:
> 6 *slices bacon*
> 2 *large onions, chopped*
> 1½ *pounds pork liver*
> *Salt and pepper*
> *Sage or thyme*
> 6 *medium potatoes*
> 1 *cup beef bouillon (from a cube)*
> *A little butter*

Fry the bacon until crisp in a skillet. Remove it and fry the chopped onions in the same fat until pale gold. Then add to them the liver cut in strips and stir until it loses its red color. Return the bacon, drained and crumbled, to the pan and mix well. Season with little salt, plenty of pepper and a light dusting of powdered sage. The sage adds a little different taste and goes well with the onions, but you can use thyme if you prefer.

Pour this liver mixture in a deep casserole or baking dish. Peel the potatoes and slice them thinly. Arrange them in a good thick layer on top of the liver. Dissolve a bouillon cube in a cup of hot water and pour over the potatoes. Salt them lightly and dust them with a little more sage and pepper. Dot with butter here and there. Bake in preheated oven at 375°F. for about 1 hour or until the potatoes are tender and lightly browned. Smells and tastes absolutely delicious!

CHOUCROUTE GARNIE

Embellished Sauerkraut!

The Choucroute Garnie, literally "embellished sauerkraut," originated in Alsace and consists of sauerkraut slowly simmered for hours with white wine and an apple. This is served with a mountain of fluffy mashed potatoes and the "garnish": frankfurters, slices of ham, slices of fresh pork chops and thick slabs of bacon. Good cold beer or dry German wine and an assortment of mustards and you could just sit and eat, and eat, and eat. . . . Make this for a crowd:

FOR 6 TO 8 PEOPLE:

2 to 3 pounds canned sauerkraut
3 tablespoons fat or bacon drippings
1 apple
2 large onions, chopped
2 bay leaves
3 or 4 peppercorns
1 cup dry white wine
6 pork chops
2 large slices ham or picnic ham or
  "cottage roll" (boned shoulder) ham
Salt and pepper
8 to 10 frankfurters
Mashed potatoes

Drain the sauerkraut, the canned kind does not require any rinsing. Heat a little fat or bacon drippings in a large heavy pot and add to it the apple and onions. Cook a few minutes until they get soft but not brown. Add the sauerkraut, bay leaves and peppercorns and pour in the wine. Stir well to mix, cover the pot tightly and leave it to simmer gently for about 1 hour. Peek in once in a while and add a little water if it seems to be in danger of sticking to the pot. At the end of an hour, stir well and place all the meat, except the frankfurters, on top of the sauerkraut. If you use a "cottage roll," which is simply boned shoulder ham, slice it in inch thick slices. Continue cooking for another hour, adding a little more water or wine if it seems to dry. You can add pepper to the meat but be cautious about salt, the ham already adds quite a lot.

Try to get frankfurters with a good smoky taste and without the bright red coloring. The coloring runs and makes the dish unappetizing. Place the franks on top of the other meats about 20 minutes before serving so they have time to heat thoroughly.

Arrange all the meat on a large platter, pile the sauerkraut in a ring and make a mountain of fluffy mashed potatoes in the center.

CASSOULET

French Baked Beans!

Cassoulet should certainly cook a very long time. Anatole France mentions somewhere with love a cassoulet which cooked without interruptions for about twenty years, replenished from time to time.

Poems have been written about this dish, so, if you are thinking about canned pork and beans, forget it. This is something quite different!

The success of this dish lies in a good variety of meats. In some parts of France they add pieces of goose preserved in its own fat for extra richness. You can't get anything similar here, but you can use not too lean meat and different kinds of sausage. In Louisiana, for instance, there is a kind of very spicy sausage called "andouille," which goes wonderfully in this dish. Different kinds of highly seasoned smoked sausage are available in various parts of the country, so use whatever kind you can get in your area.

Call up a few good friends who love to eat, and start your cassoulet at least a day before the party!

FOR 6 HEARTY EATERS:
> 1 *pound dried navy beans*
> *Salt*
> ½-*pound slice bacon*
> 2 *large onions*
> 3 *large fresh tomatoes or* 1 1-*pound can whole peeled*
>   *tomatoes, drained*
> 2 *large cloves garlic, finely chopped*
> *Thyme*
> *Sweet Basil*
> *Bay leaf*
> *Pepper*
> 6 *small rather fat pork chops*
> 6 *lamb chops or pieces of lamb stew*
> 1 *pound fresh pork sausage*
> 1 *pound smoked pork sausage*

Soak the beans several hours or overnight in cold water. Put them to cook in fresh water to cover without any seasoning and leave them to simmer for about 1 hour. At that time they should begin to get tender but not be fully cooked. French cooks take a few out on a spoon and blow on them: if the skin peels back by itself, they are just right! Season the pot with a little salt and set them aside, still in their liquid.

Take a large heavy pot, fry the bacon, cut into inch strips, until it renders a little of its fat. Set it aside, while you fry the rest of the meats in the bacon drippings, a few pieces at a time, until all are gently browned. Set them aside with the bacon.

Chop the onions coarsely and fry them in the same fat until golden, then add the tomatoes, cut in pieces also, the garlic and a goodly pinch of thyme, basil and a bay leaf. Season generously with salt and pepper and leave to cook until the tomatoes form a rather thick purée. Drain the beans, reserving the liquid, and mix them well with the tomatoes.

You can finish cooking the cassoulet in the oven or on top of the stove. In the oven, you take a very large, deep casserole, or one of those French earthenware pots, and arrange in it a layer of meats, a layer of beans and repeat until the pot is filled and all is used, finishing with beans. Season each layer of meat with a little salt, pepper and thyme and basil. Pour on enough bean liquid to moisten to the top and bake for 3 to 4 hours in preheated oven at about 300°F. As a thick crust forms on top, mash it down with a spoon.

On top of the stove, you mix all the meats with the beans and cook, covered, for 2 or 3 hours, adding bean liquid as necessary. In both cases the result is creamy, fragrant, almost a purée of beans with very tender, melt in your mouth meats.

SAUCISSE DE CAMPAGNE À LA PURÉE DE LÉGUMES

Country Sausage with Mashed Vegetables

This recipe plays up the artless goodness of pork sausage by cooking it on a bed of country vegetables. This is a simple homely dish but one which can make a husband and children glad to be there. Play it up all the way and have apple pie for dessert!

FOR 4 PEOPLE:
  4 or 5 large potatoes
  2 onions
  6 medium carrots
  1 heart of celery
  1 or 2 leeks (optional)
  Salt and pepper
  Thyme
  Bay leaf
  Parsley
  1½ pounds pork sausage (large country style)

Clean and peel all the vegetables, cut them in large pieces and cook them in water to cover with a good seasoning of salt and pepper, thyme, a bay leaf, and the parsley.

Fry the sausage lightly in a little oil or lard until golden on one side. Or better still if you have trouble preventing it from popping open and breaking to pieces, do this: put about ¼ inch of water in the skillet, then add the sausage, pricking it well all over with a fork or pointed knife. Bring to a boil and simmer over medium heat. After a while the water will completely evaporate and the sausage will start to sizzle and brown but won't pop.

Drain the vegetables when they are tender. Mash them either with a fork or put them through a food mill. Pour into them the fat rendered by the sausage and beat well, just as for mashed potatoes. Taste and correct the seasoning if necessary.

Spoon this purée into a well-greased casserole and arrange the sausage on top of it. Bake in a preheated oven at 375°F. for about 30 minutes or until the sausage and the top of the vegetables are a delightful golden brown.

JAMBON À LA CRÈME

Ham in Cream and Sherry

If you are preparing this ham for a small party, you may decide to use one of the small canned hams. For a larger gathering, use a whole ham. If you are really an epicure, get a whole country ham. Boil it first as directed on the label and then give the sherry treatment (see below) to the choicest part. This is the nice, rounded part, which is completely boneless. The rest of the ham can be used in any usual way.

FOR 6 PEOPLE:
   2 pounds (about) cooked, ready-to-eat ham
   1 cup sherry
   1 cup heavy cream
   Pepper

Trim the ham nicely of most of its apparent fat. Place it in a pot just large enough to hold it. Pour the sherry over it and cook very slowly, turning the ham once or twice until the wine is almost completely absorbed. This should take about 20 to 25 minutes, for a small ham. For a whole ham, use at least 2 cups sherry and cook for at least 1 hour. The ham must not cook fast; it must imbibe the sherry flavor slowly and savor it a while.

When done, there will be a few tablespoonfuls of fragrant juice at the bottom of the pan. Remove the ham and slice it. Keep warm. Pour the cream into the juices and heat, seasoning with pepper. Salt should not be necessary. Don't let the sauce boil, just allow it to heat and blend well with the ham gravy. Pour a little over the sliced ham and pass the rest separately.

JAMBON SAUCE MADÈRE

Ham in Madeira Sauce

Ham in Madeira sauce is a French classic. It is always served with spinach, beautifully creamed and buttered. If it seems to you that the French are unimaginative by always sticking to this same combination, wait until you have tasted it, you could not improve on a perfect thing!

Sauce Madère is one of those sauces which are simple for French chefs to make in restaurants and a lot more difficult at home. It is simply a good dark meat sauce to which the Madeira wine is added. The best way to make it is to plan ahead: serve a good roast or pot roast of beef a few days ahead of time and save some of the juices. With some good meat extract and butter you will come up with a sensational sauce.

FOR 4 PEOPLE:
> A *little fat or oil*
> 1 *onion, chopped*
> 1 *tablespoon tomato paste*
> 1 *tablespoon beef extract and*
>> 1 *cup beef gravy (from a roast)* OR
>> 2 *tablespoons beef extract and pinch thyme and bay leaf*
> 3 *tablespoons butter*
> 3 *tablespoons flour*
> 1 *cup Madeira wine*
> 4 *nice thick juicy slices of ham cooked, ready to eat*
> *Pepper*

Start by heating a little fat or oil in a small pot, add the chopped onion and let it get good and brown. Stir in the tomato paste and let it cook until it loses its bright red color and becomes almost brown. Add a tablespoonful of good liquid beef extract and the beef gravy. If you don't have any, add 2 tablespoons of the beef extract, instead of one, and enough water to make 2 cups of liquid. Add a good pinch of thyme and a bay leaf. Leave this to simmer until it has cooked down to about 1 cup, it will be very rich and a pretty dark color.

Melt 3 tablespoons butter in another small pan, add the flour and cook it, stirring, until it gets a pretty golden color. Cool slightly and add first the beef sauce, stirring well as you go, then the cupful of Madeira. Cook until bubbly and slightly thickened, and simmer, stirring once in a while, while you cook the ham.

Brown the ham slightly on both sides in a large skillet in a little fat or oil. Pour the Madeira sauce over it, stirring to blend it with the ham juices in the pan. Leave for a few minutes for the flavors to blend but don't let the ham boil in the sauce, or it will toughen. Taste the sauce and add a little pepper, it should not need any salt. Serve this fragrant ham with the sauce over it and don't forget a dish of spinach.

JAMBON PERSILLÉ

Parsley Ham

This is a recipe from the Southwest of France, the Bordeaux wine region. In that area, it is as much a part of Easter as Easter eggs, but I can find no reason why you should limit it to that time of year! The texture of this dish is much like head cheese and it is eaten the same way—either sliced with a salad or in sandwiches. There the resemblance ends. This dish is made from ham long simmered in a fragrant wine broth and then mashed with lots and lots of parsley. A really superb combination of flavors.

The old-fashioned recipe starts with a whole ham but, unless you are planning to feed a small army, I suggest you use one of the small picnic hams available at the supermarket. Also, this would be a very good way to finish off a baked ham.

FOR 1 SMALL 3 TO 4 POUND HAM:
  1 picnic ham
  1 bottle dry white wine
  1 carrot
  1 or 2 onions
  2 or 3 ribs celery with leaves
  1 clove garlic
  Bay leaf
  Pepper
  1 envelope plain gelatin
  1 cup finely chopped parsley
  A little good wine vinegar

Wipe the picnic ham and place it in a large pot with water to cover. Bring to a boil and simmer for about half an hour. If you are using leftover baked ham, you can omit this step. Remove the ham from water, let it cool a little, then cut off the skin with a sharp knife and trim some of the fat. You should leave a little fat but not a thick layer.

Set aside about ¼ cup of wine.

Discard the first water, place the ham back in the pot, add the wine and enough water just to cover the ham. Add the carrot, onions and celery, left whole, the clove of garlic, the bay leaf and a little pepper. Bring to a boil, cover and simmer gently until the meat is so tender you can break it with a fork. This should take around 2 hours, but it needs no watching.

Remove the ham from the broth, place it in a large bowl and chop it while it is hot. Remove any bones or cartilage you find as you go.

· Let the broth cool until the fat congeals on top. The refrigerator will hasten the process. Remove this layer of fat and taste the broth; it should have a good if somewhat salty flavor. If it is really too salty, dilute it with a little water. Measure 2 cups of it and heat it with the reserved wine and the gelatin, stirring until the gelatin is completely disssolved. Add the chopped parsley to the hot liquid but don't let it cook, just wilt a little. Add this fragrant mixture to the ham and mix well. Add just enough wine vinegar to give it a little tang, taste as you go, and a little freshly ground black pepper.

Pour into a pretty bowl and chill in the refrigerator until set. Well covered, this dish will keep quite a few days.

CURRY D'AGNEAU

Lamb Curry

If you have ever tried it, you'll have found out that very hot and peppery food does not go with wine very well, one kills the other somehow. Which is certainly the reason why French food is seldom very peppery. So don't tell me this is no real curry, hot and fiery as it is in India. This is a French version of the dish, more delicate in flavor and much milder!

You can use good, lean lamb stew for this dish, or you can use little lamb chops, two per person, and have a gala meal. But if you happen to have leftover leg of lamb, it will be exceedingly good and very different from the first meal. So if a whole leg of lamb seems too much for your family, you could easily plan to roast it one day and use the leftovers for curry a few days later.

FOR 4 PEOPLE:
- ¼ cup dried raisins
- 4 tablespoons butter
- 2 large onions, coarsely chopped
- 1 to 1½ pounds raw or leftover cooked lamb
- 2 apples
- 2 or 3 tender stalks celery
- 1 clove garlic, minced
- 2 teaspoons curry powder
- Salt and pepper
- Lemon juice
- 1 tablespoon flour, if needed
- 1 cup heavy cream

Start by pouring a little boiling water over the raisins and leaving them to plump. Melt the butter in a nice heavy pot and brown the onions in it. Add the lamb and, if it is raw, let it brown well on all sides. If you are using leftover cooked meat, let it just absorb a little of the onion and butter flavor for a few minutes.

Peel, core and chop the apples and add them to the lamb. Chop the celery finely also, and add it, the raisins, the clove of garlic and the curry powder to the meat. Any Frenchman would not dare to add more than 2 teaspoons of the curry; you can add more than that but don't forget that it is easy to add and rather hard to take away. Season with salt and a little black pepper and add water. If you are starting with raw meat, add water to cover the meat and leave to cook for about 1 hour or until the meat is tender. With cooked meat, add only about 2 cups, since it will not need to cook very long.

When the meat is tender and the apples have practically disappeared into the sauce, taste and correct seasoning if necessary. It should be very well seasoned, because the cream will tone it down. Add a few drops of lemon juice to sharpen the flavor. If the sauce is quite thin, you can mix a tablespoonful of flour to a thin paste with water, add it to the meat and boil up, stirring, a few minutes.

At serving time, with the dish very hot, remove from the fire and stir in the cream. Serve with boiled rice. You can, if you wish, garnish this dish with the usual curry accompaniments, such as chutney, sliced tomatoes and cucumbers. If you serve wine, try a not-too-dry white Bordeaux.

GIGOT OU GIGUE GRAND VENEUR

Leg of Lamb or Venison Grand Veneur

This is one of the dishes which make the reputation of French cooking. If you can get a leg, even better, a saddle of venison (which is the two fillets and the most tender part), you can prepare the finest, noblest dish ever put before a hunter. If you can't get venison, substitute with a leg of lamb. With this preparation, a gentle lamb acquires enough of the aristocratic qualities of venison so that only the initiated can tell the difference.

Ideally, the wine you use in the marinade should be the same as the one you plan to serve with the meal. You need 2 bottles of the best rich old Burgundy you can afford. If you cannot afford it in such large quantities, keep the finest wine for the table and give the venison the lesser one.

Three days before the party, start with this:

Saddle or leg of venison or leg of lamb, 6 to 7 pounds

For the marinade:
2 *medium onions*
2 *medium carrots*
1 *stalk celery*
2 *cloves garlic*
3 *or 4 sprigs parsley*
Salt and pepper
2 *pinches whole thyme (1 teaspoon)*
2 *bay leaves*
1 *bottle good Burgundy*
1 *cup good red wine vinegar*
½ *cup olive or cooking oil*

On the appointed day you will need in addition for the sauce:
¼ *pound (1 stick) butter*
Salt and pepper
½ *cup red currant jelly*
Worcestershire sauce
1 *cup heavy cream*

Three days, or two if you are pressed for time, before the party, prepare the marinade and soak the meat in it. Slice the onions, carrots and celery thinly. Leave the garlic and parsley whole. Take a large dish or bowl but not a metal one. An enameled dish is all right provided it does not have the slightest chip or crack. Arrange half the sliced vegetables at the bottom of it. Rub the meat well with salt and pepper, place it in the dish and cover it with the rest of the vegetables and herbs.

Pour on the wine, the vinegar and the oil. Cover with wax paper and store in the refrigerator. Turn the meat at least twice a day so that every part of it will have a chance to absorb all the goodness of this mixture.

On the day of the party:
Heat the oven to 325°F. Take the meat out of the marinade and sponge it dry with paper towels. Reserve the marinade. Place the lamb or venison in a roasting dish, on a rack if you have one, dot it generously with butter and a very light seasoning of salt and pepper.

Roast it uncovered, counting 30 minutes per pound. It should not be too well done, this will give it a slight pink tinge in the center. If you can't stand the thought of pink meat, count an additional 5 minutes per pound but be careful not to overcook it.

As it cooks baste it occasionally with a few spoonfuls of marinade. Use only a little at a time and wait until it has almost completely evaporated before adding more. During this time, place the rest of the marinade in a small pot and leave it to simmer until it has reduced to about 1 cup. Strain it carefully.

When the meat is done, remove it to a serving platter and keep it warm while you finish the sauce.

Place the baking dish on top of the stove, pour in a little of the marinade and stir and scrape until you have melted every last bit of browned juices in the pan. Pour into a small pan with the rest of the marinade. Add to this the red currant jelly and heat and stir until it has completely melted. Season very sharply with Worcestershire sauce; you can use a tablespoonful and add more if necessary. Taste, it should be really very sharp and peppery. Bring it to a simmer, remove the sauce from the fire and stir in the cream. It should be absolutely perfect!

Slice the meat, which will be juicy and tender, and pass the sauce separately. A purée of chestnuts is the traditional accompaniment of game with this sauce. I have found that mashed sweet potatoes go beautifully with it also. Pass some red currant jelly, or cranberry jelly, with the meat also.

LAPIN BRABANÇONNE

Rabbit Cooked in Beer

This is a delicious rabbit stew. Thyme grows wild in the Western Europe countryside and it is said that it gives wild rabbits their wonderful flavor, as they are particularly fond of it. To approximate this flavor, be sure to add a generous pinch of thyme to the stew.

FOR 1 RABBIT TO SERVE ABOUT 4 PEOPLE:
> *1 rabbit*
> *A little flour*
> *½ pound slab bacon*
> *12 very small onions*
> *1 can beer*
> *3 tablespoons mustard, if possible Dijon*
> *Salt and pepper*
> *Thyme*
> *Bay leaf*
> *½ cup heavy cream*

Cut the rabbit into pieces and shake them in a paper bag with a little flour, just as you would fried chicken, or simply thaw a frozen rabbit already cut up.

Cut the bacon into small cubes. Slab bacon is better since regular sliced bacon, cut in pieces, practically disappears in the gravy. Take a large heavy pot and cook the pieces of bacon until golden on all sides. Remove it with a slotted spoon and brown the onions in the same fat. If you cannot get the very small ones, cut up some larger ones. Set the onions aside with the bacon and brown the pieces of rabbit. There should be enough fat from the bacon but add a little butter if necessary.

When the pieces of rabbit are golden, return the bacon and onions to the pot, pour in the beer, stir in the mustard, season with salt and pepper and a good pinch of thyme. Drop in the bay leaf. Cover the pot and simmer very gently until the meat is quite tender. Peek in once in a while and do not let it burn, but you should not have to add any more liquid.

Cooking time is dependent upon the age of the rabbit. One hour should be plenty unless you got the great-granddaddy of them all!

At serving time, taste the sauce and add more salt and pepper if necessary. Remove the pieces of meat to a serving dish, stir the cream into the sauce, pour over the meat and serve. For a true Belgian feast, you should serve this with plain boiled potatoes and lots of cold beer!

LAPIN RÔTI À LA MOUTARDE

Roast Rabbit with Mustard

Rabbit used to be so plentiful it was at one time a very cheap meat. Alas, it is now practically a luxury dish unless you have a hunter in the family and wild rabbits nearby!

If such is the case, however, you can make this dish at its finest. This means having really young rabbit to start with. If you have two of them, use only the *râble*, which is what the French call the fillet or back of the rabbit with its two long and tender pieces of meat. The rest of the rabbit will make very good stew. If your hunter husband assures you, however, that the rabbit is really a very young one, men seem to know about such things, you can roast the whole thing with excellent results.

FOR 4 PEOPLE:
  Backs or râbles *of 2 rabbits or 1 whole very young one,*
    or frozen ones
  Salt and pepper
  ¼ pound (1 stick) butter
  French Dijon mustard
  1 onion
  Bay leaf
  Thyme
  1 cup heavy cream

Wipe the rabbit, salt and pepper it all over, and place it in a well-buttered roasting dish. Paint it all over with a good even layer of French Dijon mustard.

Place pats of butter evenly over the meat and add the onion, left whole, a bay leaf and a pinch of thyme in the pan. These will flavor the butter as it cooks. Place in a preheated 375°F. oven and roast, basting very frequently with the butter in the pan, until the meat is golden and done. This should not take much more than half an hour for just the backs, a little more for a whole rabbit. Test the meat with a fork, and if the juices show no trace of pink but are clear, the meat is done.

Remove the meat to a serving dish, add the cream to the juices in the pan, stir and scrape over very gentle heat on top of the stove until all is well mixed and hot. It should not boil fiercely. Add another tablespoonful of mustard to the sauce, and season to taste with salt and pepper. Pour over the meat and serve immediately, discarding the onion and bay leaf.

LAPIN AUX PRUNEAUX

Rabbit with Prunes

Have you ever thought of cooking a rabbit with prunes? It is a savory stew, I assure you, and a favorite way of cooking rabbit in Belgium. When Maria decided judiciously that the rabbit brought home by my father was not young enough to roast with cream and mustard, she turned it into this stew, and smacked her lips in anticipation!

FOR 4 PEOPLE:

10 or 12 prunes, soaked overnight
½ pound slab bacon
2 tablespoons butter
1 dozen very small onions or chopped large ones
1 large rabbit, or 3 pounds frozen, cut into pieces
Salt and pepper
Thyme
Bay leaf
¼ cup dried raisins
1 tablespoon flour
1 tablespoon vinegar

Soak the prunes overnight to plump them. If you can soak them in cold tea, it gives them an excellent flavor; try it!

Cut the bacon into little cubes, pour a little boiling water over it, soak a few minutes and drain. Dry it on paper towels.

Heat the butter in a large pot or Dutch oven. Gently fry the bacon in it until golden. Remove it with a slotted spoon and add the onions. Fry them until well browned. Add a little more butter if necessary and fry the pieces of rabbit to a golden brown also. By now the juices at the bottom of the pot should be quite dark. Return the onions and bacon to the pot, add enough water to cover and season well with salt and pepper, thyme and a bay leaf.

Simmer until the rabbit is almost tender, about 45 minutes, then add the prunes and the raisins. Cook until the meat is really very tender for at least another half hour, perhaps more.

Some of the prunes will break up and flavor the sauce deliciously. Thicken the gravy with 1 tablespoon of flour mixed to a thin paste with a little vinegar. Taste and season the sauce well with additional salt and pepper and a little more vinegar, if it seems to need it.

By now the meat is tender and the sauce a rich lustrous brown. If it looks somewhat pale, here is a trick used by French cooks: melt 1 tablespoon of sugar with about 1 teaspoon of vinegar in a large iron spoon or a very small pan. Cook over high heat until the sugar turns to a dark, almost black, caramel. Stir into the sauce, which will take immediately a rich brown color. Strangely enough, in small amounts, this caramel is completely tasteless, but we eat with our eyes also. . . .

TERRINE DE LAPIN OU POULET
MÈRE GRAND

Grandmother's Rabbit or Chicken Pâté

Terrines are country cousins of the fine French pâtés. Very often they are made with whole pieces of meat hidden in the ground ones. When you slice this kind of pâté, you have the pleasure of finding these delicious tidbits.

Terrine takes its name from *terre*, earth, after the earthenware dishes they are usually baked in. These dishes are particularly good as they are thick and whatever is in them cooks evenly without burning. There is something delightfully appetizing and homelike about their shiny brown glaze. Of course, the new miracle baking dishes are excellent also but don't try to bake a terrine in a thin metal dish. The outside would be too crusty before the center is done.

This terrine is good hot or cold. It bakes very slowly for a long time. So that it won't dry out, you need a close-fitting lid or several layers of aluminum foil. Another good and appetizing trick is to seal the lid to the pot with a ribbon of dough. Simply mix a cupful of flour, 2 tablespoons of salt and enough water to make a soft dough. Roll this between your hands to make a long sausage-like piece and stick this all around the dish. Break it only at the table and all the heavenly fragrance of the dish will pour out.

FOR 1 LARGE PÂTÉ (2- TO 2½-QUART DISH):
1 rabbit or large chicken
½ pound veal
½ pound lean pork meat
Salt and pepper
A little allspice
Thyme
1 onion
1 carrot
Bay leaf
1 cup sherry or dry white wine
Slices of pork fat or bacon to line the dish
½ pound slab bacon
2 pounds ground pork or country sausage

This kind of terrine can be made with many different kinds of meats, if you can't get rabbit, try chicken. At other times you may want to use such delicacies as wild goose, pheasant or any kind of game. The process is the same.

Cut the rabbit in nice large pieces, removing as many of the bones as you can during the process. A good sharp, pointed knife makes this easy. Cut the veal and pork into long strips. Place all these meats in a shallow bowl, season them generously with salt and pepper and a pinch of allspice and thyme. Slice the onion and carrot, place them over the meat with the bay leaf, pour on the sherry or white wine and marinate for several hours or even overnight.

Line a casserole with thin slices of pork fat or bacon, reserving a few slices for the top of the casserole. Cut the slab bacon into strips also.

Place a good layer of pork sausage, removed from its casing, at the bottom of the dish. On this arrange a layer of the rabbit meat, and strips of veal, pork and bacon. Keep all the strips going the same way. Dust with a little allspice and thyme and repeat the layers of sausage meat, rabbit, etc., finishing with sausage. Pat all tightly. Arrange the reserved slices of fat or bacon on top in the same direction as the strips of meat inside the dish. This will serve to remind you how to slice the pâté. You want to do this across the strips so everybody gets some! Arrange a few slices of the marinated onion and carrot on top, pour in as much as you can of the marinade and cover the dish.

Bake in preheated 300°F. oven for 2½ hours. This long slow cooking is what makes all the meats tender and the flavors blend. If the pâté seems to be getting too dark or sizzles too hard (if you can't see through the dish), turn the oven down even lower and place a pan of water in the oven.

If you eat the terrine hot, remove the lid at the table. If it is to be eaten cold, chill it and scrape off some of the fat before serving.

TERRINE DE CAMPAGNE

Liver Pâté Country Style

The French pâté de foie gras, which comes in terribly expensive little cans, is definitely not the only pâté eaten in France. This fine pâté made with fattened goose liver is reserved for very special occasions. Pâtés, though, and their country cousins,"terrines," are very much an everyday dish.

Every *charcuterie* (pork store) makes its own pâtés, and so there is a wide and delightful variety. They are also frequently made at home: sometimes very fancy with truffles and mushrooms, sometimes with just pork liver beautifully seasoned. French pâtés and terrines are baked slowly in large earthenware dishes and then covered with a thick layer of melted lard to exclude all the air. They are sometimes kept this way for very great lengths of time, although I think that with modern refrigeration, it is much safer to keep them cold. If you want to, though, you can freeze pâtés very well, and in that case the layer of lard keeps them from drying out.

Pâté can be served in many ways: in small pieces as appetizers, in thick slices with a good salad for a delicious hot weather meal. A thick slice on crusty French bread makes a wonderful *casse-croûte*, the French equivalent of a light lunch.

FOR 1 PÂTÉ BAKED IN A 1½- OR 2-QUART
ROUND CASSEROLE:

>   *2 pounds pork liver* OR
>   *1 pound pork liver—1 pound ham*
>   *Salt and pepper*
>   *Pinch thyme*
>   *Allspice*
>   *Nutmeg if liked*
>   *½ pound fresh fat pork*
>   *1 cup fine dry bread crumbs*
>   *1 egg*
>   *1 bay leaf*
>   *4 tablespoons brandy (optional)*
>   *A few thin slices pork fat*

Ask the butcher very politely and nicely if he will give you a few
very thin slices of pork fat which he has trimmed off various roasts,
etc. Or perhaps he will consent to give you a thick chunk of it which
you can slice yourself. If you are a really good customer, he may not
even charge you much or at all.

The next absolute requisite for a pâté is a meat grinder, so borrow
one if you must. You are now all set.

Take a nice heavy pot, cut the fresh pork MEAT (not the sliced
fat), into inch cubes and fry them until they have rendered enough
fat to cover the bottom of the pot. Now add all the other meats, such
as liver or liver and ham, cut also into inch pieces. Season with salt
and pepper, a light dusting of thyme and any other spices you favor.
Keep in mind, though, that the spices should enhance and not mask
the flavor of the meat. Cook very slowly, stirring and tossing the
meats, until it is uniformly grayish in color but not brown. Let it cool.

Put the meat through the meat grinder twice, since the mixture
should be very fine. Place it in a large bowl, add the bread crumbs
and the egg, and the brandy, if you are using it. Port, Madeira or
sherry can be used instead with good results also. Knead with your
hands until the mixture is really quite smooth.

Line a casserole with thin slices of the pork fat. If you can't get
any, you may use thin slices of bacon or simply grease the casserole
very generously. Cover the casserole tightly with two layers of foil
after you have packed the meat mixture in it. Place the casserole in
a dish containing about an inch of water and bake it for about 1 hour

and 45 minutes in a preheated oven at 375°F. Test the pâté by inserting a knife near the middle; if it comes out clean, all is done. Take the pâté out of the oven and place a small plate or board over it and a weight on top of that. An unopened bag of sugar, the iron, anything good and heavy. This will give the pâté a close, fine texture. Leave until cold and chill before serving.

CERVELLE AUX CHAMPIGNONS

Brains with Mushrooms

There is really no part of an animal that the French can be said to despise! I am always pleasantly surprised to see such things as marrow bones, sweetbreads, kidneys and brains sold cheaply in this country. All of these are expensive in France and very highly prized. The French even eat the spinal cord of beef, which tastes almost exactly like brains, under the name of *amourettes*!

In France, brains are usually one of the first meats given to babies as they are considered so digestible. Lovingly prepared and served with mushrooms, the adults thoroughly enjoy them also.

FOR 4 PEOPLE:
> 2 large calf brains or about 2 containers from the
>   supermarket
> Salt
> 5 tablespoons vinegar
> ½ pound fresh or frozen mushrooms
> 4 tablespoons butter
> 1 large onion
> Pepper

Soak the brains in cold salted water for a few hours and then carefully remove as much as you can of the membrane which covers it. It pulls off quite easily. Soak the brains a little longer in cold water and they will be a pretty pale pink without a trace of blood.

Cook them in boiling salted water to which you have added about 3 tablespoons of vinegar. This should take about 10 minutes, depending on the size of the pieces. They should just be firm enough to handle. Drain and cool.

Clean and slice the mushrooms. Melt half the butter in a large skillet, add the mushrooms when the butter sizzles and then the pieces of brains. Cook slowly, over a rather slow fire until the brains are beginning to turn golden and the mushrooms are cooked. Remove both to a hot dish and keep warm.

Add the rest of the butter to the skillet and let it turn golden. Add the finely chopped onion to it and cook just a few minutes. The onion should not be really cooked, just sort of wilted. Pour in 2 tablespoons of vinegar, add a little salt and plenty of black pepper, stir and pour over the brains and mushrooms.

Absolutely delicious served with little green peas, plain boiled potatoes and a deliciously chilled dry white wine!

CERVELLE SAUCE TARTARE

Brains with Tartar Sauce

The Belgians have a particular fondness for cold dishes served with hot French fries. It is a really delicious combination, the French fries made rather large, crisp on the outside, mealy inside and burning to the tongue, contrasting perfectly with some cold and creamy dish, spicy with mayonnaise or tartar sauce.

The idea of serving hot potatoes with cold dishes is a pretty good one. The potatoes do not take long to fix, particularly in this country where you can buy frozen French fries, but they give added body to a cold meal. In this case, the brains well flavored with wine are served thoroughly chilled with the tartar sauce.

FOR 4 PEOPLE:

> *2 large fresh brains (1½ to 2 pounds)*
> *1 large onion, sliced*
> *1 carrot, sliced*
> *1 stalk celery, sliced*
> *Salt and pepper*
> *Thyme*
> *Bay leaf*
> *1 cup dry white wine*
> *Tartar sauce for garnish*
> *Parsley or lettuce leaves*

Clean the brains well as indicated for Brains with Mushrooms. Make a well-flavored broth with the sliced vegetables, salt and pepper, thyme, a bay leaf and 1 cup of wine. Add water to make enough broth to cover the brains but don't add them yet. Simmer gently for about half an hour. Add the brains and cook them until firm all the way through. Depending on the size of the pieces, cook about 15 to 20 minutes. Drain well and cool.

Slice the brains in ½ inch slices and arrange these on a serving dish. Garnish with a thick ribbon of well-flavored tartar sauce. Parsley or lettuce leaves look pretty around it. Chill well before serving.

ROGNONS FLAMBÉS À LA LIÉGEOISE

Flambéd Kidneys Liégeoise

Either you love kidneys or you hate them! Few people can just take them or leave them without strong feelings about it.

This recipe originates from the Ardennes part of Belgium where they make a kind of gin called Genievre. Dutch "Bols" or good gin such as you use in your favorite martini will do very well also for this recipe. What you really need are juniper berries to give this dish its real flavor. If you absolutely cannot find them, try allspice.

FOR 4 PEOPLE:
    2 veal kidneys
    4 slices bacon
    4 tablespoons butter
    Salt and pepper
    A little thyme
    2 or 3 crushed juniper berries OR
        2 or 3 berries allspice
    Small glass (1½ ounces) gin

Split the kidneys in two and remove as much as possible of the tough white inner parts with a small sharp pointed knife. Soak the kidneys in cold water for several hours or overnight, changing the water once or twice. Wipe them well and slice them approximately ½ an inch thick.

In the Ardennes they have small earthenware pots which are always used to prepare this dish. If you have a casserole that can go on top of the stove, use it.

Fry the bacon, cut into small strips, until almost crisp. Drain off the bacon fat and replace it by the butter. As soon as it sizzles, add the kidney slices, season them with salt and pepper and a little pinch of thyme. Crush the juniper berries between your fingers and add them to the kidneys. Heat the gin in a large spoon or small pan for a second. Actually the best way to do this is to heat the pan or spoon first, not too hot, pour in the gin and touch a match to it. Pour it flaming over the kidneys.

Stir well to mix and close the dish tightly. You can now finish cooking on top of the stove or in the oven as you prefer. On top of the stove, it takes about 40 minutes over a very, very low fire. Keep the lid on, shake the pan occasionally but open it as little as possible and only add a little water if it seems to dry out.

Kidney fanciers will prefer the oven method: place the dish, covered tightly, in a preheated 375°F. oven (if you have an earthenware casserole; 350°F., if not), for about 1 hour. Bring the dish to the table and lift the lid *only* when ready to serve.

ROGNONS AU MADÈRE ET CHAMPIGNONS

Kidneys with Madeira and Mushrooms

Kidneys fixed this way, with mushrooms and Madeira or port wine, are considered quite a delicacy in France. Young veal kidneys are eminently suited to this dish which is quite quick and easy to prepare.

There is one thing to remember about the cooking of kidneys: they must cook very quickly or very long. In between times, they are just tough pieces of rubber, hard to chew and rather unpleasant. In this recipe, they should cook very quickly, just long enough to make the redness disappear and no more. Served this way, over rice or with toast, they will be absolutely delicious.

FOR 4 PEOPLE:

2 or 3 small veal kidneys
6 tablespoons butter
½ pound fresh or frozen mushrooms
Salt and pepper
2 tablespoons tomato paste
1 tablespoon liquid beef extract
½ cup water
½ cup Madeira or port wine
2 tablespoons chopped parsley, 2 tablespoons butter

Split the kidneys, remove as much as you can of the tough white inner parts with a sharp knife and put them to soak in cold water for several hours or overnight. Change the water once or twice.

Wipe the kidneys with paper towels and slice them thinly, about ¼ to ½ inch thick. Heat 4 tablespoons of butter in a skillet and when it sizzles add the sliced kidneys. Toss and turn over high heat until all trace of redness is gone; this should take about 5 minutes or so. Keep stirring, though, so all the slices will cook evenly, and season with salt and pepper as you go.

This is the only unpleasant time about cooking kidneys. During these first few minutes, no matter how well you soaked them, they do give off a rather unpleasant odor. If this bothers you, or if you fear that it will bother your guests, you can do this early in the morning and finish later; by then the aroma of the wine will take over!

Remove the kidney slices to a bowl as soon as done. Remember that now they must not cook anymore; they are still tender if you cooked them really fast. Add the sliced and cleaned or thawed mushrooms to the juices in the pan, cook a few minutes until the juices are greatly reduced and beginning to dry out. Add the tomato paste; cook a little longer until it begins to brown. Now add the beef extract and about ½ cup of water. Stir and mix well, then add the wine. Simmer a few minutes for the flavors to blend. The sauce should be about as thick as thin tomato sauce.

Mix 2 tablespoons of butter with about an equal amount of chopped parsley. Just before serving, return the kidney slices to the sauce and heat very gently until just hot, but don't let it boil. Stir in the butter and parsley just until melted and serve.

8. SAUCES

SAUCES ARE WHAT TURN PLAIN STEAK into Tournedos Béarnaise, plain chicken into Poulet aux Champignons and a simple fish fillet into a creation! The French say *"C'est la sauce qui fait le poisson,"* or that fish is only as good as its sauce.

Sauces, in a way, *are* French cooking. Many have been handed down for generations with very little change. Some are at their best only in the cuisine of great restaurants: they are to cooking what the couturiers are to dressmaking. You can make fairly good imitations but you can't copy them entirely. When you understand what goes into these sauces, you'll know why! Great cooks will take a simple piece of meat or fish and prepare it very simply: Sauté it in a little butter perhaps, or simmer it in a little wine. So far so good, you can do that at home easily. Then comes the sauce: its base may contain enough ingredients to feed a family of four for a week; it may start out as a kind of soup or broth, using several pounds of meat, bones, chickens, and be cooked down to a pint of a rich, thick, lustrous extract. This you cannot duplicate exactly! The French housewife doesn't try to: she uses a number of substitutes and comes up with very good results. When she wants the absolutely real thing, she coaxes her husband into taking her out to dinner!

Real French sauces are never, never gooey! The secret lies in using very little, if any, flour. Most French cream sauces are just that: heavy cream added to the natural juices of whatever they go with! You get a fairly thin sauce which does not mask, just enhances the flavor. Most white sauces which do use flour will be made with broth instead of milk and then thinned down with cream also.

Basically there are about four different sauces, and from these stems an infinite variety. Master these four, and you can duplicate almost anything! The basic ones are white sauce thickened with flour, cream sauces thickened with egg yolks, emulsions of egg yolks and oil or butter such as mayonnaise, béarnaise, etc., and the dark meaty sauces which would come in this country under the name of gravies. So I'll give some examples of each and you'll be able to take it from there.

VELOUTÉ

Velouté means velvety, which is exactly what this is! The velouté is not really a sauce, just the beginning of one. With it as a base, you can concoct all kinds of sauces, limited only by your imagination. Starting with flour and butter, you add bouillon, vegetable juices or water, fish broth, etc. The velouté constitutes about half or two-thirds of the amount of sauce you eventually want. Here are the proportions for 1 cup:

FOR 1 CUP VELOUTÉ BASE:
   2 tablespoons flour
   2 tablespoons butter
   1 cup broth

Melt the butter in a small pan, add the flour and cook until frothy but don't let it brown. Gradually add the broth, hot preferably, letting it be absorbed before you add more. A wire whisk is most helpful for this, practically a guarantee against lumps. Let the mixture come to a rolling boil, still stirring.

The broth is, of course, the deciding factor as far as the flavor of the finished sauce. That's why the broth is very important. If you are boiling a chicken, take about 2 cups of chicken broth, add to it the neck, and any pieces you have trimmed off the chicken, the skin for instance, after the bird is cooked, the bones, if the chicken is to be served boned. Let this simmer down to 1 cup of the richest broth you have ever tasted.

With fish, it will probably be first cooked in wine or wine and water and herbs. If there is just a little liquid, you may add a little wine to it to make 1 cup. If the fish was first boiled, do the same as for chicken, adding bones, heads, skin, to the broth and cooking it down. Some cooks will even get a couple of small fishes as extras for the broth.

With vegetables, you can use for a start the water they cooked in. To this you can add wine, a bouillon cube, or make it half water, half milk.

So you now have your velouté, smooth, velvety and already good-tasting if a little thin. If it is really very well flavored, you can add from half to 1 cup of good heavy cream. Correct the seasoning if necessary. Once the cream has been added, take care not to let the sauce boil fiercely, as it can curdle. You can flavor it further by the addition of mushrooms, shrimp, grated cheese, even truffles. A spoonful of wine, port, or sherry, or brandy or cognac, will also add flavor. Just be sure it is something that will go well with the dish.

SAUCE À LA CRÈME

Sauce à la Crème is more a sauce with cream than a cream sauce! Poulet à la Crème is simply a roast chicken to start with. After it is cooked, remove it from the pan and skim off a little of the fat. Heat the drippings with a tablespoonful of water, or better brandy or wine. Stir and scrape until you have a fragrant, dark brown gravy. Simply pour in 1 cup of heavy cream, taste and correct the seasoning if necessary and serve as soon as the cream is hot. Don't boil it though. You can do the same thing with roast veal, even roast beef if you add a dash of something spicy, like a steak sauce or Worcestershire sauce and/or brandy or cognac.

Another good use for this sauce is simply to pour the cream in the skillet in which you have cooked chops or steak. Any browned bits in the pan should also first be loosened and melted with a little liquid, water or wine! This sauce is made excellent by the addition of mushrooms or truffles also. Completely gourmet and the simplest to prepare at the last moment.

SAUCE À LA CRÈME AUX OEUFS

This sauce is a little thicker in texture than the Sauce à la Crème, by the addition of egg yolks to the cream. It requires a little more care, after the eggs are added, since it must on no account boil or they will curdle and spoil completely the appearance and even the taste of the sauce. It can be used in two ways: to thicken and make even richer a good velouté and cream sauce. This is the easiest, as the flour in the velouté prevents it from curdling to a certain extent. Or simply by adding egg yolks to cream and using this with the juices of the meat or fish you are cooking. It can be used to thicken soups deliciously also. Here are some examples:

For creamed soups:
3 cups good flavorful soup
3 egg yolks
1 cup heavy cream

This is a very quick and easy way to finish a soup at the last minute. It turns a merely good soup into a gourmet *potage.* Make sure the soup is quite well seasoned. Take a good chicken soup for instance. You could add a dash of sherry or dry white wine to it. At serving time, heat the soup to boiling. Beat the egg yolks and the cream into a soup tureen or large bowl. Very slowly pour ½ cup of the hot soup into the cream and eggs, stirring vigorously with a whisk. Then gently add the rest of the soup, pouring not too fast and stirring all the time. Keep stirring for a minute after all is added. That's all there is to it, but wait till you taste it!

For stews:
4 servings hot cooked veal, chicken stews
3 egg yolks
1 cup heavy cream

This sauce is particularly good with veal or chicken stews. The stew will probably have already been thickened a little with flour. The procedure is about the same: beat the egg yolks and the cream, pour in a little of the hot gravy from the stew, stirring very well; return all to the pot, still stirring and off the fire. Don't boil! Marvelous with mushrooms added.

For fish:
½ to 1 cup fish juices
1 cup cream
3 egg yolks

If the fish is to be rebaked or browned in the oven after the sauce is added, make a cup of velouté, using the juices in which the fish cooked. Add this to the cream and eggs, pour over the fish and brown in the oven lightly. This is the beginning of the classics: Sauce Normande, Marguery, etc. You can add to this sauce mushrooms, shrimp, poached oysters, mussels, anything good! You can also make it by adding the cream and eggs directly to the fish juices: cook as carefully as you would any custard. On top of the stove with a very, very low heat or preferably in the top of the double boiler, just until creamy and slightly thickened.

MAYONNAISE

Mayonnaise has many sisters and the whole family is quite glamorous! Their names are Béarnaise, hollandaise, tartar and mousseline, which is the most delicate of them all! Master mayonnaise and you will have no trouble with any of them.

These sauces are emulsions. This may sound like a course in chemistry, but simply mix oil, vinegar and egg yolk and you get a kind of French dressing, quite thin and uncreamy. Beat them right, and you get a bowl of shimmering, fluffy, yellow creamy mayonnaise, delicious and glamorous with many dishes.

HERE ARE THE PROPORTIONS FOR 1½ CUPS:
>   *2 egg yolks*
>   *Salt*
>   *1 teaspoon or so prepared mustard*
>   *1 cup oil*
>   *Vinegar or lemon juice to taste*
>   *Salt and pepper*

First a word about the mustard. Many recipes for mayonnaise use dry mustard as an ingredient. Dry mustard in France is used solely (and not very much anymore) for foot baths and poultices! A source of astonishment to all Frenchmen is to find the English eating it. The English themselves admit that the mustard manufacturer's fortune has been made by what people leave on their plates and not what they eat. Dry mustard is indubitably hot but has very little real flavor. It really adds nothing to mayonnaise; prepared mustard does! Try a good French mustard—some are deliciously flavored with herbs and wine —or any good brand of American mustard.

Place the egg yolks in a bowl with a pinch of salt, a teaspoon of mustard and beat with a wire whisk until well mixed and slightly thickened. It will take just a second or two. Pour on a couple of drops of oil, literally a couple of drops, but you don't really need an eye dropper! Beat until mixed before adding more, drop by drop at first, then increasing gradually until you are pouring a thin stream of oil. Beat hard and fast, the mayonnaise will get quite thick. When you have added about half the oil, add a little vinegar or lemon juice, just a few drops, which will thin down the mayonnaise. Then add more oil, and a little more vinegar; finish with oil, always beating hard. When you are sure the mayonnaise is "taking," i.e., getting creamy and fluffy, you can switch from a whisk to an electric egg beater. It is no better but less tiring, especially if you plan on doubling the recipe for a large party, maybe.

Taste and season the mayonnaise well with salt and pepper and more vinegar if necessary. Don't make it too sour, though, mayonnaise should be creamy.

Even for the best of cooks mayonnaise sometimes decides to act up! Here is what to do in case of accidents. French cooks blame heat for unsuccessful mayonnaise, and many swear it is most difficult to make mayonnaise in hot weather. I make it successfully in New Orleans, which is hotter than France! Americans, on the other hand, blame cold, having refrigerators. I make it with eggs straight from the refrigerator! Through the years everything has been blamed: adding salt at the beginning, adding it later, the type of oil, the kind of vinegar, even the way you stir (always in the same direction), and the state of your health.

Personally, I blame the eggs! After all, I have to blame something. Perhaps if an egg is not fresh, it does not absorb the oil as well. Also, 2 yolks are easier than one. Adding the right amount of mustard also helps. And I firmly believe in starting right: drop by drop. If in spite of everything the mayonnaise does curdle, try taking a fresh bowl, a teaspoon of mustard and adding the curdled mayonnaise by teaspoonfuls, beating as hard as you can until it becomes fluffy again. Instead of additional mustard, you can use an extra egg yolk. I find a French wire whisk invaluable, while some people swear by a fork. Maria used an old wooden spoon worn down to fit the bowl exactly.

A good trick, when making mayonnaise or other things which have to be stirred a lot, is to place a damp paper towel or dish rag under the bowl. It holds the bowl firmly in place and makes beating much easier. Mayonnaise made this way has to be used fairly quickly.

If you have to store it in the refrigerator, be sure you let it reach room temperature before you stir it; it will separate if it is very cold. If you plan to garnish dishes with it, do so as soon as the mayonnaise is made. They can then be left in the refrigerator without trouble. This mayonnaise can be piped and used as a border on many cold dishes. It is marvelous in salads, with cold fish, shrimp, etc.

With it, you can also make several delicious sauces:

Tartar Sauce

The real tartar sauce is made by mashing finely 2 hard-boiled egg yolks with 2 raw ones and then making a mayonnaise. This will give you the very finest flavor. You can, however, make it by first making a regular mayonnaise and adding to it the finely mashed yolks when it is finished. If you are a real whiz at mayonnaise, the first method is quite easy. If not, use the second. Next add to the sauce a very little chopped onion, some finely chopped pickles and/or capers, and the chopped white of 1 egg. If available, add fresh parsley and chives. Tartar sauce is out of this world with fried foods. Try serving it also with such things as boiled tongue (hot) or to accompany a good boiled beef dinner. This recipe will yield ½ cup.

Cocktail Sauce

This incredible sauce is best served very, very cold. Plan to serve it in individual glasses, it looks very pretty that way. Line the bottom of the glass with shredded lettuce first. Have the shrimp, lobster or crab meat ready.

FOR 4 SERVINGS:
* 1 cup homemade mayonnaise
* 1 tablespoon tomato paste
* 1 tablespoon Worcestershire sauce
* 1 tablespoon gin
* ⅓ cup whipped cream

Make the mayonnaise with lemon juice instead of vinegar and make it quite spicy with plenty of salt, pepper and good mustard. Season with 1 tablespoon of tomato paste, not tomato sauce, and

1 tablespoon of Worcestershire sauce. The mixture should be really quite hot and tangy. Sprinkle the gin, 1 tablespoon or so, on shrimp. Measure the cream already whipped, and fold it into the mayonnaise sauce gently. Arrange the shrimp over the lettuce in the glasses, pour the sauce over them and chill thoroughly. Do not stir until eating it! You can garnish each serving additionally with quarters of fresh lemons to squeeze on as desired and a little bunch of curly parsley.

BÉARNAISE

Béarnaise gets its very special taste from herbs which are cooked in vinegar. The most necessary ones are tarragon, parsley, a little onion or best of all a small real eschalot.

FOR 4 GENEROUS SERVINGS:
½ pound (2 sticks) butter
1 eschalot, minced finely
1 tablespoon minced parsley
1 teaspoon dried tarragon
¼ cup white wine (optional)
¼ cup white or red vinegar
Salt and pepper
3 egg yolks

Melt about 1 tablespoon of the butter in a very small pan, add to it the eschalot, parsley and tarragon and cook until the eschalot is transparent but not brown. Pour in the wine and the vinegar (or you can use only the vinegar), season with just a pinch of salt and bring to a simmer. Cook until the liquid has almost completely evaporated; there should just be a tablespoonful of it left. Chefs usually strain this, pressing all the juice out of the herbs and using only the vinegar. They then chop some more herbs to add to the sauce later. This is delicious when you can get fresh tarragon, otherwise just use the herbs and the vinegar without bothering to strain them.

Melt the remaining butter in a small pan, it should be melted but not sizzling. Beat the egg yolks in the top of the double boiler, add the vinegar and herbs to them and beat over hot water, not boiling, until slightly thickened. Creamy is the word, then; still beating add the melted butter much as you would oil in making mayonnaise—

a few drops at a time at first, gradually increasing to a small stream. Don't let it get really hot, it curdles quickly. Taste and add pepper as needed. When the sauce is nice and fluffy, keep just barely warm until serving time. What it does to steak is unbelievable!

You can sometimes add a tablespoonful of rich meat gravy or steak juices to this sauce. It then takes the name of Sauce Choron.

The above is the classic French recipe for béarnaise and it works very well! On the other hand, I am always experimenting to find ways of preparing things more easily. One day I invented the following method for making béarnaise, which would make Henri IV (its namesake) turn over in his grave! The results were excellent!

Beat together in a bowl the eggs and the vinegar, using the same proportions as above. Gradually stir in the butter, melted and not too hot. Beat well, the sauce should be creamy and show no signs of separating but will be quite thin. Pour this into a small pan and heat, stirring wildly, over a very low heat or a double boiler. Remove from the fire as soon as it begins to thicken and keep stirring a few minutes longer. Almost instant béarnaise! Cook it in the pan you used for the vinegar and you have one less pot to wash!

HOLLANDAISE

Hollandaise is almost the same as béarnaise but you use a little lemon juice instead of vinegar and you don't use herbs. You need:

3 egg yolks
1 tablespoon water
½ pound (2 sticks) butter
2 teaspoons lemon juice (or more)
Salt and pepper

You can use the double-boiler method or the quick Béarnaise method. Beat the egg yolks with the water, gradually add the melted butter as usual. Season with a little lemon juice, salt and pepper. Be cautious with salt, the butter is generally quite salty already.

Mousseline

Mousseline is a lighter, creamier version of hollandaise. It is usually served with asparagus in France. Delicious also as a salad dressing for a cold chicken salad on a hot summer day. Simply make the hollandaise and very gently fold in one-third of its volume of whipped cream. Measure the cream already whipped.

SAUCES BRUNES

Brown Sauces

These are the sauces which often go with chops and steaks and which make French restaurants famous. They most often start with Espagnole, a greatly reduced meat extract with many good things and perhaps the most difficult to duplicate at home.

The French housewife turns to substitutes to make these sauces. First of all, she carefully saves all the juices and gravies from roasts. To these, she adds good commercial beef extract. The brands vary immensely. I find that bouillon cubes are generally good for just that: bouillon or soups. They are much too salty to use in sauces, which will have only a little liquid added. When buying extract check the list of ingredients carefully; some of them are strictly vegetable, and although they add good flavor, they can't replace the good beef ones. Thus forewarned, let's look at some of these sauces!

Sauce Bordelaise

Sauce Bordelaise is wonderful with steak. It is hearty and flavorful and a great favorite in the small restaurants near the Halles in Paris where the butchers sell their meat. You have to start with a good steak and cook it to your liking. Then make sure to get some marrow bones from your butcher when you purchase the steak and you'll have most of the makings of:

Sauce Bordelaise for Steak:
2 tablespoons chopped eschalots or onions
2 tablespoons chopped parsley
1 tablespoon butter or beef drippings
1 cup dry red wine
Pinch thyme
Small part of one bay leaf
4 to 6 (1-inch) slices marrow bone
A little flour
2 tablespoons liquid beef extract
½ cup water
1 tablespoon tomato paste
Pepper
A little lemon juice
1 teaspoon cornstarch mixed with 1 tablespoon water,
    if needed

Chop the eschalots and parsley finely, cook them in 1 tablespoon butter or beef drippings until the eschalot (or onion) is soft and transparent. Pour on the wine, add thyme and bay leaf, simmer for about ½ hour or until the wine is reduced by half.

While the wine is simmering, take a sharp pointed knife and slip it between the marrow and the bone, then gently push out the marrow and cut it in small ½ inch cubes. Roll them in a little flour, just enough to coat them. Place 1 tablespoon beef extract with half a cup of water in another pan and gently poach the marrow in it. It should take just a few minutes of gentle simmering, being careful not to break it.

Remove the bay leaf from the wine; leave or strain the vegetables as you prefer. I like to leave them in! Add to the wine the other spoonful of beef extract, the tomato paste and any crusty browned bits from the pan in which you cooked the steak. If necessary, you can pour a little of the wine into the skillet and heat, stirring and scraping, then return to the rest of the wine. Add this to the marrow and its broth and taste. You should need very little salt, if any, but you can add pepper to taste and just a dash of lemon juice. The sauce should be rather thin but rich and glossy. The tomato paste and the flour, having adhered to the marrow, thicken it just a little. If it really is watery, you can thicken it slightly with a teaspoon of cornstarch mixed with a tablespoon of water. Pour over the steak and serve immediately.

You can vary this Sauce Bordelaise by adding to it mushrooms cooked in a little butter or for supreme occasions, a sliced truffle. At other times, a little more tomato paste will make it very good with something like pork chops. Makes you feel very creative! You can have the sauce about ready long before you cook the steak and just add the steak juices to it at the last moment.

SAUCE CHASSEUR

This is a marvelous tomato sauce with mushrooms, flavorful with a little white wine. It is excellent with chicken, with veal roast or veal chops. And try using it instead of regular tomato sauce with noodles or spaghetti.

FOR ABOUT 2 CUPS SAUCE:
  ½ pound fresh mushrooms
  ¼ pound (1 stick) butter
  1 eschalot, finely chopped
  Salt and pepper
  1 cup dry white wine
  1 (6 ounce) can tomato paste plus 1 can water
  2 tablespoons good liquid beef extract
  2 teaspoons dry tarragon
  1 teaspoon dry chervil (if available)
  2 tablespoons chopped parsley

Clean the mushrooms and slice them. Brown them in half the butter and when they are almost ready, add to them the finely chopped eschalot and cook until it is transparent. Season with a little salt and pepper, pour in the wine and leave to cook until reduced by half.

Add to this fragrant brew 1 small (6 ounce) can tomato paste

1 can water, 2 tablespoons beef extract. Stir well to mix and add the dried herbs and the freshly chopped parsley. Bring to a simmer and leave to cook for a few minutes for the flavors to blend. Taste and season with more salt and pepper if necessary. When the sauce already tastes so good you want to keep right on tasting, stir in the rest of the butter in small pieces, which makes it even better!

The sauce is now ready but you should add to it any drippings, well skimmed of fat, from whatever you intend serving it with. At times, add a tablespoonful of cognac or Brandy to make it even more flavorful!

SAUCE MADÈRE

This sauce is a classic to serve generally with ham and veal. The Madeira wine gives it its name, but you can vary it with other wines, such as port or sherry. It starts simply as a superb gravy to which is added the wine that gives it its name. Now don't get the idea that you can simply open a can of brown gravy, add wine to it and be done! It may be edible but it won't come close to a true Sauce Madère.

This is one sauce which depends upon your ingenuity. Plan on having a good pot roast a couple of days before you will need the sauce. Serve the pot roast with a tomato sauce perhaps and save the rich, brown beef gravy. Add the wine to it and just let it simmer until reduced as in the last paragraph. Failing this, or if you have just a little gravy, go to work like this:

FOR 1½ TO 2 CUPS SAUCE:

1 carrot
1 onion
1 stalk celery
3 tablespoons beef drippings or butter
Salt and pepper
3 tablespoons flour
1½ cups water
3 tablespoons good beef extract
1 tablespoon tomato paste
Thyme
Bay leaf
½ cup good beef gravy if available
  (or chicken, veal or pork gravy)
½ cup Madeira wine

Finely chop the carrot, onion, celery, and cook them until soft and slightly browned in about 2 tablespoons of the drippings or butter. Season with just very little salt and pepper. Add the last spoonful of butter or drippings and sprinkle the flour over the vegetables. Let it cook until it gets a pretty toasty brown color. Now add 1½ cups of water, the beef extract, the tomato paste (you won't taste it really, but it will give the sauce an appetizing color), thyme, bay leaf, and stir well to mix all intimately. Simmer gently uncovered until reduced to about 1 cup. Stir just once in a while. Strain the mixture and taste. It should have a good flavor and be thick enough to coat a spoon well. If necessary add more beef extract to make it really very rich. Be careful, though, the extract is very salty. Add to this any gravy you have on hand. I mean of course, real meat juices, the part which turns to jelly after it has cooled and from which you have removed the fat. It can be chicken, veal, even pork, if you don't have beef gravy.

All you do now is add the wine. The sauce should be thin, like unthickened gravy really, just barely glazing a spoon. Simmer just a few minutes to develop flavors and serve. What it does to a ham steak with spinach is simply incredible!

You can, of course, add something to this sauce, like mushrooms or truffles for really grand occasions. Imagine, for instance, little pastry shells filled with mushrooms, cubes of ham and chicken. Add sliced truffles and this sauce, and serve only to your most cherished friends!

BUTTERS

In addition to all the marvelous complicated sauces, French cooks use very simple seasoned "butters" to great advantage. These give a gourmet touch to the very simplest foods. All you need is good fresh butter, slightly softened. Add to it a few herbs and add to the dish just as you serve; you'll be amazed at the flavors.

For instance, serve with plain boiled potatoes well drained and dried further on top of the stove by shaking them over high heat to get every last drop of moisture out. Now add a good pat of butter you have mashed with finely chopped parsley and just a drop of lemon juice. Marvelous! These are Maître d'hôtel potatoes.

Cook young green beans until tender but firm in very little boiling salted water. If you don't cover the pot, they will stay greener, by the way! Drain thoroughly and toss with a pat of softened butter mixed with chopped parsley and just a tiny piece of garlic, the size of a small pea. Don't let the butter cook, the heat of the vegetables will melt it and spread it through the whole dish. Not so high in calories, either; you only need a tablespoonful or so for an average dish for 4 people.

Grilled steaks take kindly to being served with just a small pat of lemon-parsley butter melting over each serving. Or try mixing the butter with a spoonful of Worcestershire or other steak sauce.

Veal chops simply grilled or fried in a skillet are utterly delicious with a pat of butter mixed with tarragon and lemon.

Small party sandwiches are extra good when spread with one of these butters. Butter and finely chopped watercress are excellent also.

Finally, a pat of butter, with or without herbs, floating on a bowl of soup looks mighty appetizing!

9. DESSERTS AND PASTRIES

DESSERTS ET PÂTISSERIE

The words "French pastries" are usually enough to make anyone's mouth water! The variety of cakes in a French *pâtisserie* is absolutely unbelievable the first time you see it. Cream puffs ready to burst with whipped cream, éclairs dark with chocolate and so named because they disappear like lightning, babas so drunk with rum you expect them to collapse, and the little fruit tarts, one apricot glossy in the center of its own little tart, cherries crowding together in theirs, strawberries riding proudly in their *barquettes* of pastry so fine it crumbles at a touch. The large cakes too: St.-Honoré, patron saint of pastry cooks, honored by a large cake of layer upon layer of little cream puffs with a cloud-like filling, *mokas* of pale beige coffee-flavored butter cream, as elegant as ladies going to a fashion showing at a *grand couturier, nougatines* with almonds peeking through rich shiny caramel, cakes topped with chestnuts, candied cherries, flowers made of spun sugar, so delicate you cannot bear to eat them, you can go on and on. . . .

Many of these marvels can be made fairly easily at home: take such things as éclairs; the pastry is the first one to be taught to apprentice pastry cooks because it is so simple. Once you know how, you have the basis of not only éclairs, but cream puffs, profiterolles, St. Honoré, rich glamorous-looking cakes or desserts all of them.

French fruit pies are easy too; the pastry is made from a cookytype dough, baked empty and filled with fresh or canned fruit with a light glaze. Add whipped cream and you have quite a production!

The most difficult to make at home is the *pâté feuilletée*, that multi-layered pastry from which Napoleons are made. French housewives usually buy it ready-prepared and you can do the same if you buy the frozen puff pastry shells available at the supermarket. For certain dishes, though, you can use a very good substitute that is fairly easy to make as we shall see. So let's have a look at these different pastries and what we can do with them.

Start with the easiest, the

PÂTE À CHOU

Believe it or not, you could almost prepare an entire meal from chou pastry. It can be used for everything from appetizers to desserts with a few main dishes in between. Monotonous no doubt if all served at the same meal, but entirely feasible.

BASIC CHOU PASTE FOR APPROXIMATELY
6 ÉCLAIRS:

   ¼ cup (½ stick) butter or margarine
   ½ cup water
   ½ cup unsifted flour
   3 medium eggs

Place the butter and water in a 2 quart pan, bring to a boil. When the butter has completely melted, add the flour *all at once* and stir vigorously until the mixture forms a smooth ball which leaves the sides of the pan. I know this sounds silly and that you expect to get nothing but a gooey mess full of lumps! You won't! But the proportions must be exact and you must cook it over a rather high fire. A wooden spoon helps.

Let the mixture cool a little, then beat in the eggs one by one, beating until each is completely absorbed before adding the next one. Voilà the base!

Éclairs and Cream Puffs: Heat the oven to 475°F. Now decide if you want "éclairs" long and filled with *crème pâtissière** and topped with chocolate glaze or cream puffs, round and traditionally filled with whipped cream. For the éclairs form cigar-sized and -shaped oblongs of dough on a well-greased cooky sheet. For the puffs, make nice round balls the size of a small egg. You can use a spoon or a cooky press with the large tip.

Place the shaped dough in the hot oven and bake 10 minutes,

after which you may peek, but only peek, opening and closing the door very gently. The dough will be all puffed up and beginning to brown. Turn the oven down to 325°F. and bake an additional 20 to 25 minutes or until the pastry is well browned and completely firm and crisp. If you take it out too soon, it will look beautiful as it comes out of the oven but will flop down miserably a few moments later. The pastry has to be a deep rich toasty brown everywhere, even in the cracks.

After baking and cooling, slice off the tops of the pastries with a sharp knife and scrape out any soft bits of dough inside. These shells can be baked ahead of time and kept in an airtight container before filling.

Fill éclairs with the crème pâtissière, plain or any flavor you prefer. Cream puffs are generally filled simply with whipped cream, lightly sweetened and flavored with a little vanilla or instant coffee to taste. The cream puffs or *choux*, to give them their French name, freeze beautifully. You can serve them icy cold with a hot chocolate sauce for a sumptuous dessert. I often make a large batch of them just before the holidays, freeze them on a cooky sheet and store them in bags when they are quite hard. Remove from the freezer 10 to 15 minutes before serving so they will not be rock hard.

Éclairs or puffs can be iced very simply by mixing confectioners' sugar with just enough water to make a stiff paste. Count 1 cup sugar to ice 4 to 6 éclairs or choux. Flavor the sugar with 1 teaspoon vanilla or 1 square (1 ounce) melted semi-sweet chocolate. Heat very gently just until the mixture pours. Brush immediately on the tops of the pastries and leave to set for a few minutes. The glaze hardens as it cools.

Chou Pastry Swans

Besides the usual puffs and éclairs you can make very pretty "swans" filled with whipped cream.

Place balls of dough the size and shape of an egg on a greased cooky sheet. For each ball make a thin strip of dough about the size of a pencil and 4 inches long, shaped like an "S." You need a cake decorator, or make a cone of paper, fill with dough and cut off the tip. These strips will be the necks of the swans. Remove them with a spatula when they are crisp and brown, leaving the bodies to bake longer as for ordinary puffs.

When the puffs are done, remove a slice off the top neatly. Fill them to overflowing with stiffly whipped cream. Push the necks into the cream at one end. Cut the little "lids" in two lengthwise and stick them into the cream to form the wings. You can, if you wish, drizzle a little white icing on top, but the "swan" effect is unmistakable and very pretty.

Fritters

Chou pastry can also be used to make fritters, or *Beignets soufflés*, which puff up deliciously. Add an extra egg to the dough to make it soft enough to coat slices of apple, banana, orange, pineapple, etc. Have the fruit dry or rolled in flour to make sure the paste sticks to it nicely. Good with vegetables too! Deep fry in hot fat at 375°F. until golden. Drain on paper towels.

Doughnuts

You can also make a delicious kind of doughnut the French call *Paix de Nonnes*. There is a little story attached to this name. It is said that two convents, many hundred years ago, had been feuding in gentle nun-like fashion over some piece of property. When an agreement was finally reached the superiors of both convents decided to celebrate by serving this delicious dessert, hence its name of "Nuns' Peace." However, over the years the French spelling of the word has been altered to that of a similar sounding word which changes its meaning completely. Strangely enough it is a quite innocent English word, but just ask a French friend (and an intimate one at that) for his translation of "Pet."

To make the dessert: simply drop teaspoonfuls of chou paste into hot deep fat (375°F.) and fry until golden and puffed up, 5 minutes or so. Drain on paper towels. Serve sprinkled with confectioners' sugar or filled with a spoonful of jam.

PÂTE SABLÉE

Piecrust

French fruit tarts are extremely delicate and light to eat. They are usually served at room temperature; the pastry's full buttery flavor is not improved by being chilled. The fruit filling is barely cooked or, as for strawberries for instance, left raw. Over this goes a light glaze of fruit juices, sugar and a little cornstarch. The top of the pie is liberally garnished with whipped cream, sometimes a kind of custard fills the bottom of the pie with the fruit on top of it. This is called *crème pâtissière** or pastry cream and is simply a good, vanilla-flavored pudding or boiled custard!

Here is the basic pie dough recipe:

FOR ONE 9- TO 10-INCH PIECRUST:
> 1 cup flour (unsifted)
> ¼ pound (1 stick) butter OR
> > ½ butter and ½ good margarine (not shortening)
> 1 egg yolk
> 6 tablespoons sugar
> A little flour for rolling dough

If you can get a French pie pan, you'll be blessed! The bottom comes off and the sides are quite low and fluted, saving you a lot of work and making it extra easy to remove the pie shell from the pan without breaking it! Whatever the pan, though, butter it generously.

Place the flour in a large bowl, make a hole in the middle; this is called a "well" technically. In this hole place the softened butter, the egg yolk and the sugar. American butter being generally salty, don't add any salt. With a fork or the tips of your fingers, work the butter, sugar and egg yolk into a smooth mixture. Then gradually work in the flour until you have a ball of rather soft dough. If your kitchen is very hot in summer and the dough is really very soft, place it in the refrigerator for about 1 hour. You can then roll it out between two sheets of floured wax paper. This is an American trick I find marvelous for handling dough easily. Line the pie pan with the dough. Don't be afraid of handling it, this dough will not get tough no matter what you do to it. You can even press it into shape in the pan with your fingers and not bother rolling it out. If it tears, press a little piece onto the hole.

The shell now has to be baked empty. To keep it in shape, prick it well all over, line it with foil, and fill it with dried beans. French cooks generally keep cherry pits and use them over and over again to bake pie shells. Dried beans work just as well and you can store them in an airtight tin or jar to use over and over also.

Bake the pie shell in preheated oven at 400°F. for about 10 to 15 minutes or until it is dry and just beginning to turn golden around the edges. Pour out the beans, remove foil, and cook it a few minutes more until it is golden all over.

In a pinch, you can do without the beans. You will have to look into the oven after about 5 minutes, though, and poke at the dough with a sharp knife to make it lie down, it will probably rise in the center! If you wait too long, it will harden this way and you will be stuck with a dome-shaped pie, almost impossible to fill!

You will find that this kind of pie shell is very easy to take out of the pan. It has a sugar-cooky taste which is delicious no matter what you fill it with.

DEMI-FEUILLETAGE

Flaky Pastry

Here is a last pastry recipe for a good imitation of French flaky pastry. Only the most hardened purist would find fault with it! Most French cookbooks have recipes for real *pâte feuilletée*, which takes quite a few hours to make as it seems to spend most of its time taking rests between rolling-outs! This kind can be made in 5 minutes. It is absolutely marvelous for those little salty tidbits served at cocktail parties. Try little breakfast sausages, anchovies, etc., besides the usual sweet fillings.

FOR 1 LARGE PIE OR 12 SMALL PASTRIES:
>   1 cup unsifted flour
>   ¼ pound (1 stick) butter (or margarine)
>   3 tablespoons ice water

The trick to this pastry is to have everything cold. The butter or margarine must be hard, the water really ice water: i.e., place a few cubes of ice in a cup or glass to melt into water before you start measuring the flour (in another cup). If the kitchen is very warm in summer, chill the bowl and use a thick one which will stay cold.

Do not make too large a batch of pastry at a time. It is made so quickly it is better to mix more as you need it if you are planning a large party.

Place the flour in the bowl, roll the stick of butter in it to coat it on all sides with flour. Slice the butter with two knives, chop it really, until the largest pieces are about the size of a pea. Some will be smaller, of course, but you should end up with a bowl of small pieces of butter coated in flour, larger than the usual "texture of corn meal" given in many pastry recipes.

Pour about 3 tablespoons of ice water over the dough and bring it together with the tip of a knife. If you can't get it all into a ball, add a few drops more water. Handle the dough as little as possible and do not knead it at all. Flour a pastry board or cloth generously and flour the roller also. Roll out the dough to ¼ inch thick or even a little less for small pastries. Cut into shape and bake on greased pie pans or cooky sheets in preheated oven at 400°F. for about 7 minutes or until golden all over. If you are baking little sausages, for instance, you can then turn the oven down to 350°F. and bake until the inside is thoroughly done.

Crisp, golden, flaky, buttery, all these adjectives and more will run through your mind with the first bite! This is a pastry which is best served warm and can be reheated beautifully.

CRÈMES

Creams or Puddings

The French use relatively little cornstarch except as baby food! Creams for desserts or as pie and pastry filling are therefore usually made with eggs and a little plain flour. They are very good made that way, anyhow, and the addition of flour precludes accidents such as eggs curdling. If you have children, don't forget that eggs are good for them in addition to the milk, and such desserts should be counted part of the meal.

Vanilla flavoring of good quality is delicious in this country. You can sometimes obtain vanilla beans or pods for an even more delicious flavor. I have seen recipes telling you to split the bean and scrape it.

No doubt you get a good bit of flavor that way but I have never seen this done in France. The look of all those little black seeds seems to me most unappealing! We usually simply let a whole bean or a piece of one steep in warm milk for a while. The vanilla aroma develops fully that way. Another good trick is to place a vanilla bean in a tin or jar of sugar and forget about it for about one month. Shake the jar occasionally when you happen to see it on the shelf. Then every time you use a cup of that fragrant sugar, replace it with fresh sugar and shake. This is wonderful in cakes and pastries.

Here is the basic recipe for Crème Pâtissière:

FOR ABOUT 1½ CUPS THICK CREAM:

3 large eggs
3 tablespoons flour
½ cup sugar
1½ cups rich milk
1 teaspoon vanilla or ½ vanilla bean

If you are using a vanilla bean, scald the milk an hour or so before making the cream, place the bean in it and forget it!

Place the eggs, flour and sugar in a small bowl. Beat to a thin cream with a little of the cooled milk. Return the rest of the milk to the fire and as soon as it comes to a boil, pour it onto the egg mixture, beating all the time with a whisk. Return all to the fire and cook, stirring until it breaks to big fat bubbles. The flour will prevent it from curdling, have no fear. Stir in liquid vanilla extract; the flavor will be fresher and stronger if you add it last.

As the mixture cools, stir it once in a while or, which is easier, place a sheet of wax paper or thick plastic film right onto the cream. This crème pâtissière makes a wonderful filling for éclairs, in pies under a layer of fresh fruit, or simply as a pudding. Now that you know how to make it, you can easily make Crème St.-Honoré.

Crème St.-Honoré

Use the same ingredients as for Crème Pâtissière but with one extra egg. Separate all 4 eggs. Make a crème pâtissière using the yolks only and half the sugar. Beat the egg whites, at room temperature and with a pinch of salt until frothy. Gradually add the rest of the sugar, 2 tablespoons at a time, beating well after each addition, just as for meringue. When the meringue is nice and stiff and holds stiff peaks, fold it gently into the crème pâtissière—very light and fluffy and delicious. On a very hot day, or if you want to make this cream far ahead of time, like the day before, you can ensure its keeping light and fluffy with the addition of gelatin. Simply soften an envelope of plain gelatin in a little cold water and add to the cream before cooking. The gelatin will have melted by the time the cream has thickened well. Stir and fold in the meringue mixture before the crème pâtissière sets.

This cream is used traditionally to garnish a cake made up of layers of chou paste rings. Delicious and very pretty. You can also serve it simply as a pudding with lightly cooked fruit and crisp cookies for a sumptuous dessert.

Still starting with the crème pâtissière, you can make plain *crème au chocolat* by adding 2 ounces semi-sweet chocolate to the milk as it heats. Stir until melted. Or you can make the most delicious caramel or butterscotch-flavored *crème caramel* this way.

Place 4 tablespoons sugar with just a few drops of water in a very heavy saucepan. Stir over high heat until the sugar melts. Then leave it to cook until it starts to turn golden and gives off a delicious caramel aroma. Remove from the fire and leave it to cool in the pan. If it seems to be getting too brown, it *will* go on cooking for a few minutes after you remove it from the fire, you can simply stand the pan in a little cold water. Pour the milk you will use for the cream over this caramel and heat it, stirring until the caramel melts. Don't add the milk until the caramel has cooled, though; it would bubble up, make an awful mess and probably curdle! Make the *crème* as usual with the delicately flavored milk, adding more sugar if you deem it necessary. Superb filling for éclairs as is or with the addition of a little rum!

There remains a delicate almond-flavored cream known as *crème Frangipane.* This is wonderful as a filling for a plain cake, such as pound cake or sponge cake. Simply make the crème pâtissière but add to it a few drops almond extract along with the vanilla. Crumble finely 4 or 5 small almond macaroons and add them to the cream before it cools. If you can find almond paste, which is simply finely pounded almonds mixed with sugar, you can add a couple of table-spoonfuls of it instead of the almond flavoring. This makes a wonderful pie filling particularly under pear halves or apricots. These fruits are definitely enhanced by the almond taste.

CRÈME AU BEURRE

Butter Cream

Now that you know all the variations of crème pâtissière, let's look at the more sophisticated Crème au Beurre.

Crème au Beurre is a fantastic concoction made simply of butter, eggs and sugar! It is so rich you can't eat very much of it, but it has the most unique taste and texture. Just imagine: it is smoother than cream and richer than butter!

Crème au Beurre reaches absolute perfection flavored with rich dark coffee. You can make it also with vanilla or chocolate, but to my mind, nothing beats coffee. French coffee is roasted much darker than American coffee, with the exception of New Orleans coffee. For the finest taste, you should make your own coffee extract starting with a rich dark blend. If you cannot get dark coffee, however, you may be able to find espresso-type instant coffee; it will be better than ground light roast coffee. Next on the list of preference is regular instant coffee and lots of it! The taste will be a little milder, sort of coffee and cream compared to dark roast but excellent all the same. Here is the standard recipe after which you will find what to do with this incredible cream.

FOR AT LEAST 8 PEOPLE:

    1 cup freshly ground dark roast coffee
    1 cup boiling water
    2 cups sugar
    8 egg yolks
    1 pound plus ¼ pound butter OR
      ½ butter and ½ margarine
    1 pound vanilla wafers or plain cake

Start with the extract: pour about 1 cup of boiling water over the coffee grounds. If you have a drip pot, you can use that, of course. Failing that, place the grounds into a small pitcher, pour the water over them and leave to stand for about 10 minutes. Strain through several layers of fine cloth, squeezing out every last fragrant drop. You need altogether about 1 cup of very strong coffee, so add more water, boiling, as needed. Measure ½ cup of this witches' brew and set the rest aside.

Add ½ cup of coffee to the 2 cups sugar, stir until the sugar is melted, and cook over fairly high heat until the sugar reaches the thick syrup stage. To test it, drop a little into cold water; it should settle at the bottom thickly. Remove from the fire and leave to cool slightly.

Beat the egg yolks. Be sure that you remove all the little white thread-like bits which usually adhere to them, and gradually pour on the sugar-coffee syrup. Now leave the whole thing to cool thoroughly, stirring once in a while so no skin forms on top.

Set aside 1 stick of butter, letting it soften at room temperature, for emergency use later if needed! Place the pound in a large bowl and work it to a smooth cream. If you have never done it, you won't believe this, but butter almost always has lumps in it! Work with your fingers until the butter is relatively soft, then start beating it with a fork or, better still, a French wire whisk.

Gradually add the sugar-egg mixture, a few tablespoonfuls at a time, beating until it is completely absorbed before adding more. Butters vary a little, and so you may not be able to add all the sugar. Beat firmly though. If at the end you see that the mixture shows definite signs of separating, don't panic, just beat in the reserved butter!

You will probably have been tasting all along, at the end the cream should be of incredible smoothness with a strong coffee flavor. You can now use it to make the traditional Moka described below or simply use it to fill and ice a good layer cake. It makes the most wonderful icing you ever tasted. For the Moka:

Take a 1 quart mold, preferably a plain one. A 9 inch layer cake pan holds about 1 quart by the way, or a small loaf pan. Combine American ingenuity and French cooking and line it with plastic film, leaving several inches hanging out on the sides. This cake used to be a minor nightmare to turn out before I discovered plastic film! Press the film so it will stick well to the pan.

Spread a ¼ inch layer of cream evenly over the bottom and sides of the mold. Pour the reserved coffee into a soup plate, quickly dip one by one the vanilla wafers and arrange them neatly in a layer at the bottom and on the sides. Press them down lightly into the cream so they stay in place. Break up a few of them and fill the cracks. Spread a ½ inch layer of cream over the bottom cookies, another layer of cookies, more cream and so on until the mold is tightly filled, ending with a layer of cookies. Don't let the cookies soak in the coffee, just a quick dip. Cover the mold with the film which hangs over the sides, then with a plate and place a weight over that to press every-thing down firmly. Store in the refrigerator several hours or overnight. The weight can be an unopened carton of milk, no need to clutter up the refrigerator!

You should have about 1 cup of cream left over, refrigerate that also. When you are ready to finish the cake, peel off the plastic film from the top, turn the cake onto a pretty plate. The mold will lift off quite easily. You can grab the film and give it a tug if necessary. Peel off all the rest of the plastic film, and smooth any wrinkles in the cream with a knife. Wish my wrinkles would erase that easily!

Now decorate the cake with the rest of the cream. To do this, you must let it soften at room temperature before you touch it. If you beat it before it has softened, it will separate! So give it plenty of time. Use a cake decorator to make a pretty border or just swirl it with a knife. Return the cake to the refrigerator and keep it there until serv-ing time. Serve in very thin pieces. Your guests will think you stingy at first but will understand after a few mouthfuls!

This cake is worthy of the grandest celebrations: I don't recom-mend it for children's birthday parties, though! Unless the children possess discriminating palates, most of them won't care particularly for the coffee flavor. To make chocolate butter cream, add 3 ounces melted and cooled chocolate to the butter. For plain vanilla, simply add 2 teaspoons vanilla extract and use plain water instead of coffee.

Now if you want to add rum to the coffee you dip the vanilla wafers in, your male guests are likely to sing your praises forever but their wives may hate you!

BAVAROIS AUX FRAISES

Strawberry Bavarian Cream

Bavarian creams make wonderful desserts in summer. They are smooth and cold and creamy and particularly good made with fruit. In this case: strawberries and cream, the combination sure to please everybody; I have never heard of anyone not liking strawberries!

Raspberries are used extensively with other summer fruit in French desserts—probably because they are rather expensive to serve by themselves and also because their aroma is so definite that a little of them goes quite a long way. Mixed with strawberries, they seem to deepen the strawberry flavor. Over peaches or pears, they not only enhance those flavors but add such a pretty blush, they make the whole dish twice as appealing.

You can make this Bavarian cream well in advance, which makes it easy for parties. Use a fancy mold and garnish with berries and cream and you will have a glamorous concoction with really very little trouble.

FOR 6 TO 8 SERVINGS:

    2 *pints fresh ripe strawberries*
    1 *8-ounce box frozen raspberries, thawed*
    2 *tablespoons (2 envelopes) plain gelatin*
    1 *cup sugar (approximately)*
    ¼ *cup brandy, fruit brandy, fruit wine or orange juice*
    1 *cup heavy cream*
    Whipped cream for garnish (optional)

Rinse the strawberries briefly before hulling them. Then hull them and pick out a few nice ones to reserve for garnish. Put the rest through a food mill or blender along with the thawed raspberries. You should have around 2 cups of fragrant fruit purée. Sweeten it to taste, using about 1 cup of sugar; make it a little sweeter than you usually would, since the cream has to be added later. Soften the gelatin in a little cold water. Add it to the purée and cook the whole thing until the gelatin is completely melted, just a few minutes really: the less you heat this, the better it tastes! Stir in the brandy or wine. Cherry brandy or apricot brandy are a nice touch or you can use orange juice if you don't want anything alcoholic.

Chill the mixture in the refrigerator until it begins to set—the consistency of unbeaten egg whites is just right. Whip the cream until it forms soft peaks. Watch it now, you don't want butter but that is what you'll get if you beat the cream too much! Fold the cream gently but thoroughly into the fruit. Pour the whole thing into a pretty mold rinsed with cold water and leave it in the refrigerator until set, at least 4 hours, and you can wait until the next day if you wish.

Turn the cream out onto a pretty dish. It will come out easily if you dip the mold in hot water for a second and loosen the edges with a knife. Decorate with the reserved berries and/or whipped cream if you wish.

CERISES, FRAISES, PÊCHES, ETC. MIREILLE

Cherries, Strawberries, Peaches, etc.,
Mireille

This usually sounds crazy to most Americans, but I am not very fond of ice cream! I have to admit, though, that American ice cream is extraordinarily good and fantastically cheap compared to the French ones. Ice cream in France is usually served for fancy occasions and worth its weight in gold!

What I do like, however, perhaps because it is not quite so cold and shivery as ice cream, is simply frozen whipped cream! Sweetened whipped cream, frozen until just barely hard, could become one of my secret vices. Perhaps after you try this dessert, you will see why and become an addict also!

In this case, the cream is frozen after small pieces of macaroons or other crisp sweet cookies are folded into it. The cookies are first soaked in good liqueur and the combination is irresistible with a fruit sauce. The name Mireille applies to the cream and you can serve with it any fruit in season. This glamorous preparation takes very little time, hardly any cooking and can be made well ahead of time: what more can you want for a summer dessert!

FOR ABOUT 6 TO 8 SERVINGS:
> *12 small almond macaroons or other crisp cookies*
> *¼ cup good liqueur: Grand Marnier, brandy, or*
> *   fruit-flavored liqueurs, rum, kirsch, whatever you*
> *   like best!*
> *1 pint fresh strawberries*
> *1 small carton frozen raspberries*
> *Sugar to taste*
> *2 cups heavy cream*
> *6 tablespoons sugar plus approximately ½ cup*
> *   to sweeten fruit*
> *A few drops vanilla*

Place the cookies in a soup plate, pour the liqueur over them and let them become thoroughly drunk!

Rinse and hull the strawberries. With other fruit, such as cherries, peaches or pears, remove the pits and/or peel and slice and poach briefly in a little water and sugar. You make a little syrup with sugar and water, bring it to a simmer and add the fruit. Cook over very low heat just until the fruit is barely tender. Strawberries should never be cooked, however. They would go as limp as dish rags. So slice them and sweeten them to taste.

Thaw the raspberries and press them through a sieve to remove all those little pesky seeds. When I was a child, we were firmly convinced that there was a factory where they sliced matches thinly to make seeds for raspberry jam! Pour the raspberry purée over the fruit and mix well. You may take a taste and decide if it needs sugar. Take just one taste and put the sauce away in the refrigerator or you will want to eat it all!

Pour the cream into a deep bowl. Whip it: I prefer above all a French wire whisk for this or a plain egg beater. The electric ones scare me for whipping cream; one second too much and you get butter! As soon as the cream begins to thicken, add sugar a little at a time. I ordinarily use about 6 tablespoons for this amount of cream. Add a few drops vanilla. Continue whipping until the cream is fairly stiff and holds nice soft peaks.

Crumble the drunk cookies into not too small pieces and fold them into the cream. You can now pour the mixture into a mold, preferably one that is not too fancy so it will unmold easily. If you like you can line the mold with plastic film: makes turning out a cinch! Wax paper works well too in this case.

Freeze until the cream is just hard. I like it best that way and freeze it only for about 1½ hours. You can, of course, freeze it much longer and take it out of the freezer and place it into the refrigerator about 1 hour before serving. Unmold onto a pretty dish, pour just a little of the fruit sauce over it and pass the rest of the sauce separately.

For convenience you could freeze the cream into an ice tray and cut it into individual slices if you prefer. Just think: after the strawberry season, you can have cherries Mireille, peaches, pears, and why not pineapple? I told you it was easy to become an addict to frozen whipped cream!

CHARLOTTE AUX POMMES

Have you ever noticed how men seem to like apple desserts? I wonder sometimes how much coaxing Eve really had to do! This dessert is very simple and good, sort of a bread pudding with baked apples, and it has that elusive quality which makes you feel like a good mother when you serve it! For one thing, the aroma of baking apples on a cold winter day is one which enchants young and old and makes them happy to be home.

For fancy occasions, you can turn this pudding out of its mold, provided you bake it in something like a loaf pan, with straight sides. If you have one of those pretty baking dishes which can come to the table, though, use it. Makes everything much simpler.

FOR 4 GENEROUS SERVINGS:
  6 to 8 slices day-old bread
  6 tablespoons butter (or butter and margarine)
  4 to 6 cooking apples
  1 cup (approximately) sugar
  A little cinnamon

Trim the crusts off the slices of bread. Cut the slices into wide strips, such as halves or thirds. Butter very generously the baking dish and dust it with sugar. Butter the slices of bread also and use the strips to line the bottom and the sides of the baking dish, cutting some of the pieces to fit if necessary. Fill the dish with the peeled, cored and sliced apples. Place a layer of apple slices, dust with sugar and cinnamon, a few dots of butter and repeat until the dish is full. The amount of sugar depends on the tartness of the apples, of course. Cover the dish with more strips of bread, buttered on both sides if you are so inclined, or at least on the outside if you are thrifty and don't believe in such extravagance!

Bake the dish in preheated oven at 350°F. for about 1 hour or until the bread is golden and crisp on the outside and the apples tender when you poke at them with a pointed knife. Serve warm, and if you pass a little pitcher of cream along with it, your children will have wonderful memories of their childhood!

CHIPOLATA

*Belgian Custard Dessert with Candied
Fruit*

Ask for Chipolata in France and in Belgium and you will get two completely different things! In France they are savory little sausages bought at the *charcuterie* and in Belgium, a luscious creamy dessert, usually from the *pâtisserie*. This is the one I want to talk about here. It starts with a wonderfully rich vanilla custard to which is added chopped candied fruit and maraschino cherries. Then comes whipped cream or egg whites, depending on how calorie conscious you are!

FOR 4 PEOPLE:
   4 egg yolks
   8 tablespoons sugar
   1 cup rich milk
   2 teaspoons vanilla extract
   1 envelope plain gelatin
   4 ounces chopped candied fruit
   1 cup heavy cream OR
      4 egg whites
   Maraschino cherries for garnish

Make the custard by beating the 4 egg yolks with 4 tablespoons sugar and a little of the milk. Scald the rest of the milk, pour gently, stirring vigorously over the egg yolks and stir in the vanilla. If the mixture coats a spoon, stop right there; if it doesn't, cook it in the double boiler over hot water until it does. Just a regular creamy custard! Soften the gelatin in a little cold water, add it to the hot custard and stir until completely dissolved. Now stir in the chopped candied fruit, mixing it in well. Chill, stirring once in a while so the fruit is evenly distributed until the custard is beginning to set.

Now whip the cream, adding the remaining sugar as the cream begins to thicken, or beat the egg whites until they form soft peaks and add the sugar gradually, beating until it has completely dissolved. Fold gently but thoroughly into the custard. The egg whites will give a much greater volume: you not only get less calories, you get more dessert! The cream, however, gives a smoothness and taste which is heavenly. Maybe your husband likes you a little plump anyhow!

Pour the mixture into a mold rinsed with cold water, or into individual serving dishes. To unmold: dip the mold briefly into hot water and turn out on a pretty dish. Garnish with maraschino cherries. If you decorate the dessert with more whipped cream, you are either too thin and trying to gain weight or past caring! Unless you have Belgian ancestors. . . .

CLAFOUTI AUX CERISES

Cherry Pudding

This is a marvelous Alsatian dessert made with fresh, luscious red cherries. Or juicy black ones, maybe, just bursting with juice! It's a kind of custard with the cherries baked right into it. If you have a little kirsch or brandy on hand, you could add it to the batter—a couple of tablespoonfuls do wonders.

FOR 4 PEOPLE:
> 1½ to 2 cups pitted fresh cherries
> > or 1 1-pound can sweet dark cherries
> 3 eggs
> ⅓ cup (approximately) sugar
> 3 tablespoons flour
> 1 cup milk
> 2 or 3 tablespoons brandy or kirsch (optional)
> Powdered or confectioners' sugar for garnish

If you are using fresh cherries, remove the pits. You can do this easily and quickly with a special little tool or with a pointed knife. With canned or frozen cherries, be sure they are thoroughly drained.

Beat the eggs and the sugar together. You need about ⅓ cup sugar with sweet fresh cherries, more if they are sour, less if you are using canned cherries in syrup. Make a thin paste with the flour and a little of the milk, stir into the eggs with the rest of the milk. Add the brandy or kirsch, if you are using it. If you have the slightest suspicion of a lump, strain the whole thing. Place the cherries in a shallow, well-buttered dish and pour the batter over them. Bake in preheated oven at 350°F. for about 30 to 40 minutes, or until the custard is set. Sprinkle with a little powdered or confectioners' sugar just before serving, warm or cold, as you prefer.

If you wish, you can thicken the cherry juice from canned cherries with a teaspoon of cornstarch, bring it to a boil, and serve it as a sauce. Seems a shame to waste it!

CRÊPES

Thin French Pancakes

Thin lacy French pancakes make all kinds of glamorous dishes and are very easy to make, believe me! Don't think for a moment that you need all kinds of special pans or implements, either. I have made them with equal success in everything from cast-iron skillets to Teflon-lined pans. Pans with slanted sides, straight sides, high and low sides! As to the principle that you must reserve one pan exclusively for pancakes, well . . . being an average housewife with lots of children, all the pans are used for anything from hamburgers in gravy to fried eggs depending on the size exclusively!

The secret of this batter is simply to add melted butter or oil right into it. This way the pancakes won't stick, except maybe the first one! When Maria made pancakes, she always called the first one the cat's pancake: it generally did not flip as well as the next ones. Besides our cat loved pancakes as long as they were plain. He did not like apple ones.

Pancakes are delicious as desserts, simply with sugar or with various fillings. You can also work magic with a little brandy and *flambez* them right at the table for glamorous occasions. Salty pancakes are wonderful filled with such delicacies as crab meat, lobster or mushrooms. They solve neatly the problem of what to do with that last little bit of chicken which is not sufficient for a whole meal and too much to throw away. Moreover, they are quite inexpensive to make. You can have a wonderful pancake party for a great many people, offering a variety of fillings, for a really small amount of money. Fun and different and not too much work at the last moment.

In many parts of France and Belgium, pancakes are traditionally served for Mardi Gras, the Tuesday before the beginning of Lent. Everyone has to flip his own pancake, holding a silver coin in his left hand, to ensure good fortune all year. At one time, one pancake was flipped to the top of the highest cupboard and left there all year: this made sure there would always be food in the house! Probably made the mice happy, too.

Flipping pancakes is not nearly as difficult as it looks. All it takes is a little nerve! Keep in mind that even if it falls on the floor, the loss is not great and the mess negligible: one paper towel takes care of it. It is a wonderful morale booster and great for the ego! If you are making pancakes for a group of adults, prepare them ahead of time, except for the last 4 or 5. Invite everyone in the kitchen while you "finish the pancakes"; everyone will think you're a great cook even if your previous accomplishments were just being superb at thawing things fast. I cannot recommend this trick too highly to mothers of children who are taking new math: it will improve your image no end if you have no idea of what an infinite set is! (It does not mean dishes that can be replaced one by one for more than five years.)

Practice this in privacy, you'll see how easy it is: when the pancake is lightly brown on the bottom and dry on top, shake the pan to make sure the pancake does not stick anywhere. Grasp the handle firmly at the very end. Slide the pancake back and forth a few times by shaking the pan away and toward you. Now when the pancake reaches the edge of the pan farthest from you and is about to slide right out, give a firm flick of the wrist. It will obligingly turn over and slide right back into the pan. With a little practice you will make them sail high wide and handsome with considerable satisfaction.

Now for the recipe for basic crêpes and some ideas of fillings:

FOR ABOUT 12 TO 15 SMALL PANCAKES:
> *1 cup sifted flour*
> *3 eggs*
> *Pinch salt*
> *2 cups (approximately) milk*
> *4 tablespoons melted butter*

Place the flour in a deep bowl, make a well in the middle. Into this, place the eggs, a pinch of salt, and about half the milk. With a rotary egg beater or a fork, start beating the eggs and milk together, the flour will gradually be absorbed. When the mixture is smooth, add enough of the rest of the milk to make a batter the consistency of light cream. It should just coat the spoon. Cover and let the mixture rest for a couple of hours or longer. This gives the flour a chance to swell. Before using, stir well and add a tablespoonful more milk if it seems too thick.

Melt the butter in the pan you plan on using. An 8 inch one is about right. Pour the melted butter into the batter and stir well. Heat the pan and pour in just enough batter to cover the bottom with a thin coat, the edges of the crêpe should be so thin they are lacy. I have a large kitchen spoon which holds just the right amount, about 3½ tablespoons. Maybe you have one too.

Cook the pancake until it is dry on top and flecked with dark brown on the bottom. Turn it with a pancake turner or spatula if you're chicken about tossing it, it will taste as good! Brown the other side lightly. Stack the pancakes in a warm place if you plan on eating them soon. If not, you can stack them with a layer of wax paper between them and reheat them later, even the next day. If you stir the batter a little each time you make a pancake, you should not have to grease the pan at all. If the pancakes seem to have a vague idea of sticking toward the end, grease the pan with just a few drops of oil or a dab of butter. When all are ready serve them in one of these ways: Sprinkle with sugar and a few drops of lemon juice and hand to the nearest child. Or spread them with jam, jelly or honey. A dab of butter is delicious with honey.

For glamorous occasions, when you want to impress people a little, try the Crêpes Suzettes recipe.

CRÊPES SUZETTES

To the French, Crêpes Suzettes are always orange-flavored. There are, of course, other fillings and sauces you can use but technically you should then call them Crêpes Flambées.

You will find below the recipe for the orange Crêpes Suzettes. Don't stop there, though. At times you can think up many delicious variations. I love apricot jam. Often I use it instead of the marmalade, make the sauce with it and rum and *flamber* the whole thing with rum. If you sprinkle the dish with toasted slivered almonds, the results are delicious.

For Crêpes Suzettes:
4 ounces (½ glass) orange marmalade
2 or 3 tablespoons Grand Marnier or Cointreau
12 pancakes
3 or 4 tablespoons butter
2 tablespoons sugar
½ teaspoon (approximately) grated orange rind
¼ cup brandy

This will serve 4 to 6 people. Mix the orange marmalade with a little Grand Marnier or other orange liqueur or brandy. Spread the pancakes thinly with a little of this and fold them in four, like little fans. Melt 3 or 4 tablespoons butter in a large skillet or chafing dish. There should be enough to cover the bottom of the pan thinly. Arrange the little folded pancakes in the butter and sprinkle them with 2 tablespoons sugar mixed with about ½ teaspoon of freshly grated orange rind. Heat very gently until the pancakes are really hot. Turn them over once, to be sure. You can do this in the kitchen if you like, leaving them on very low heat while you eat the main course. At the table, just before serving, pour in the brandy, which will warm immediately from the heat of the pan, and set a match to it. Stand back and watch the blue flames whoooosh! Serve as soon as the flames die down.

Crêpes Fourrées

12 pancakes
1½ or 2 cups Crème Pâtissière*
4 tablespoons good rum
Butter and sugar

Stuff the pancakes with a generous spoonful of good crème pâtissière or vanilla pudding which you have flavored with 2 tablespoons good rum. Roll the pancakes and arrange them in a baking dish. Butter the dish generously, of course, and dot the pancakes with a little more butter. Sprinkle a little sugar over all. Heat covered with a lid or foil in a low preheated oven. At 250°F. allow about 30 minutes; you can have the oven lower and leave it longer if convenient. Drizzle the rest of the rum over the hot pancakes just before serving. The pancakes can be stuffed this way with other flavors of cream, other liqueurs and/or fruit. Or you can do this:

Crêpes à la Chartreuse

12 pancakes
A little sugar
2 finely crumbled almond macaroons (about 4 tablespoons)
¼ pound butter
¼ cup chartreuse liqueur
Powdered sugar

Make the pancakes, roll them up with a little sugar sprinkled on them. If you wish, you can wrap them up tightly in aluminum foil and refrigerate them until later. Near serving time, place the package, still well wrapped, in the oven to warm up. Allow about 20 minutes at 375°F.

Crumble the macaroons finely. Their size varies—use enough to make about 4 generous tablespoonfuls. The sauce is simply made by melting the butter with the macaroon crumbs and the liqueur. Don't cook it, just heat it through. If you like, you can have the pancakes on a hot serving dish and make the sauce right at the table in a small chafing dish. Unroll the pancake in the sauce, then fold it in four, place it on a plate and pass it to the lucky guest along with powdered sugar to use as he pleases.

Without a chafing dish, simply dip the unrolled pancakes in the sauce, fold them and return them to a hot serving dish and pour the rest of the sauce over them. If you don't care for chartreuse, think of Benedictine or any fruit-flavored liqueur. Count 2 pancakes per serving.

CRÊPES FARCIES

The thin French pancakes called crêpes are marvelous eaten with salty fillings. Great for using up little bits of leftovers such as chicken, shrimp, crab meat or many vegetables.

See the recipe for basic crêpes, and here are a few ideas for fillings.

Any kind of seafood will be delicious in a cream sauce flavored with a little tomato paste and a dash of sherry. A good spoonful of Worcestershire sauce will add a pleasant pepperiness.

Cheese can be added to any cream sauce as a seasoning for vegetables. For a more interesting taste, try mixing several kinds of cheese. Cheddar and Swiss, half and half, go well together. Domestic Swiss is usually rather bland and a couple of tablespoons of grated Parmesan or Romano cheese do wonders for it.

Count about 2 cups of filling for 12 crêpes. Use a generous spoonful on each crêpe and keep about ½ cup of the filling in reserve. Dilute this with a little cream or sherry to make it a thin sauce consistency.

Arrange the filled crêpes in a well-buttered baking dish. Pour the sauce in a wide ribbon across the top of the dish. Dot with butter and/or bread crumbs or a little grated cheese. The dish now has simply to be reheated until piping hot. Count about 25 minutes at 375°F. If you prefer, you may cover the dish with foil and bake it longer at a lower temperature. Stuffed crêpes are very patient.

You can have a delightful crêpe party if you prepare a great stack of crêpes and wrap them in foil in packages of 10 or so. Reheat in the oven, 375°F. for about 25 minutes, opening the foil a little during the last 10 minutes so the steam can escape.

Have ready various types of fillings, salty and sweet, hot and fragrant on a hot plate or chafing dishes. Let each guest decide the kind of filling he wants. Very easy on the hostess and a different kind of buffet supper.

DIABLE EN CHEMISE

Devil in His Night Shirt!

In spite of its silly name, this dessert is so simple and so delicious you'li wonder why you did not think of it before! It is simply sweetened whipped cream, slightly hardened in the freezer and covered with a dark, rich chocolate sauce. Glamorous enough for any party and easy to prepare ahead of time and forget until serving.

FOR 6 PEOPLE:
> 2 cups heavy cream
> 4 to 6 tablespoons sugar
> 4 ounces semi-sweet or sweet dark chocolate
> 2 tablespoons butter
> 4 tablespoons water or coffee
> 2 egg yolks

Whip the cream, adding about 4 to 6 tablespoons of sugar to it as soon as it begins to thicken. Continue beating until it is quite stiff, but don't make butter! Mound the cream in a shallow bowl, the one you will serve it in, giving it a smooth dome shape. Reserve about 4 tablespoons for garnish later. About 1½ hours before serving place it in the freezer or freezing compartment of the refrigerator. You just want to get it very cold and slightly hardened, not frozen hard. Until that time it can stay in the refrigerator, of course.

Make the chocolate sauce by placing the chocolate, broken in pieces, the butter and 4 tablespoons water (or coffee) in a small pan. Melt over low heat, stirring, and don't let it boil, just melt. Cool a little then stir in the 2 egg yolks. You should have a smooth, glossy rather thick sauce that will just pour. Stir in a few drops more water or coffee if necessary. Let it get thoroughly cool but not chilled.

At serving time, remove the dome of cream from the freezer, pour the chocolate evenly all over it to cover it completely. With a small spoon or a knife, draw devilish eyes, nose and mouth: the cream will show white under the chocolate! Pipe or spoon the reserved cream around the base of the dome, this is the collar of the nightshirt! Who would have suspected that the devil could be so white inside!

FONTAINEBLEAU

France is famous for its cheeses even though very few of them are exported. There are Camembert, of course, and Roquefort, both strong cheeses which leave no one indifferent: you love them or hate them! What is less known is that France produces innumerable cream cheeses also. One of these, served in the spring with fresh berries, is the Fontainebleau. This one is actually whipped cream left to drain until only the thickest, creamiest part remains. It is served as is with just a little powdered sugar or with plump fresh strawberries or, if you can find them, fresh raspberries, velvety and red!

This recipe is the closest I can come to the real thing. You have to whip the cream until it is really very thick, almost to the point of separating into butter! The best thing to do is to beat it by hand; to come that close to butter, you have to stop at just the right time: an electric beater just might be a little too fast for you!

FOR 4 PEOPLE (OR 6!):
2 cups heavy cream
Fresh berries and sugar

Whip the cream until really very stiff; looking at it closely, you should see it nearly ready to turn to butter. The cream will have a pretty, definitely "creamy" color, not stark white as at first.

Line a strainer or colander with several layers of cheesecloth, place it over a bowl or plate and spoon the cream into it. Leave the cream to drain for several hours or even overnight in the refrigerator. The extra fluid will drain and the cream will be really very thick and hold its shape by then. Spoon it into individual dishes or a large bowl; pass sugar and berries separately. This must be as close to heaven as we can hope to get on this earth!

GÂTEAU DE SEMOULE

Farina Dessert

It took me over a year to discover that the semolina I was hunting for in supermarkets was called farina in this country or sold as a breakfast cereal under the name of "Cream of . . ." wheat or rice as the case may be! My "English" English did give me trouble at first: I used to ask for biscuits, which is what the English call cookies, and get biscuits . . . which I called "scones"!

To get back to semolina or farina, we use it in France to make delicious desserts or puddings you might like to try. These are very light and delicate in taste and go excellently with any kind of stewed fruit. A compote of dried apricots, for instance, goes with this one perfectly. Good for the small fry too, but don't be surprised if the adults ask for more!

FOR 6 TO 8 SERVINGS:

3 eggs, separated
¾ cup sugar
4 cups milk
½ cup farina (cream of wheat)
1 teaspoon vanilla

Beat the egg whites into stiff but not dry meringue, using about 4 tablespoons of the sugar.

Heat the milk to boiling and sprinkle in the farina. stirring as you go to avoid lumps. Add the rest of the sugar to this and cook approximately 10 minutes, less if you are using the instant kind of cereal. The mixture should be good and thick and the farina soft. Beat the egg yolks; stir a little of the hot farina into them then return all to the pot, stirring well. Now pour this over the egg whites and fold in gently just until all is well mixed. Add the vanilla.

Rinse a bowl or plain mold with cold water, pour the farina into it and chill until set, about 4 hours. Unmold on a pretty plate to serve. You can garnish the pudding with whipped cream and fruit, if you wish, or sometimes add mixed, chopped candied fruit before the pudding sets. Raisins are good too! You will be surprised just how good this pudding is!

Other delightful variations, fit for company any time, are almond and coffee farina! For the almond, try adding just a few drops of almond flavoring to the pudding along with the vanilla. Get a package of blanched slivered almonds—you need about 4 tablespoons—and toast them slightly. You can do this on a cooky sheet in the oven or simply in a skillet on top of the stove. Keep shaking them so they brown evenly, they burn very quickly. Sprinkle over the pudding before serving.

You can stir about 2 teaspoons of instant coffee into the milk and stir before adding the farina. Serve this delicately flavored pudding ice cold with a warm chocolate sauce and wait for raves!

HÉRISSON

Apple Hedgehog

This is a really delicious apple dessert, fit for company anytime but sure to delight the family. Whole apples, cooked in brown sugar, covered with a sauce of apricots and a thick layer of meringue.

As you only use the egg whites in the meringue, you could make a custard with the egg yolks and pass it alongside. This dish is very sweet, so if the custard is only lightly sweetened, it makes a nice contrast.

FOR 4 TO 6 SERVINGS:
½ cup water
1 cup brown sugar
6 nice firm apples
2 cups fresh or canned applesauce
1 glass (8 ounces) apricot jam
A little cinnamon
3 eggs, separated
¾ cup sugar
Slivered almonds (4 tablespoons)
1½ cups milk
1 tablespoon cornstarch

Make a syrup by adding about ½ cup of water to the brown sugar in a shallow pan just big enough to hold the 6 whole apples. Peel and core these but leave them whole. Cook them in the hot syrup, watching them so they stay whole. Turn them over so all sides have a chance to imbibe the brown sugar flavor. The time varies immensely with the apples, just don't let them fall to bits. Remove them gently with a slotted spoon when they are done and place them in a well-buttered baking dish.

Cook down the remaining syrup until very thick and add to it the applesauce, the apricot jam and a dusting of cinnamon. Let this cook slowly until very thick. It will get a dark, appetizing color. Cool slightly and spoon over the whole apples.

Make a meringue by beating the 3 egg whites with about 6 table-spoons sugar. Add the sugar gradually, 2 tablespoons at a time, and beat until the meringue is thick and holds stiff peaks. Cover the apples with it and stick the slivered almonds all over to give the prickly hedgehog effect. This isn't solely for decoration, the almonds taste delicious!

Bake the whole thing for about 30 minutes at 375°F. or until heated through and the tips of the almonds are a pretty toasty color.

Make the custard sauce by using the 3 egg yolks, beaten with a little sugar and 1 tablespoon cornstarch and just enough cold milk to make a smooth paste. Heat the rest of the milk and pour over the eggs. Stir well. If the milk is hot enough, it may not need any further cooking, thickening immediately. If not, return to the pan and cook until thick and creamy. Don't let it boil fiercely!

KOEKEBAKKEN

Flemish Pancakes

The Flemish people in the northwest part of Belgium are a robust breed like their neighbors of the Netherlands. They have to be. For centuries they have fought the sea to keep it from their land. The summers are short and the winters long and hard. The land is flat, below the level of the sea in many places, offering no protection against the cold north wind, which, somehow, never seems to stop blowing. The trees which line the roads are all bent in the same direction.

As in Holland, bicycles are the usual mode of transportation and after pedaling against the wind for a few miles, I can assure you that you work up a tremendous appetite. The Flemings love good stick-to-the-ribs kinds of foods and plenty of it as can be readily seen by their round rosy cheeks. These pancakes, made with a yeast dough and with bacon cooked right into them, are a favorite farm-house supper. The Belgians eat them sprinkled generously with brown sugar and drink beer or coffee with them. Try them also with honey or maple syrup.

FOR ABOUT 12 LARGE PANCAKES:

8 to 10 slices bacon, cut in half
2 cups flour
1 envelope yeast dissolved in ¼ cup warm water
4 eggs
1½ cups milk OR
1 cup milk and ½ cup beer
Brown sugar or syrup

Fry the bacon until slightly crisp but not crumbly. Drain and set it aside on a plate and pour off the fat into a small bowl.

Have all the ingredients at room temperature. Place the flour into a large bowl, make a well in the middle, and pour into this the yeast dissolved in warm water, the eggs and about ½ cup of the milk or beer. Beat until you get a smooth thick batter, then gradually stir in enough milk to thin it to a thick cream consistency. It should be just a little thinner than the usual American pancake batter. Cover the bowl with a cloth and leave the batter to rise in a warm place for about 1 to 1½ hours or until it is quite bubbly on top.

Heat about 1 tablespoon bacon drippings in a large skillet, pour in enough batter to cover the bottom of the pan with a thin, even layer. Add a few pieces of bacon and cook until the bottom is nicely browned and the top dry looking. Turn the pancake and cook until brown on both sides. Keep warm while you make the others and serve with brown sugar to sprinkle on.

Have a large pot of coffee ready and some hot milk; steaming mugs of *café au lait* make this perfect when the wind is howling outside!

MELON EN COMPOTE

Compote of Cantaloupe

How do you pick a cantaloupe to be sure of getting a good one? One way is to press the stem end lightly: it should yield slightly. But mostly I trust my nose, sniff the round spot opposite the stem end, the aroma of cantaloupe should permeate the rind noticeably over and above the assorted smells of the vegetable counter. To err is human, though, and sooner or later, we cut into a cantaloupe to find that it is hard and practically tasteless. Don't serve it with a thick layer of apologies, it still won't taste good. Instead turn it this way into a delight:

FOR 4 PEOPLE:

> *1 large or 2 small decidedly unripe cantaloupes*
> *1 cup sugar*
> *½ cup water, if needed*
> *¼ cup port, cream sherry, sweet white wine or just*
>   *orange juice*
> *¼ cup dried raisins*
> *Sour cream*

Cut the cantaloupe, discard the seeds, and dice the flesh into ½ inch cubes. Add the sugar and leave to stand for about half an hour to draw out the juices. If at the end of that time there is still no juice, reread the first paragraph for another time when you choose a cantaloupe, add half a cup of water and the wine or orange juice. Add the raisins too and simmer over a low fire until the melon is tender but not mushy. Add more water or wine if necessary but there should be just a little syrupy juice when you have finished.

Serve well chilled with large dollops of sour cream.

MELON PARFAIT

Melon always means "cantaloupe" in France. Have you tried serving it as an appetizer? Delicious way to start a summer meal and good for the calorie conscious too! Small perfect cantaloupe halves, the seeds scraped out, and a little good port wine poured in the cavity make a delicious hors d'oeuvre. Let them stand for about 1 hour so the port can permeate the whole melon. To my mind, you lose a lot of the aroma and flavor of cantaloupe by chilling it. It should be cool but never really icy.

A "parfait" though, means a rather soft ice cream in French cuisine. In this case, you will find it is a perfect way to serve cantaloupe which is very ripe. I don't mean to imply that you are completely incapable of picking a good cantaloupe at the peak of perfection! Simply that it is nice to know what to do with one that is slightly, just very slightly mind you, too ripe!

FOR 4 PEOPLE:
> *1 large cantaloupe, very ripe*
> *4 tablespoons sugar*
> *2 or 3 tablespoons Madeira or red port*
> *1 cup heavy cream*

Remove the rind and seeds from the cantaloupe and mash it finely through a food mill or with a fork. You should have approximately 2 cups of purée. Sweeten this with the sugar and flavor it with the wine. Taste and make sure the flavor is perfect. Whip the cream until it forms soft peaks. About 1 to 1½ hours before serving combine the cream with the melon and pour into ice-cube tray. Freeze until not too hard and spoon in sherbet glasses. You can garnish with additional whipped cream if you wish.

MELON EN SURPRISE

This way of serving cantaloupe is almost an ode to summer! It combines all the fresh flavors of ripe fruit. You simply need as large a cantaloupe as you can find and as many varieties of fresh fruit as are available. Try using peaches, strawberries, cherries, pears, bananas, oranges, seedless grapes, pineapple, etc.

With a sharp knife cut a slice off the top of the cantaloupe. Scrape out all the seeds. With a sharp old teaspoon or one of those handy little ball cutters, carefully remove all the flesh of the melon, taking great care not to cut into the rind. Combine the melon balls with the other fruit, sugar to taste and a little good aromatic liqueur. Kirsch for instance, or rum, or one of the delicious orange-flavored French liqueurs such as Grand Marnier or Cointreau. Refill the melon with this fruit salad and leave in a cold place for several hours for the flavors to blend. You may have to place extra salad in a bowl but it will not be quite as good. The melon rind will impart an incredible aroma to the other fruit. If you have cut the top slice off carefully and replaced it exactly, you can surprise your guests who will think you are serving plain cantaloupe.

You can also serve small cantaloupes, really small ones at one per person, filled with just strawberries or, that supreme delight, fresh raspberries. Just add sugar and a little liqueur.

Sometime try a Melon à la Glace: cut small cantaloupes in two, remove the seeds and dice the flesh. Mix with sugar and a little good brandy. Return to the shells. At serving time, add a scoop of ice cream, vanilla or fruit-flavored, and cover the whole thing with swirls of whipped cream.

Pretty hard to make up your mind which way you like cantaloupe best!

MOUSSE AU CHOCOLAT

Chocolate Mousse

Mousse au Chocolat is generally the first thing little French girls learn how to make in the kitchen. Much like little American girls make fudge!

This is deliciously light and really melts on your tongue. Serve it well chilled after a simple but elegant meal. Real chocolate lovers will prefer it plain. If your taste runs more to milk chocolate, try folding into the mousse an equal amount of whipped cream before chilling it.

The following proportions used to be given per person. I find this a little too generous; try using a 3 egg base for 4 or 5 people and multiply accordingly.

FOR 4 PEOPLE:

   3 ounces (3 squares) semi-sweet chocolate
   3 tablespoons coffee
   6 tablespoons sugar
   3 eggs, separated

Melt the chocolate with the coffee in a small pan over a very low heat. Stir until melted and smooth. Cool slightly.

Beat the egg whites as for meringue, adding the sugar gradually when the whites are in soft peaks. Continue beating until the meringue is very stiff and you cannot feel or taste a single grain of sugar.

Stir the egg yolks into the chocolate mixture and blend in about ½ cup of the whites. Pour this over the rest of the whites and fold gently but thoroughly. You will get a thick creamy mixture which will just pour. Choose your prettiest little individual dishes or one large dish and pour the mousse into it. Chill for 4 hours or overnight, covered, in the refrigerator.

Even though this contains no gelatin, it will set quite firmly. Serve with thin crisp cookies.

MOUSSE DORÉE

Cream Cheese Mousse (or Cold Soufflé!)

This is a delicious dessert usually made in France with a little cream cheese called *Petit Suisse*. This is something like slightly hardened sour cream, softer than packaged cream cheese in this country and I wish some American dairy would start to make it!

You can make this dessert quite successfully though with the brick-type cream cheese, sour cream and fresh eggs. It has the prettiest golden color and a fresh, uncloying taste. If you have friends with ulcers, you can safely offer it to them and give them the recipe; it should make life a little brighter!

If you feel like being tricky, you can also pretend this dessert is a soufflé! It isn't though, but if you pass it under the broiler for a few seconds after pouring it into a nice ovenproof bowl, you can brown the top and it will look as though you carefully baked it!

FOR 4 PEOPLE:

  1 8-ounce package cream cheese
  4 tablespoons sour cream
  3 eggs, separated
  6 tablespoons sugar
  1 or 2 tablespoons milk or cream
  1 teaspoon vanilla

Let the cream cheese soften at room temperature. Place it in a bowl with the sour cream and mash it with a fork until the whole thing is getting creamy. Add the egg yolks, 3 tablespoons sugar and the vanilla and beat until you get a soft thick cream. You may have to add a tablespoonful or two of milk or cream to get it that way.

Beat the egg whites in another bowl, gradually adding the rest of the sugar when they get frothy. Beat as for meringue until you get nice, glossy peaks. Gently fold into the cream cheese mixture, mixing only until well blended. Pour into a bowl, pop under the broiler for just a few seconds to get the top flecked with brown, and chill for 2 hours or more.

Even if you ordinarily hate cream cheese, try it: you won't know it!

MOUSSE À L'ORANGE

Here is another mousse light and fluffy and fruit-flavored! Again, as for the Mousse Dorée, you can pretend it is a soufflé and impress people. This one can be made with orange juice, fresh or frozen, but don't stop there. Almost any kind of fruit juice would be delicious: pineapple, lemon diluted to strong lemonade; or instead of juice you can use a thin fruit purée, such as strained strawberries, raspberries or a mixture! Endless combinations; and don't tell anyone, but eggs and fruit are very good for them!

FOR 4 PEOPLE:

   3 tablespoons cornstarch
   2 cups orange juice
   3 eggs, separated
   ⅓ cup (approximately) sugar
   Whipped cream, for garnish (optional)

Make a thin paste of the cornstarch, a little of the cold juice and the egg yolks, in that order. Reserve 4 tablespoons sugar and add the rest to the juice unless you are using a very sweet kind of juice. In that case omit it.

Beat the egg whites into a very stiff meringue, adding the reserved sugar gradually. Use a large bowl.

Bring the juice to a boil in a small saucepan, pour a little over the cornstarch mixture, return all to the pot and cook, stirring well, until very thick. Don't worry about curdling, the starch will prevent that. Pour, boiling hot, over the meringue and immediately start folding it in, gently but thoroughly until all is well mixed. Pour into a bowl or serving dishes and chill until set. You can garnish it with whipped cream if you like.

To pretend this is a soufflé: make a collar of aluminum foil extending about 1 inch above a small baking dish with straight sides. Tie it securely and fasten the opening with paper clips. Pour the mousse into this so that it protrudes above the edge of the dish almost to the top of the collar. Pop under a very hot broiler for just a few seconds to fleck the top with brown. Chill for several hours. Remove the collar when the mousse is set! Very glamorous! Pass whipped cream separately.

OEUFS À LA REINE

Glamorous Floating Island

Remember floating island pudding? Even if you have never made it, you probably remember your mother or grandmother making it. It is a delicious concoction of vanilla custard and meringue served well chilled. This pudding is basically the same thing but glamorized a little for party occasions: we shall mold it in a pretty ring mold and pour over it a delicious pink syrup made with strawberries and raspberries. And if you want to garnish it additionally with whipped cream well . . .

FOR 6 TO 8 SERVINGS:

   6 eggs
   1 cup sugar
   1 quart (approximately) milk
   2 envelopes plain gelatin
   2 teaspoons pure vanilla
   1 pint fresh or 1 10-ounce box frozen strawberries, thawed
   4 ounces (1 small box) frozen raspberries, thawed
   Dash Cointreau (optional)

Separate the eggs into 6 yolks and 4 whites, reserving two of the whites for another occasion (lemon meringue pie tomorrow maybe?). Beat the other 4 whites into a meringue, sweetening it with 4 tablespoons sugar added gradually. Beat until stiff and glossy. Heat the milk to simmering in a wide pan. Watch it so it doesn't boil over and make that dreadful mess milk just loves to make as soon as you turn your back on it. Drop teaspoonfuls of the meringue into the hot milk, a few at a time, and cook them until just set: a minute or two on each side. Don't cook them too much or you'll get a leathery mess. Remove them with a slotted spoon as soon as done. Set aside to cool.

Soften the gelatin in a little cold water. Measure the milk and, if necessary, add enough more to make 3½ cups. Add the gelatin to the hot milk and stir until completely dissolved. Beat the 6 egg yolks with the rest of the sugar, add just a little of the hot milk, stirring wildly, then add the rest of the milk. It should thicken slightly immediately. If it doesn't, return it to the pan and cook a few minutes more, stirring. You should do this over hot water unless you are a really very experienced cook. It can curdle if it gets too hot. Add the vanilla and leave to cool until it is just beginning to set: the consistency of unbeaten egg whites.

Rinse a 1½-quart ring mold with cold water and pour about 1 inch of custard into it. Arrange a layer of the little egg white balls over it and pop the mold in the coldest spot in the refrigerator to set. Repeat the operation until the mold is full, finishing with a layer of custard. If you pour in the whole thing at once, the meringue will rise to the top and you will not get the layered effect, which is very pretty. Chill several hours or overnight. To unmold: dip the mold in hot water very briefly, loosen the edges with a knife, cover with a pretty plate or shallow bowl and turn the whole thing upside down or right side up depending on which way you look at it! A gentle shake and the pudding should slip out quite easily.

For the sauce, simply buzz the thawed or fresh fruit in a blender or press it through a sieve or food mill. Add sugar to taste and maybe a dash of Cointreau if you have any. Drizzle a little over the pudding and pass the rest separately. Luscious is the word for it!

OMELETTE AUX BANANES

Banana Omelet

Sweet omelets are not served much in this country and I wonder why! A jam omelet for instance is a delicious thing and a very good way to get eggs into small children. Quite glamorous too for a brunch on a lazy Sunday morning. The reason it is not served more often may be the butter here in America. Sounds crazy? For some reason a sweet omelet tastes best made with sweet, unsalted butter. You do add a pinch of salt to the omelet, of course, but the golden part is definitely better tasting if it is not too salty from the butter. So get a little pat of sweet butter from the supermarket and keep it for sweet omelets!

FOR 4 PEOPLE:
> 3 bananas
> 1 lemon
> ½ cup sugar
> 3 tablespoons good rum or water with a little
>   rum flavoring added
> 6 fresh eggs
> Dash salt
> 3 tablespoons unsalted butter

Slice the bananas not too thinly and sprinkle them with lemon juice as you go so they don't turn black. Use firm and white bananas —but not too ripe. In a small pan, make a syrup with the sugar and the rum and add the bananas to it. Let them get good and hot, then drain them and keep them and the syrup hot. I do this by putting the bananas in a strainer and the strainer over the syrup, over very low heat.

Beat the eggs in a bowl with a dash of salt until they are well mixed, but don't beat them to death. (See remarks on omelets in general.) Melt the butter in a large skillet and as soon as it is frothy, pour in the eggs and make the omelet as usual. Put the sliced bananas in the middle and fold over the right-hand side of the omelet. Slide it onto a dish, flipping the pan over at the last second. This gives you the classic folded-in-three omelet of the French chefs! Gives you a great sense of achievement. Pour the syrup over and serve with speed.

OMELETTE À LA MARIÉE

Bride's Omelet

Here is another sweet omelet you may want to try. This one is fit for any party: the egg whites are beaten to a meringue, giving the omelet a very fluffy texture almost like a soufflé. At the last moment, the omelet is *flambée* with a little brandy, preferably cognac. Make sure the lights are turned out in the dining room when you bring it in. Where does the name come from? I have no idea but any girl who serves this to her beau can be pretty sure of becoming a bride soon.

FOR 4 PEOPLE:
   4 tablespoons chopped pecans
   2 tablespoons chopped candied orange peel
   2 tablespoons finely crushed macaroons
   2 tablespoons orange juice or Cointreau
   4 tablespoons sugar
   6 eggs
   Dash salt
   3 tablespoons sweet butter
   4 tablespoons brandy, preferably cognac

Combine the nuts, candied peel and macaroon crumbs with the orange juice or Cointreau and sugar in a small bowl. Leave them to become thoroughly acquainted for several hours if possible. Separate three of the eggs. Place the 3 yolks and remaining eggs in a bowl. Beat as for any omelet* with a dash of salt. Mix in the nuts, candied peel, macaroon crumbs and orange juice. Beat the remaining 3 whites until stiff but not dry and gently fold them into the rest of the eggs.

Heat the butter in a large skillet and swish it around until frothy. Pour in the eggs and cook until the omelet is golden at the bottom and the top puffy and light and not quite runny. Fold in two and slide onto a hot dish. The dish MUST be hot! Pour on the brandy and touch a match to it. Serve immediately.

PÊCHES MELBA

Peach Melba

Peaches Melba were named, like the toast, after the famous singer Nellie Melba. If her voice was indeed as sweet as this delicious concoction, it must have been wonderful to hear! You can buy ready frozen Melba sauce but for the most delicious dessert, try making your own by putting fresh or thawed frozen raspberries through a strainer. To about 1 cup of this fragrant purée, add ½ glass (4 ounces) of raspberry jelly and let it melt over low heat.

Now place a generous serving of good vanilla ice cream in an individual dish. Over this a ripe, fresh peach, pitted and peeled. Pour the sauce over the peach, which will blush prettily at being so complemented. A dollop of whipped cream over all. Cool and delicious!

For another slightly different version of this dessert try this with fresh peaches or pears:

FOR 6 SERVINGS:
  ½ cup sugar
  1½ cups water
  6 nice, juicy, ripe peaches or pears
  A few drops red food coloring
  1 quart vanilla ice cream
  1 8-ounce glass raspberry jelly
  1 pound fresh or canned cherries
  1 cup whipped cream (½ cup heavy cream before
    whipping)

Make a syrup by adding the sugar to about 1½ cups water and gently poach the peeled and pitted peaches or peeled whole pears. A few drops of red food coloring will give them a dainty pink color. They should be barely cooked, so simmer very gently until just tender.

Soften the ice cream slightly and spoon it in an even layer at the bottom of a large shallow dish. Make six indentations or depressions for the fruit so it will rest firmly later and return the dish to the freezer to firm.

Melt the jelly over a low fire and add the fresh or drained canned cherries to it. Whip the cream and sweeten it lightly. Place all these ingredients, in separate bowls, in the refrigerator until just before serving time. Now take out the ice cream, place a pear or peach in each indentation, spoon cherries in raspberry syrup over and around them. Stir about 2 tablespoons of the raspberry syrup into the whipped cream to give it a pretty light pink color. Swirl or pipe the whipped cream all around the dish. Serve immediately!

MONT BLANC

Maybe this recipe should be called Pike's Peak in this country! It looks exactly like a snow-capped mountain! It is actually so simple a combination it is hardly a recipe, but it tastes delicious.

The hardest part of the job may be getting fresh chestnuts! They are not too widely available. If you can't, maybe you can find a can of chestnut purée. The dessert won't be quite as light and fluffy but it will be much less work!

FOR 4 PEOPLE:

2 pounds chestnuts OR
   1 pound (1 large can) chestnut purée
2 cups milk
¾ cup sugar
1 teaspoon vanilla
2 cups heavy cream

Make a slit in each chestnut with a sharp knife. To succeed in peeling them, you may then either plunge the chestnuts in boiling water to cover and leave them until they are beginning to pop open, about 5 minutes over rather high heat. This makes them easy to peel but tends to make the chestnuts a little soggy. Better to my mind is to place them in the oven in a large pan with only ½ inch or so of water at the bottom. Bake at 400°F. for 10 to 15 minutes or until the skins crack wide. In either case, as soon as the chestnuts are cool enough to handle, remove the thick husk and the brown peel.

Place the peeled chestnuts in a pan with about 2 cups of milk, enough to just cover them. Add ½ cup of sugar and the vanilla. Cook the chestnuts gently until they are quite tender and easy to crumble. Drain them if necessary; they may have absorbed most of the milk by now!

Whip the cream until it begins to thicken, add the rest of the sugar, and finish whipping it until it forms nice firm peaks.

Now take a large flat dish. Place the chestnuts in a coarse sieve or food mill and press them through onto the dish. They will fall to the dish in soft, fluffy little grains. Don't touch them, just push them gently with a fork to make a nice mound if they spread too much over the dish. This lightness is what we are after. Over this mound, spoon or pipe the cream into a "snow cap," making a nice, high peak. That is all there is to it but the mouthfuls of fluffy chestnuts with the cool cream make a superb combination.

All you can get is canned chestnut purée? Or, perhaps, you don't exactly feel like peeling all those chestnuts! Put the purée in a pastry bag or decorator with the smallest plain tip. Press it through in a kind of thin spaghetti and garnish the mound with whipped cream as above. Not quite as fluffy maybe, but still excellent.

POMMES MERINGUÉES

Apple Custard with Meringue

This is another of those "Mama-is-a-great-cook" kind of apple desserts! It used to be my favorite as a child: baked apples, creamy custard and a thick fluffy meringue. Don't keep it just for the family, it will do very nicely for company also.

You can cook this dessert in a large dish or individual ones but adjust the cooking time as indicated below, so that the apples don't cook to pieces. You know, of course, about baked custards: they must cook slowly in order not to separate or be full of bubbles. So go gently, we eat with our eyes also!

FOR 6 SERVINGS:
  6 eggs
  ⅔ cup sugar
  1 teaspoon vanilla
  2 cups milk
  6 small apples, peeled and cored

Separate four of the eggs. In a bowl, beat the 4 yolks, the 2 remaining whole eggs, half the sugar and the vanilla. Scald the milk and pour it gradually on the egg mixture, beating vigorously.

Butter a baking dish very generously. Arrange the apples in it and pour the custard over them; it should come about half or two-thirds of the way up the apples. Bake in preheated oven at 300°F. for about 35 minutes for 1 large dish (or 20 minutes for individual ones) or until the custard is set and the apples tender when pierced with a fork.

While the apples are cooking make a meringue with the egg whites and the rest of the sugar, adding it gradually and beating until glossy. Swirl this on top of the cooked apples and return to the oven, turned up to 400°F. to brown the top slightly. Serve warm or chilled as you prefer.

To decorate this dish beautifully, swirl the meringue prettily and make very small indentations in a pattern with the back of a spoon. After browning the meringue fill the indentations with a little apple or raspberry jelly. They will glow against the white meringue like topaz or rubies!

RIZ À LA CONDÉ

Super Rice Pudding

You may have had Riz à l'Impératrice. This Riz à la Condé is an even more glamorous version of creamy rice pudding. Imagine rice cooked right in the milk, thickened with egg yolks for a creamy custard, whipped cream added to this, fruit, liqueur, and finally surrounded by apricots!

FOR 4 TO 6 PEOPLE:

1 cup raw rice
2 cups water
Pinch salt
2 cups milk
1 cup sugar, approximately
4 egg yolks
1 envelope plain gelatin
1 cup mixed, chopped candied fruit
¼ cup kirsch or fruit liqueur or rum
1 cup heavy cream
12 dried apricots, cooked

The nicest way to make this pudding is definitely to cook the rice in milk. It does take time, however, so plan ahead! Most good brands of rice do not require washing. Check the package. Place 1 cup of rice in 2 cups water with a pinch of salt. Bring to a boil and drain immediately in a sieve. Now return the rice to a double boiler, add the milk, cover and cook over simmering water until the rice is quite tender and soft and most of the milk absorbed. This varies a little with different rices, but you should count at least 1 hour, maybe 1½.

You may start with 2 cups cooked rice and decrease the milk to 1 cup. It will cook much faster, right on top of the stove, but you lose a little creaminess!

As soon as the rice is done, sweeten it with about ½ cup of sugar, taste and add a little more if necessary, it should be quite sweet. Beat the egg yolks in a bowl, add a little of the rice to them, stirring well, then return all to the pan, stirring vigorously. It will turn very creamy immediately. Add the gelatin softened in a little cold water to the still hot rice and stir until dissolved. Set aside to cool.

Place the candied fruit in a small bowl with the liqueur. Kirsch is the usual one because it goes beautifully with fruit, but you can use a fruit brandy, Cointreau, Grand Marnier, cognac or rum! Each adds its particular goodness!

Whip the cream until thick and glossy, sweetening it to taste when it is beginning to thicken. Now fold the cream and fruit into the cooled rice, pour into a mold rinsed with cold water and chill for several hours in the refrigerator.

Have about a dozen apricot halves cooked and sweetened nicely. You can pour a little more liqueur over them if you like. Unmold the rice on a pretty dish and surround it with the apricots. Simply glorious!

SABAYON

This is a marvelous, heady dessert definitely not for children! Try serving it at the end of a rather large meal in very small glasses or cups, just what you need to revive you! It is served generally hot, a potent mixture of wine, sugar and egg yolks combined to make fluffy custard.

You should also think of this Sabayon as a sauce over a steamed pudding. Make it a little less thick so it can be poured and you will find it a delicious change from hard sauce. It is also good with fruit compotes and crisp cookies.

For a spectacularly different ice cream, try the Sabayon glace at the end of the recipe. The quantities are fairly small; this is rich remember, you don't want to overdo it!

FOR 4 PEOPLE:

  5 *egg yolks*
  ½ *cup sugar*
  1 *cup wine: fine sherry, good port or a good dry*
    white wine, the quality of the wine makes a great
    difference

For the ice cream: 1 cup heavy cream

Beat the egg yolks with the sugar in a small bowl. Drop by drop, at first, add the wine, beating well, with a wire whisk preferably. The beginning is the only tricky part: if you add the wine too fast you get lumps!

Place this mélange (mixture sounds too medicinal here!) in the top of the double boiler over hot, not boiling water. Beat fast, with the whisk or an electric egg beater, until the eggs get fluffy and light and the cream gets quite thick, to soft peaks, almost! To eat hot, pour this in small glasses or punch cups and serve immediately with crisp cookies. One serving should make you feel like dancing a jig!

For the ice cream: whip the cream until glossy and thick and sweeten it to taste. Chill it. Continue beating the Sabayon after removing it from the heat, until quite cold. The easiest way is to have a bowl of cracked ice to place it in. When cold, gently fold in the whipped cream and freeze for at least 2 hours.

SOUFFLÉ AU CHOCOLAT

Chocolate Soufflé

Just the word "soufflé" evokes fine eating. Most cooks are a little shy of them, though; the word also evokes something very difficult and complicated to prepare. Not so!

There are, of course, soufflés and soufflés! The true soufflé, loved by the French, light and creamy, has a bad reputation of falling flat on its face. The reputation is totally undeserved if you realize that it is expected to do so! It should, for eye appeal, reach the table high and puffy but as soon as you start serving it, it will fall. If it keeps its shape and doesn't, well it is a very nice kind of pudding, no doubt, but it is not a real soufflé. I remember eating at my grandmother's as a child when the cook appeared, crestfallen and almost in tears, to announce that the soufflé had fallen. Grandmother cheerfully told her not to worry and go ahead and serve it but was not prepared for the next announcement: "But it fell on the floor, Madame!" From that kind of fall, no soufflé recovers!

A good soufflé, therefore, cannot be kept waiting. In this case allow from 30 to 35 minutes: this is a dessert; you can remember to place it in the oven as you start the main course probably. If your guests have to wait just a few minutes, it will only serve to whet their appetites anyhow.

FOR 6 PEOPLE:
4 tablespoons butter
4 tablespoons flour
1 cup milk
4 ounces (4 squares) semi-sweet or sweet dark chocolate
A little sugar (optional)
2 tablespoons rum or Grand Marnier or brandy
4 egg yolks
Sugar
6 egg whites
Pinch cream of tartar
Heavy cream, whipped or plain as a sauce

Melt the butter in a saucepan, add the flour and cook, stirring, until frothy but not browned. Gradually add the milk, beating it in with a wire whisk is a guarantee against lumps. When the mixture is smooth and bubbly, something like a very thick cream sauce, add the chocolate, remove from the fire and stir until the chocolate has melted.

I prefer my desserts not too sweet. To me semi-sweet chocolate is perfect without any additional sugar. You may however add a little sugar to the mixture if you feel it is really not sweet enough or use the sweet dark chocolate instead. Don't try to use the melted chocolate which comes in little packages, it really won't taste the same.

You may now flavor this chocolate base with a little liqueur such as rum or brandy. Grand Marnier or other orange-flavored liqueur will give a deliciously evanescent orange taste to the chocolate.

Stir the egg yolks into the slightly cooled base. Take a 1½-quart soufflé dish or other ovenproof casserole and butter the bottom and halfway up the sides. Sprinkle a little sugar into the dish and shake out what does not stick to the butter.

You could do all this ahead of time if you wish. The chocolate base can be refrigerated as well as the 6 egg whites. Just be sure you let everything reach room temperature again before you proceed.

Heat the oven to 400°F. Add a pinch of cream of tartar to the egg whites and beat them until light and fluffy but not too stiff, soft peaks in other words. The volume of whites will be greater if you beat them by hand with a wire whisk. Pour about 1 cupful of whites into the chocolate base. Fold them in gently but thoroughly. Pour the chocolate back over the rest of the whites and fold very, very gently. A spatula does a good job but the best instrument is simply your gently cupped hand. It allows you to feel exactly where the heavier chocolate part is. Don't mix too much, a few little dabs of whites here and there won't hurt.

Pour the mixture into the prepared dish. Dip your finger into the soufflé about 1 inch deep and 1 inch from the edge and draw a circle. This will make the high rising "hat" in the middle of the soufflé. Lick the finger; it is a good way to taste the delicious chocolate mixture anyhow!

Pop the soufflé into the oven and bake at 400°F. for 30 minutes. At that time it should be puffed up and a lovely dark brown. The center will be still creamy and soft and will set completely as you serve it. If necessary, an extra 5 minutes in the oven will not ruin it, just set it a little more firmly.

Ovens vary a little. The first time you cook a soufflé, make a good note of the time. You can test for doneness by giving the dish a gentle shake as you take it out of the oven. If the "hat" wobbles from side to side, pop the soufflé right back in the oven and count an extra 5 minutes. Note this for next time.

Pass a bowl of whipped cream or pitcher of heavy cream to pour on each serving as desired.

Note: You may notice that the temperature given for this chocolate soufflé is slightly lower than for the other soufflés mentioned in this chapter. Chocolate burns quicker than other ingredients and we don't want the top too brown!

SOUFFLÉ À LA VANILLE, AU GRAND MARNIER, ETC.

Vanilla, Grand Marnier and other Soufflés

Dessert soufflés are a beautiful way to end a meal. They are light as can be after a heavy meal. Think of them also when you plan on serving a cold meal in summer. A hot soufflé for dessert is the perfect answer to what to have for one hot dish.

Soufflés are essentially composed of two parts: the base, which is simply a thick cream sauce to which you add the flavoring from which the soufflé takes its name, and egg whites beaten as for a rather soft meringue.

Here is the basic recipe for a vanilla soufflé. Add a little orange peel (1 teaspoon), freshly grated, and 4 tablespoons Grand Marnier and you have the classic Grand Marnier soufflé.

FOR 6 PEOPLE:

4 tablespoons butter
4 tablespoons flour
1 cup milk
½ cup sugar
1 tablespoon vanilla extract
4 egg yolks
6 egg whites
Pinch cream of tartar

You may, of course, use a vanilla bean in place of the vanilla extract. If so, scald the milk, drop the vanilla bean in it and leave for about an hour. Omit the vanilla extract.

Melt the butter in a small saucepan, add the flour to it and stir until frothy but not browned. Gradually add the milk, stirring well, add the sugar and cook, still stirring, until bubbly and very thick. Cool slightly.

Now is the time to add vanilla or Grand Marnier and a little orange peel if you so desire. Taste and make sure the flavor is very pronounced; the whites will tone down the taste quite a bit later.

Butter a soufflé dish, 1½ quart size, on the bottom and halfway up the sides. Dust it with sugar and shake out the excess. Heat the oven to 425°F.

Stir the egg yolks into the base, beating them in so they are thoroughly mixed.

Beat the egg whites with a pinch of cream of tartar until fluffy and light and in soft peaks. Mix about 1 cup of the whites with the base, folding them in gently but thoroughly. Pour back over the rest of the whites and fold very gently (see Chocolate Soufflé) just until mixed. Pour into the dish and bake for 25 minutes or until the soufflé is high and puffy and a beautiful gold on top.

Any soufflé can be baked in individual dishes if you prefer. I find the easiest way to do this is to pour the soufflé mixture into a very wide-mouthed pitcher or use a bowl with a lip to mix the whites. Pour into the small dishes up to ½ inch from the edge. The baking time will vary from 7 to 10 minutes, depending on the thickness and the size of your dishes.

TARTES AUX FRUITS

Fruit Tarts

French fruit pies are so light and fresh that you could eat and eat and eat them forever! As a rule, the pastry crust is cooked first. This is then filled with the fruit, lightly poached in syrup, sometimes over a layer of *crème pâtissière*, the whole is then covered with a light fruit glaze. It is almost like gilding the lily to then add whipped cream!

Canned fruit, such as peaches, apricots, cherries, pears, pineapple, does about as well as fresh. Simply drain it and arrange it over the cooled pie shell. Pears and pineapple usually have the *crème pâtissière* filling, lightly flavored with almond. Fresh fruit should be peeled, pitted and cooked in very little water with enough sugar to sweeten it nicely.

To make the glaze, measure the syrup from the can or from cooking the fresh fruit. Count 1 teaspoon of cornstarch to each ½ cup of syrup. Mix it in a thin paste with a little cold syrup or water, add it to the rest of the syrup and cook until thickened and clear. Sometimes you may add a little lemon juice to very sweet fruit, like pears, and a drop of red food coloring turns the glaze a dainty pink. Pour while hot evenly all over the pie. *Voilà!* When it has cooled you can pipe a border of whipped cream all around the pie.

Strawberries should never but never be cooked! Hull them after washing them so they don't have a chance to get watery. Reserve the smallest sorriest ones for the glaze. You can now, if they are perfectly ripe and sweet, simply arrange them in the cooled piecrust. If not utterly perfect, place them in a bowl and sprinkle them with sugar. Leave them to absorb the sugar for at least an hour. A nice touch is to pour a little Cointreau over them too. Arrange them on the pie and save the juices for the glaze, as follows:

Strawberry pie glaze:
½ cup (approximately) sliced strawberries
½ cup sugar or sugar which already served to sweeten
    the berries
4 tablespoons red raspberry jelly

Mash the strawberries with the sugar and cook them in a small pan until the sugar has completely dissolved and strawberries have turned into small pieces of something like red flannel. Strain but don't press it, you need only the clear juice. Add this to the raspberry jelly and stir over low heat until it has completely melted. Pour this over the strawberries in their pie shell, drizzling it evenly from the tip of a spoon. You should now garnish the pie with a circle of stiffly whipped cream, mounding it high all around the edges.

Served early in the spring this can practically guarantee you a new spring wardrobe or whatever your heart desires.

FLAN AUX POMMES

The French version of apple pie is very different from the American one. For one thing, the pie is open-faced and the apples arranged neatly in rows brown most temptingly. Here is one delicious and glamorous version:

1 recipe Flaky Pastry*
3 or 4 large tart apples
A little sugar (optional)
1½ cups Crème Pâtissière*
½ glass (4 ounces) apple jelly

Make up a recipe of flaky pastry, roll it out to about ¼ inch or a shade more. Grease generously a large cooky sheet. Cut the dough into a large 12-inch square and place it on the cooky sheet. Don't ask me why, but this type of pie is always square! Carefully place the trimmings on top of one another and roll out again (do not knead this dough, remember). Cut into ½-inch wide strips.

Brush a little water along the edges of the pastry square and place the strips so as to form a little edge or rim. Bake the pastry in preheated oven at 400°F. until pale gold and not quite done through, about 5 minutes.

Peel and slice the apples very thinly. If they are really very tart, sprinkle them with a little sugar, but a little tartness will make a nice contrast. Spread a layer of the crème pâtissière all over the crust up to the rim. Arrange the apple slices over it in neat overlapping rows so as to cover the cream completely. Melt the apple jelly over a low fire and drizzle evenly over the whole pie.

Return to the oven at 375°F. for 15 to 20 minutes or until the apple slices are edged with brown and the pastry a deep gold. Slide onto a dish and serve warm rather than chilled.

TARTE AUX POMMES PAYSANNE

Country Apple Tart

Another apple pie recipe is made with a completely different kind of dough. A yeast dough this time, very thin, soft in the center and crisp and crusty around the edges. A friend of mine calls these "fruit pizzas" and in a sense, she is right!

This is a specialty of the Ardennes region of Belgium. They come in all sizes, the largest going by the name of *"roue de charette"* or wagon wheel! If you have a 12- or 14-inch pizza pan, it will do fine for this pie. Don't be afraid of making it large. It is so light and delicious to eat, it disappears like lightning!

Besides apples, you can use cherries, plums or fresh apricots. The fruit must be raw, however, and not too juicy. Don't try it with strawberries, they would be cooked to a mush!

FOR 1 LARGE PIE:
¼ cup warm water
1½ teaspoons (about ½ envelope) dry yeast
½ cup sugar

For the dough:
2 ounces (½ stick) butter
1 egg
½ cup milk, scalded and cooled to lukewarm
1½ cups (approximately) flour

For the filling:
3 or 4 large apples, peeled and sliced
½ cup sugar
Cinnamon
2 tablespoons butter

Rinse a bowl with hot water. Pour in ¼ cup warm water and dissolve the yeast in it. Add the sugar, butter and egg to the warm milk and stir into the yeast with about 1 cup unsifted flour. Mix until smooth, then add enough additional flour to make a very soft dough.

Oil or butter your pizza pan or cooky sheet and your hands at the same time. With your fingers, gently pat and spread the dough until it covers the bottom of the pizza pan or makes a 12-inch circle on the cooky sheet with a small rim at the edge. Exactly as for pizza!

Peel, core and slice the apples thinly. Arrange a circle of apple slices all around the edge of the dough, leaving a small rim of dough, then keep arranging circles until the whole pie is filled with slightly overlapping slices. Sprinkle the sugar evenly over all and a light dusting of cinnamon. Dot with butter.

Cover the whole pie with a clean dish towel and leave it to rise in a warm place for about half an hour. The top of the stove while the oven is warming up is a good place.

Bake at 375°F. for about 25 minutes or until the whole pie is golden around the rim and the apples lightly browned. I warn you: this smells so good as you take it out of the oven that it will be hard to resist the temptation to cut a wedge and eat it right there, even if it spoils your dinner.

GÂTEAU AU CAFÉ

Cream Cake

This is an absolutely luscious concoction which combines the best of cream puffs and éclairs. It is the perfect thing to make for a party, such as a tea party or afternoon coffee. It is easier almost to make a really large one and it disappears so fast, it is worth it.

The filling for this cake can be varied. It requires two kinds: one a custard or crème pâtissière filling for the éclair circle, and a whipped cream one for the center. If you are intent on saving yourself trouble, you can use one of several variations: the éclair filling can be made from a package of vanilla pudding for instance. I suggest, though, that you add an egg yolk to it and a little extra vanilla for extra flavor. For the center, you can use real whipped cream, ice cream or one of the whipped cream substitutes. These last taste very good and offer the advantage of staying beautifully fluffy and thick for a long time! A nice idea for a hot day when you would prefer to have the cake ready in advance!

FOR ONE 12-INCH CAKE TO SERVE 10
(OR EVEN 12!):

    1 recipe pie dough*
    1 recipe chou pastry*
    3 cups crème pâtissière* or vanilla pudding, not instant
    3 cups heavy cream and ½ cup sugar OR
      3 envelopes substitute made according to package
      directions
    1 tablespoon instant coffee
    1 cup confectioners' sugar
    Vanilla extract
    Slivered almonds or chocolate shot

You can judge from this impressive list of ingredients that this is going to be a king-size cake! It will make a fantastic centerpiece for the party!

Make up a batch of the sweet pie dough, roll it out to fit a large 12-inch or even 14-inch pizza pan. If you don't have one and cannot borrow one from a friend, make a circle this size from heavy aluminum foil and place it on a cooky sheet. You need it as a measurement.

Butter the pan or foil and cooky sheet generously, arrange the pastry over it and prick it all over with a fork. Bake it as directed, peeking in after the first few minutes to prick again with a sharp knife or fork. You want a flat circle of crust, like a huge cooky!

When this is done, place it on its serving plate. Grease or butter the plate or sheet of foil again. While the piecrust was baking, you have made a batch of the chou pastry. With a spoon, now make a thick circle of chou pastry all around the pie plate or circle of foil. It should be about 1½ inches thick; a spoon does well or you can use a cooky press with the largest tip and go slowly so the strip is thick. Bake this as directed for éclairs, first at 475°F. for about 15 minutes as it is quite large, then at 325°F. for at least 30 minutes. It must get quite crisp and dry. If it gets too brown, turn the oven lower and leave even longer. Remove it from the oven, let it cool thoroughly. Slice a thin layer off the top, all around. A serrated bread knife does a beautiful job. Scrape off any soft bits inside. If you wish, you can now wrap both the pastries separately in foil or plastic film and leave them until the next day.

You can make the custard filling or the crème pâtissière the day before also. Simply refrigerate in a bowl. The whipped cream or substitute should be done shortly before putting the cake together, though.

Whip the cream, if it is real cream, adding sugar to taste just as it begins to thicken and also about 1 tablespoon instant coffee. You have no idea how good the coffee flavor is with the whipped cream. Pretty color too! Whip until thick and holding stiff peaks. The whipped substitute does not need sugar and you just flavor it nicely with instant coffee also as you finish beating it. It can't be overbeaten like the whipped cream.

Fill the éclair part of the cake, simply placed over the cooky part on a large plate, with the vanilla pudding or crème pâtissière. Replace the top. Add just enough water to the confectioners' sugar to make a smooth paste that will just pour or spread very easily. Flavor it with a little vanilla extract and/or instant coffee. Glaze the top of the éclair with it, spreading it evenly and quickly.

Fill the center of the cake with the whipped cream, mounding it high into a peak. Oh! Yes, it takes quite a lot, doesn't it! More than you ever suspected! Garnish this with a sprinkling of chocolate shot or a few blanched slivered almonds. This really looks like the creation of a fine French pastry cook, and aren't you proud of yourself! Refrigerate if serving time is several hours away.

Cut into fairly thin wedges to serve, using a sharp knife and being sure to cut right through the bottom crust. A long, flat cake server or spatula will make serving much easier!

TARTE AU RIZ

Rice Pie

This is a very popular kind of pie in Belgium even if it sounds rather surprising! It is simply a good piecrust filled with rice pudding and a few macaroons, baked again until golden on top. With a good cup of coffee, it really is good and you could try serving it instead of coffeecake sometime.

The Belgians have several unusual pies besides this rice one; most of them, though, are rather surprising to the uninitiated! There is a kind of cheese pie called Tarte au Maton, which to my mind is not as good as American cheesecake so we won't bother with it. As to the Walloon Tarte à l'djotte, which is a kind of green cabbage tart, you have to be a native to enjoy it! But try the Tarte au Riz, at least it is not extravagant!

FOR ONE 9-INCH PIE:
*1 recipe piecrust**
1 cup rich milk
2 cups cooked rice
3 eggs
½ cup sugar
A little vanilla
3 or 4 tablespoons apricot jam
3 or 4 macaroons

Make up a recipe of piecrust and use it to line a rather deep pie pan. Bake it filled with beans until the pastry is dry and white but not quite cooked—just crisp. Place the milk and the rice in a small pan and leave to cook very gently until most of the milk has been absorbed. Beat the eggs and sugar together, add a little of the rice-milk, stirring well, then return all to the pan. Stir in the vanilla.

Cover the bottom of the piecrust with a thin layer of apricot jam. Over this crumble the macaroons, then pour the rice pudding. Return to the oven, set at 350°F., and bake for about 35 minutes or until the rice is quite set. Try it with a knife in the middle: if it comes out clean, the pie is ready. Serve warm or chilled. Very filling but delicious!

FLAN AUX FRUITS CONFITS

Candied Fruit Pie

This is actually a very glamorous version of bread pudding. In Belgium, it would be made with *Cramique*, a kind of very fine raisin bread, so you can use raisin bread here or a hamburger bun or sweet rolls. For very special occasions, try pouring a little brandy over the pudding and *flambez* it as you bring it to the table—a superb ending to any meal.

Do not roll out the pastry too thinly. A spring form is ideal to use here. It is much easier to unmold. Or you can use a layer cake pan, 8½ to 9 inches, if you don't have a spring form. A regular pie pan would probably be too shallow to hold the pudding filling.

FOR 1 PIE:
- *1 recipe piecrust**
- *1 large hamburger bun* OR
  - *2 or 3 slices day-old raisin bread*
- *¾ cup milk*
- *3 tablespoons sugar*
- *3 ounces chopped raisins*
- *3 ounces (about 3 rounded tablespoons) chopped mixed candied fruit*
- *3 tablespoons rum* OR
  - *1 teaspoon vanilla*
- *3 eggs*
- *2 tablespoons butter*
- *4 tablespoons brandy (optional)*

Prepare the piecrust, adding a pinch of cinnamon to it if you like, and line the pan with it. Bake it filled with dry beans until white and dry.

Soak the bread in the warm milk. Beat well with a fork and add the sugar, raisins, candied fruit and a dash of rum if you have any handy. If not, a teaspoon of vanilla will add flavor. Beat the eggs as for an omelet and stir into the bread mixture. Pour into the pie crust, dot the top with butter and bake in preheated oven at 325°F. for 30 minutes or until a knife inserted near the middle comes out clean.

To unmold: Run a knife all around, turn over onto a plate and over again onto another plate to get the pudding right side up.

To set it aflame: warm a large spoon or very small pan over the fire. Pour the brandy into it. Set a match to it and pour flaming over the pudding. Delicious as is, out of this world with whipped cream or ice cream!

GÂTEAU À L'ANANAS

Pineapple Icebox Cake

Most large supermarkets now have the delicious light cookies called "lady fingers." These are very seldom served by themselves but are widely used in France to make desserts: their light spongy texture absorbs juices and liqueurs so readily. This pineapple cake is so simple, you hardly need a recipe, just a list of ingredients:

FOR 4 TO 6 SERVINGS:
  1 1-pound can pineapple tidbits
  ¼ cup good rum, other liqueur OR
    1 teaspoon rum flavoring
  1 package (12 cookies) lady fingers, split
  1 quart good vanilla ice cream

Drain the pineapple and add the liqueur or flavoring to the juice. Line a loaf pan with wax paper or plastic film, leaving a long piece hanging over the sides. Dip the top halves of lady fingers in the flavored juice and arrange a row of them on the bottom of the pan. Over this place a layer of tidbits and then a layer of ice cream. Repeat until the pan is full, finishing with a layer of cookies. Cover with the wrap and place in the freezing compartment of the refrigerator for a couple of hours. Unmold on a pretty dish, peel off the wrap and serve in slices. For a glamorous occasion, you could pipe a border of stiffly whipped cream all around the cake. A delicious and very pretty garnish, if you are so lucky as to get them, is a row of candied violets. They go particularly well with pineapple!

DIPLOMATE AUX BANANES

You may be acquainted with the luxury French dessert called a Diplomat; this one is a family one, sort of an envoy to a very small undeveloped nation! I don't know where the name comes from but I suspect that a cook was one day stuck with a batch of stale cookies and diplomatically decided to turn them into this delicious dessert!

You can make this pudding with bread, if you wish, but the flavor will be much finer with cookies or cake. Most supermarkets have a shelf where perfectly good but not as fresh cookies and cakes are sold at a greatly reduced price. There is no reason not to save money by getting those; they will do better than fresh!

FOR 4 TO 6 SERVINGS:

1½ cups milk
½ cup sugar
1 teaspoon vanilla extract
*2 cups (approximately) broken lady finger or
    other cake or cookies*
3 eggs, separated
2 tablespoons butter
1 lemon
4 large ripe bananas
Salt

For the sauce:
1 8-ounce glass apricot or peach preserves
2 or 3 tablespoons rum OR
    2 or 3 tablespoons water and rum flavoring
A little cinnamon

Scald the milk to which you have added the sugar and the vanilla. Break the cake or cookies into smallish pieces into a large bowl. Pour the milk over them and leave them to soak a few minutes. Add to this the egg yolks, butter, and a little grated lemon rind. Beat well with a fork until the cookies are completely broken up.

Slice the bananas, sprinkle them with a little lemon juice and add them to the cooky batter.

Beat the egg whites until stiff but not dry. You get the greatest volume by the way, by having them at room temperature and adding just a pinch of salt. Fold them gently into the batter and pour the whole mixture into a well-buttered baking dish.

Place this dish in another one containing about 1 inch of hot water. Diplomats seem to get into hot water sooner or later, anyhow! Bake the pudding in preheated oven at 350°F. for about 1 hour or until a knife inserted near the center comes out clean.

You can serve this pudding warm or chilled, in either case with the following sauce: Gently heat the apricot or peach preserves in a small pan with 2 or 3 tablespoons rum or the same amount of water and a little rum flavoring. The sauce should be quite runny. A light dusting of cinnamon over the pudding just before serving looks very pretty and adds a delicious flavor.

PAVE AU CHOCOLAT

Simple Chocolate Cake

Although this delicious cake goes by the name of "paving stone," it is wonderfully light and easy to make. The name comes from its shape and color, which resemble the wooden blocks used to pave Paris streets at one time. This made the noise of carriages easier to bear!

Again this cake is made from not-so-fresh cookies. The French use them quite a lot, particularly lady finger cookies. In case you wonder how the French can have so many leftover cookies, bear in mind that these are usually sold in bulk, freshly made by the pastry cooks and simply wrapped in a dainty white paper bag as you buy them. Enough jokes have been made about American packaging, but at least in most parts of Europe, you buy cookies and not just a pretty box. Nice for the children too; they usually receive a cooky from the shopkeeper, who may be hoping they will coax Mother to go there again!

FOR 1 LARGE CAKE: (9- OR 10X4-INCH)
   12 (1 package) lady finger cookies
   ½ pound butter
   1 pound confectioners' sugar
   4 egg yolks
   4 ounces sweet dark chocolate
   1 teaspoon vanilla extract
   4 tablespoons brandy or crème de cacao OR
      Sweetened strong coffee and rum or vanilla extract

Split the lady fingers in two if not already done so by the manufacturer. Let the butter soften at room temperature and beat it until fluffy and free of lumps. Oh! Yes! Butter does have lumps sometimes! Gradually beat in the sifted confectioners' sugar and then the egg yolks one by one. Melt and cool the chocolate. Beat it into the creamed butter along with 1 teaspoon vanilla extract. You now have a deliciously light and fluffy cream. Taste it, it will reward you for all that beating!

Pour the brandy or crème de cacao into a deep saucer or small bowl. If you want something quite non-alcoholic, you can substitute a little very strong coffee, sweeten it a little and flavor it with rum or vanilla extract. Take a half cooky and very briefly dip it in the saucer. Dip is not quite the word, actually; you just barely touch the cooky to the surface of the liqueur. It does not have a chance to imbibe much! You can't let them get drunk: they would get too soggy and never keep their shape!

Arrange a row of eight almost sober cookies side by side on a serving dish. Spoon a layer of fluffy cream over them, repeat, finishing with cream and use the rest of the cream to ice the sides of the cake. Use up all the cream. To live up to its name, this cake should have no decorations! Take a flat knife or spatula and dip it in water. Use this to smooth the cake as neatly as possible. You can now cover the cake loosely with plastic film. This won't stick, wax paper may! Refrigerate the cake for at least 4 hours or overnight.

If you have trouble finding lady fingers, you could use thin layers of pound cake or sponge cake. Both are very good also.

GÂTEAU AUX POIRES

This is an excellent, rather old-fashioned dessert most men are sure to like. It is a combination of cake, good custard pudding lightly flavored with almond, and a perfect half pear, ripe and juicy. This is quite hearty eating; preferably serve it after a fairly light meal.

FOR 4 PEOPLE:
> ½ cup sugar
> 1 cup water
> Few drops almond flavoring
> 4 large, ripe pears
> 1 recipe Crème Pâtissière* OR
>   2 cups vanilla pudding (not instant!)
> 4 slices pound cake
> ½ cup apricot preserves
> 2 or 3 tablespoons kirsch, brandy, rum or orange juice
> 4 tablespoons blanched slivered almonds

Make a syrup with the sugar, 1 cup water and a few drops almond flavoring. Almond flavoring is quite strong; use it sparingly, one drop at a time. Bring to a boil and leave to simmer gently for a few minutes. Peel, cut in two, and carefully core the pears. Add them to the syrup and poach them: a skillet will do well for this, so the pear halves are one layer deep and just barely cook them. The time depends on their ripeness. Perfect pears take just a few minutes. Drain and chill them.

Make up a recipe of crème pâtissière, flavored with almond also, or simply prepare a package of vanilla pudding, adding a little almond flavoring to it. Cool and chill too.

In a large bowl or individual serving dishes, arrange the slices of pound cake. Spoon on a layer of crème pâtissière or pudding and arrange the pear halves over this. Melt the preserves in a small pan with just enough liqueur or orange juice to thin it a little: 2 or 3 tablespoons. Pour this over the pears and scatter the blanched almonds over all.

If you garnish additionally with whipped cream, you are really gilding the lily!

QUATRE-QUARTS GLACÉ

Light Cake

Quatre-quarts means four quarters. This is an old-fashioned home-made cake which gets its name from the fact that you use equal amounts of flour, butter, sugar and eggs. By equal amounts, I mean weights; French kitchens to this day are usually equipped with scales —some still with the polished brass trays, the weights, from the smallest of about one-sixth of an ounce, to the largest 5-pound one, fitted into a block of wood. Children always have fun on a rainy day placing the heaviest weight on one side and seeing how many of the little ones are needed to make the needle stand absolutely straight.

If you don't own kitchen scales, you may still have baby ones somewhere or perhaps your husband has one of those little ones to weigh letters and parcels on his desk? No? Then use the cup measurements and you should have no trouble!

FOR 1 CAKE, APPROXIMATELY 9 INCHES ROUND:

> *3 large eggs*
> *their weight in:*
> *Flour (1¼ cups) plus 1 teaspoon baking powder*
> *Butter (½ cup plus 2 tablespoons)*
> *Sugar (¾ cup)*
> *2 tablespoons rum and 2 tablespoons water*
> *(or extract with 2 tablespoons water)*
> *1 8-ounce glass apricot preserves*
> *1 large slice candied pineapple*
> *6 to 8 candied cherries*
> *2 cups confectioners' sugar*

This cake can be made without the baking powder; however, better safe than sorry! Particularly if you use the cup measurements, its addition ensures a perfectly risen cake. Also, when they do use it, the French take plain baking soda; the modern baking powders are a lot more reliable!

Place the flour sifted with the baking powder in a large bowl. Make a hole in the middle and place into it the softened butter, the sugar and the eggs. Start beating from the center so that the flour is gradually absorbed. The dough will be quite stiff. Toward the end, add 1 tablespoon rum and 2 tablespoons water or rum extract and water. Pour into a well-greased and floured 9-inch layer cake pan. Bake in preheated oven at 375°F. for about 35 minutes or until the cake tests done in the center.

Turn the cake out after 5 minutes and leave it to cool completely. Cut it in two and carefully spread it with about half of the apricot preserves, then put the cake back together again.

Heat the rest of the preserves with the other tablespoonful of rum or extract and another spoonful or so of water to make the mixture quite runny. Use this to cover the top and sides of the cake. Do it with a pastry brush while the preserves are hot, if you can—quite easy that way.

Now cut the slice of candied pineapple into eighths and the cherries in two and arrange them in a pretty pattern on top of the cake. Mix the confectioners' sugar with just enough water to make a rather stiff paste. Heat it, stirring for just a minute so it will thin down considerably. Don't cook it, just heat it! Pour this evenly all over the top of the cake, smoothing it on the sides with a knife dipped in cold water as it oozes down. You have to work quite fast, this icing sets very quickly. Don't touch the top: it will set into a thin, glossy and translucent layer through which the cherries and pineapple will barely show. This is the true French way to glaze cakes and looks delicious!

You can of course, arrange other kinds of fruit before icing the cake; a large daisy of strips of orange peel, for instance, with a cherry center, or cherries and large half walnuts—a row of whole blanched almonds—whatever takes your fancy! A perfect cake for afternoon tea.

SAVARIN AUX PÊCHES

If you enjoy those blissfully drunk little cakes the French call Babas au Rhum, you should enjoy this! Babas filled with fruit and/or cream go by the name of savarin.

The true Baba or savarin dough is made with yeast. It has to rise overnight and is rather time-consuming to make. This one is made with a little baking powder and stiffly beaten egg whites as the rising agents and, truly, it could even fool an expert! Said expert anyhow would enjoy this so much, he or she would not complain.

If the only 1-quart ring mold you have is one of those aluminum ones with fancy decorations usually reserved for jellies, don't be afraid to use it. Just grease and flour it extra generously.

FOR 6 TO 8 SERVINGS:

For the cake:
¼ *pound (1 stick) butter*
½ *cup sugar*
3 eggs, separated
4 tablespoons light cream or milk
1 cup flour
1¼ *teaspoons baking powder*

½ *cup rum, peach brandy or orange juice*
6 to 8 peaches
4 tablespoons apricot or peach preserves
1 cup sugar
1 cup water
Red food coloring, if needed

Start with the pastry ring: beat together the butter and sugar until light-colored and fluffy, then beat in the egg yolks. Now beat in the cream and gradually add the flour mixed with the baking powder. Beat the egg whites separately until stiff but not dry. Be sure the beaters are quite clean; if they are slightly greasy from the butter the whites will not beat well!

Fold the whites into the batter, gently but thoroughly. Pour it into a well-buttered and floured 1-quart ring mold. Bake in preheated oven at 375°F. for 25 minutes or until the cake springs back when touched lightly. Turn onto a cake rack and lift the mold off after the cake has cooled for about 5 minutes.

Place the still warm cake onto a serving dish. You need a deep dish or shallow bowl. Drizzle about half the rum or brandy over it, piercing the cake here and there with a fork or a skewer so that it can imbibe freely.

Peel the peaches, this is a really fancy dessert. You can do this rather easily if you leave the peaches to soak in very hot water for a few minutes. Cut the peaches in two if the pits come out easily or slice them thickly.

Make a syrup with the sugar water and preserves, and gently poach the peaches in it. Let them just simmer about 5 minutes and don't overcook them. If they are rather pale-looking, you can add a few drops red food coloring to make them more appetizing. Drain and cool the peaches. Add the rest of the rum or brandy to the syrup and pour it over the cake. As the syrup drains off the cake, spoon it back on and keep piercing it with the long fork until the cake is really well soaked. If you don't care for spirits, you can substitute orange juice or a fruit wine would do well also.

Arrange the peaches in the center of the ring just before serving. If you pipe whipped cream in a crown over the cake, you are likely to blush at the compliments!

MENDIANT

Almond Custard Cake

I don't know why this delicious cake should be called a beggar unless it is because it is not iced. Maybe its lack of ornamentation makes it look a little like a poor relation among the rich pastries in the window of a *pâtisserie*. Don't let its looks fool you, though, it is excellent served with coffee or tea. The filling of rich vanilla custard is further enhanced by finely chopped nuts or almonds.

FOR A 2 LAYER 8 OR 9 INCH CAKE:
> 2 *cups sifted flour*
> 2 *teaspoons baking powder*
> ⅔ *cup butter*
> 1 *cup sugar*
> 4 *eggs*
> ¼ *cup milk*
> 1 *teaspoon vanilla and a little grated nutmeg*

> For the filling:
> ¼ *cup finely chopped almonds or nuts (walnuts, pecans, filberts)*
> 2 *cups vanilla pudding or Crème Pâtissière**
> ½ *teaspoon almond flavoring*
> ¼ *cup finely chopped almonds or nuts (walnuts, pecans or filberts)*
> *Confectioners' sugar (optional)*

Heat the oven to 375°F. Butter and flour lightly two 8 or 9 inch layer cake pans.

Sift the flour and baking powder together. Cream the butter and sugar until light and fluffy, then add three of the eggs, one at a time, beating well. Gradually add the flour, alternating with a little milk. Lastly add the fourth egg, beating until all is well blended. You can, I suppose, add all 4 eggs at the same time but this is the recipe I have always followed. Maybe the cook who first made it started with the idea of being thrifty and then could not resist making the cake extra good. Flavor with the vanilla and just a little grated nutmeg. Pour into the pans and sprinkle the tops with about half the chopped nuts. Bake at 375°F. for 25 or 30 minutes or until the top of the cake springs back when lightly touched. Cool the cakes 5 minutes or so in the pans, then turn out, and leave to cool on a rack, rounded side up.

Have 2 cups vanilla pudding or crème pâtissière ready and cooled. You will have flavored it with almond also. Take a thin slice off the top of one of the cake layers to make it perfectly flat. Spread a very, very thin layer of cream on it, just enough to make the top layer stick firmly in place.

Take a saucer or small plate as a guide. Place it on top of the cake so as to leave an edge about 1½ inches wide. With a sharp pointed knife, cut a circle out of the top layer and carefully remove it. Now dig a little deeper into the second layer to make a deep hole in the center of the cake, leaving about ½ inch of cake at the bottom. Place the cake on a serving plate, carefully cleaning it of all crumbs. Fill the center right up to the top with the cream, sprinkling in a layer of nuts as you go. Put any remaining nuts on top of the cream and cover with the "lid." It should stay up on top of the cream, press it down just a little so that some of the cream will peep through. Chill for several hours before serving.

To make this Mendiant more appealing, you can dust the top lightly with confectioners' sugar just before serving.

MRS. SMITH'S POUND CAKE

This is definitely not a French recipe: Mrs. Smith is one of the gentle Baltimoreans who enjoy good food and its preparation. She regaled me one night with a Baltimore specialty of crab cakes fit for any queen and topped them off with this marvelous pound cake. I have shared the recipe with many friends and the report has always been unanimous: the best pound cake ever eaten.

This is the recipe exactly as she gave it to me; sometimes I add a little dash of nutmeg to it. I am not sure she uses it although I seem to remember a faint aroma besides the vanilla. This cake is rich and moist, a pure delight as is or with fruit and ice cream.

½ pound butter
1 box (1 pound) confectioners' sugar
4 egg yolks
1¼ cups cake flour
1¼ cups plain flour
1 teaspoon baking powder
4 egg whites (plain)
1 tablespoon vanilla in
  1 cup milk

Cream the butter and add the sifted sugar one-third at a time. Beat in the egg yolks. Sift the flours together with the baking powder. Add one-third at a time to the butter and eggs alternately with the vanilla-flavored milk. Beat well each time. Add the 4 egg whites, previously unbeaten, half at a time, beating well after each addition.

Pour into a greased and floured 10 inch tube pan and bake in a preheated 350°F. oven for about 1 hour and 15 minutes or until the cake tests done.

TRUFFES AU CHOCOLAT

Chocolate truffles are the French answer to fudge! This is one of the creamiest, richest chocolate concoctions ever invented. Dark chocolate lovers particularly appreciate it; nothing mars the chocolate flavor, it is just as creamy as butter! You may want to double or treble the recipe, which you can do easily! These truffles can be shaped in a variety of ways and would make a very special present for a very special friend!

4 ounces sweet or semi-sweet dark chocolate, in squares or
  bars preferably, not pre-melted
3 tablespoons cream, heavy or light
2 tablespoons butter
1 egg yolk
Grated chocolate, chocolate shot, chopped nuts or walnut
  halves

Melt the chocolate in the top of the double boiler. Be absolutely sure that there is not a single drop of moisture in the pan: chocolate is very funny, just a little liquid will cause it to stiffen! When the chocolate is completely softened, stir in the cream, cool a little, then add the butter. Beat in the egg yolk. The mixture will stiffen almost immediately. Pour into a foil-lined pan and leave to set in the refrigerator.

Cut the slab into squares, the size is up to you. Pick up each square and roll it in grated chocolate, rounding it a little as you do so. This is the real truffle, it even looks like one! Fresh truffles are covered with a thin layer of sandy soil. For variations you can roll the truffles in chocolate shot or chopped nuts. Pecans, walnuts, slivered almonds all do well. You can also make a very glamorous candy by sandwiching a square of chocolate between two perfect walnut halves.

This candy melts very easily; it should be kept refrigerated as much as possible. But I guarantee it will not last long!

BRIOCHES

That the French love to eat is very much in evidence in their language. Take brioche, for instance. This delightful product halfway between bread and cake has found its way into many expressions. If a Frenchman is getting a little portly around the middle, he has a little brioche; something easy to do is as easy as brioche. When Marie Antoinette purportedly said "Let them eat cake" it came out in French as "Let them eat brioche."

Breads and products made of flour are, to my mind, the most distinctive foods in any country and the most difficult to reproduce faithfully away from their native habitat. Take croissants: they have a particular taste in France that is never duplicated elsewhere. Even in Belgium, which is right next door and should be able to look over the border and copy exactly what it is French bakers do! Same thing with biscuits—I have given my family abroad detailed recipes for this American marvel. I make them here with complete success. During one of my visits, I made some at my sister's which they found delicious but which really were not as good as here. So, don't look for a recipe for croissants here. I have found that the best croissants I make from scratch are no better than those I buy ready to bake at the supermarket. And these last are a lot less work!

Perhaps the following recipe for brioche will please you, though. I am not going to swear it is as good as the best French brioche but it is excellent. Delicious plain with butter and marvelous with all kinds of fillings, sweet or salty. One of the most important steps to get real brioche flavor is to let the dough rest overnight. So don't omit or shorten this step. For Brioche en Couronne:

FOR 2 BRIOCHES, 9-INCH CIRCLES:
> 2 packages dry yeast (2 tablespoons)
> ¼ cup warm water
> 2½ cups (approximately) flour
> 5 eggs (1 separated)
> Pinch salt
> ¼ pound (1 stick) butter or margarine
> 2 tablespoons sugar

Start by making a sponge, this is what the French call the yeast dough: dissolve the yeast in warm water to make a soft cream. Add 2 or 3 tablespoons of flour, mixing with a spoon to make a very stiff dough. Roll this dough into a small ball and place it in a pan or bowl of warm water. Not hot, just warm; test it on your wrist as you would baby's bottle. Cover the pan with a towel and leave while you prepare the rest of the dough.

Place the rest of the flour, unsifted, in a large bowl. Make a hole in the middle and break 4 eggs in it. Add a pinch of salt. Separate the last egg and set the yolk aside for tomorrow. Place it in a small cup, cover with 2 tablespoons of water and plastic film or foil and leave it in the refrigerator. Keep the white.

Start beating the four whole eggs with a fork or your fingertips and gradually work in the flour. You will eventually get a ball of stiff dough. If all the flour cannot be absorbed, gradually add the last egg white. Now comes the part where you have to go French. Most recipes I see for brioche use an electric mixer or beater. It is my belief that brioche dough prefers being slapped around rather than beaten! There is no accounting for tastes! Take the dough in your hands and slap it down on the table or pastry board until it is quite smooth and elastic. Anyhow this is rather fun and you should get rid of a lot of frustrations. Pretend it is your worst enemy and see how loving you feel after 5 minutes or so!

Now knead in the butter and sugar. When that is well mixed,

carefully lift the sponge from the water where it will now be floating. Use a slotted spoon and let excess water drip off. Spread this on the dough and knead in well. You should now have a soft, smooth dough. Place it in a greased bowl, cover with a towel and let it rise, away from drafts, for about 3 hours.

Punch the dough down, cover the bowl with aluminum foil, leaving the dough plenty of room to expand, and leave the bowl in a cool place. The French would say in the cellar—just use the bottom of the refrigerator in warm weather, in cold weather, maybe the utility room would be a good place if the cat can't get to it! Let the dough rise a second time. When I make brioche, I like to make it right after the evening meal: it can rise once in a warm place and I put it in the refrigerator at bedtime. If the idea of messing up the kitchen in the evening appalls you, make it earlier in the day but punch it down once before you both get a good night's rest.

Next day, punch it down again and shape it. Brioche en Couronne means in a crown and I find this the easiest shape to handle. Take half the dough, roll it in a ball, punch a hole in the middle with your fingers. Place it on a greased cooky sheet and work the dough into a ring approximately 9 inches across and 2 inches wide. Leave this to rise again until double in bulk, in a warm place. It takes about an hour. With a soft brush gild the top of the brioches with the egg yolk beaten with the water. You can decorate the brioches by making little snips all around with scissors. Bake in preheated oven at 400°F. for about 20 minutes or until a cake tester comes out clean. The top will get quite dark. That is as it should be, brioches are almost as dark as black coffee on top. If it seems to be burning, however, you can place a piece of foil loosely on top for the last 5 minutes of cooking.

Serve warm with plenty of butter and love in your heart. Now that you know how to make brioche dough, here some other things to make with it.

The first idea is one of the fondest memories of my childhood. Split a brioche ring in two with a sharp knife. Spread a thick layer of melted dark sweet chocolate on the bottom layer. Place the top layer back on and fill the center of the ring with slightly sweetened whipped cream. Cut in wedges, this should be the hit of any coffee party!

Brioches can also be baked in little muffin tins. Fill about halfway up. Poke a hole in the middle with your finger and place a little ball of dough, the size of a marble, in the hole. Leave to rise, gild with egg yolk and water and bake about 10 minutes. Or you can bake two large brioches with a hat with the quantity of dough given. Large or small, these brioches take kindly to salty fillings.

After the brioches are baked, let them cool a little, then remove the hat. With a sharp pointed knife scrape out a little of the inside, taking care not to pierce the shell. Fill lightly and replace the little hat. Scrambled eggs are delicious this way and you can pass crisp bacon alongside. This for a wonderful Sunday brunch with lots of *café au lait.*

Creamed chicken, fish, shrimp or anything with mushrooms will go extremely well with brioche as a base. Just be sure the sauce is fairly thin, creamy but not gooey or thick. Personally I find the ring brioche the easiest to make and serve. You can simply split them, butter them and fill the center of the ring with whatever you are using. You can fill those with a hat also but take care 1) not to dig too deeply into the brioche so it will not break and 2) to keep the filling just coated with sauce so the brioche will not get soggy. Pass more sauce separately.

Fresh fruit or a fresh fruit compote, such as lightly cooked plums, peaches or pears, served with wedges of brioche and whipped cream, will give you a not too sweet dessert particularly appreciated by most men!

Brioche dough can also make delicious doughnuts. Filled with *crème pâtissière* or preserves such as strawberry jam, they make a delicious mouthful.

FOR 24 SMALL DOUGHNUTS:
  ½ recipe for brioche
  Fat for deep frying
  1 8-ounce glass strawberry or other jam OR
    *1 cup Créme Pâtissière**
  Super-fine or confectioners' sugar

Roll small pieces of brioche dough, which has already had its night's rest, into small balls the size of a pecan. Flatten them slightly between your palms so they are egg-shaped. Place on a greased cooky sheet, cover with a towel and leave to rise in a warm place until doubled in bulk.

Heat some oil in a deep skillet or French fryer to 375°F. If you are using a skillet have the oil at least ½ inch deep. Gently lift the little doughnuts off the cooky sheet with a spatula and fry until deep gold on both sides. Do not crowd them. Split the first one to make sure it is done right through and act accordingly. Cool on paper towels to absorb extra oil.

Split the cooled doughnuts and fill with jam or custard. My preference goes to strawberry jam with lots of whole berries. Roll in sugar before serving. If this is intended for a ladies' tea party, try using super-fine powdered sugar; it does not cling to lips and hands the way confectioners' sugar does, with the resultant damage to lipstick! Husbands and children, though, usually prefer this last and plenty of it!

BOLUS

Belgian Cinnamon Rolls

Belgians, as I have often said before, love to eat. Not content with plentiful meals at noon and at night, they love a copious snack around four o'clock! School children come home to a bountiful *gouter*, which often includes bread and butter with jam or a bar of chocolate. Try this one day: simply butter generously a slice of bread or a soft roll and place a bar of sweet dark chocolate inside. Amazingly good! Besides the *tartines* of bread and butter there will also be *couques*. The French don't know these! But I think they miss a lot—they are various kinds of Danish pastries. After this, on grand occasions when Mama has friends in to tea, will come cream cakes and fruit pies. All is liberally washed down with hot chocolate or coffee served with a generous spoonful of whipped cream floating on top. Thus fortified, the average Belgian will face with equanimity the two or three hour wait until suppertime! Do you wonder that Belgium is such a happy little country with fat, rosy cheerful people?

So forget all about calorie counting and make these Bolus, which combine all the goodness of cinnamon and caramel rolls with raisins and candied fruit added!

FOR 3 TO 4 DOZEN ROLLS:
   1 cup milk
   ¼ pound (1 stick) butter or margarine
   1 cup white sugar
   2 eggs
   2 envelopes dry yeast in ½ cup warm water
   5 cups (approximately) flour

Filling:
   ¼ pound (1 stick) butter (real butter is needed here;
      margarine will burn)
   2 cups brown sugar
   ½ cup raisins mixed with
      ½ cup mixed, chopped candied fruit OR
      1 cup raisins with a little grated orange peel
Cinnamon

Scald the milk, pour it in a large bowl and add the butter to it. Stir until the butter has melted, then add the sugar and the eggs. By now the mixture should be just lukewarm, not hot. Add the yeast, softened and creamed in ½ cup warm water, and about 2 cups flour. Beat all together until you get a very soft dough, smooth and almost liquid. Now add enough flour (about 5 cups) to make a soft dough you can roll into a ball. Place it in a greased bowl and turn it over so that the top will be greased also. Cover with a cloth and leave to rise until doubled in bulk.

Divide the butter reserved for the filling into four 9-inch layer cake pans. Use two larger baking pans if you prefer, but the 9-inch ones are easy to handle. Divide 1 cup of brown sugar evenly between them also. Heat the pans on top of the stove for a minute until the butter is melted and the sugar bubbly. Leave to cool.

Punch the dough down, divide it in four equal pieces and roll it out into a large rectangle about 20 by 8 inches. Sprinkle each rectangle with brown sugar, raisins and candied fruit and a dusting of cinnamon. Roll up from the long side as a jelly roll, cut into ¾-inch slices and arrange these in the prepared pans, cut side down. Again let rise until doubled, about 45 minutes, covered with a towel in a warm place. Bake 20 to 25 minutes in preheated oven at 375°F. until well browned and turn out of the pans immediately. If necessary, you can reheat the pan on top of the stove for a minute to melt any sugar which stuck to the pan.

You can halve this recipe, if you like, but if you have children, plan on at least one panful disappearing before it ever reaches the table! The aroma will call kids from as far as two or three blocks away!

PAIN DE VERVIERS

Verviers Bread

Belgium is a tiny country which offers tremendous variety. The seacoast is absolutely flat, a lot of the land is even below sea level. Farther inland, the ground rises gently, first into rolling hills around Brussels, the capital, then more sharply into steep rocky hills. Although properly speaking these are not mountains, they give a very good imitation. Some of the peaks are so rocky and sharp that any summer Sunday you can see groups of young men practicing the art of mountain climbing complete with ropes and picks. To see some of them dangling from ropes way above the Meuse River is an awesome sight!

Verviers, in the mountainous Ardennes region, is famous for this bread. This is real homemade bread, not cake, but it is dotted with lumps of sugar not quite melted in the dough, crunchy to the teeth. Try it warm from the oven, liberally spread with butter and maybe honey or jam. Children coming home from school will really appreciate this treat! If you can manage to keep a loaf for a day or two, it will be delicious sliced thickly and toasted golden brown. This recipe makes three 9-inch round loaves—with five children I need that amount to keep everyone happy! But you can easily halve the recipe and make two smaller loaves if your family is small.

FOR THREE 9-INCH LOAVES:
  2 cups milk
  ½ pound (2 sticks) butter
  1 teaspoon salt
  1 cup sugar
  ½ cup warm water
  2 envelopes dry yeast
  8 cups (approximately) flour
  3 eggs
  ½ pound small sugar cubes

Scald the milk, add to it the butter, salt and sugar and let it cool to lukewarm. Rinse a large bowl with hot water, pour in ½ cup warm water and stir in the yeast until dissolved and creamy. Add the lukewarm milk, 4 cups of flour and the eggs, one by one. Beat with your hand until you get a smooth mixture. Add the rest of the flour, about 1 cup at a time, until you get a nice soft dough which does not stick to your hands. This can take from 3½ to 4 cups of flour.

Knead in the lumps of sugar. If you have a very sweet tooth, you may add a little more than ½ pound. In the old days, sugar was sold in large cone-shaped loaves in Belgium. It took a lot of work to pound it into powdered sugar, so this bread started, no doubt, because a cook did not take the time to pound all the sugar finely! Be glad of all the work you don't have to do!

Leave the dough to rise until almost doubled in bulk, in a warm place and with a cloth over it to protect it from drafts. Then shape it into three round loaves and place these into well-greased 9-inch layer pans. Cover with a cloth and leave to rise again until doubled. Each rising will take about 1 hour. Bake in preheated oven at 350°F. for 50 minutes to 1 hour or until the loaves are a beautiful toasty brown and sound hollow when you tap them gently. Remove them from their pans immediately: the sugar will stick if you don't. Cool and slice with a very sharp knife. Immensely satisfying with a good cup of coffee!

Do you know how they sweetened their coffee a long time ago around Verviers? Some of the sugar loaves would come with a long rope running through the middle. This would be attached to a rafter in the small cafés and everyone would simply hold his cup of hot coffee so that the tip of the cone would rest in it for as long as necessary to sweeten it to taste!

10. DRINKS AND PUNCHES

BOISSONS

We have been looking at what the French eat, let's take a look at what they drink. I know the French have the reputation of drinking nothing but wine, this is not quite true: they also drink brandy and liqueurs! Add to that coffee and, very seldom, tea, and chocolate. There is, of course, that other liquid called water, which comes in handy for washing oneself or dishes. It is said that a Frenchman on a hot summer day, afflicted with a tremendous thirst drank a glass of water. He then bemoaned the fact that he had had to spoil such a beautiful thirst! Joking aside, the French have lots of different mineral waters which are delicious. You probably know Vichy water, which has all kinds of slightly medicinal properties. There is also Perrier, which is to soda what champagne is to grape juice. And innumerable others, some of which are available here.

There are many drinks made with wine and different fruit juices. Also some marvelous concoctions to be served on a cold day. You may enjoy them as a change from the usual cocktails.

CERISES AU VIN

Here a rather unusual kind of punch, half drink—half dessert. Serve it well chilled in little punch cups with small spoons. You could serve this as a cooling summer dessert besides serving it as punch.

FOR 6 TO 8 ½-CUP SERVINGS:

1 pound dark sweet cherries, fresh or canned
Sugar
1 8-ounce glass raspberry or red currant jelly
1 lemon
1 (1-inch) stick cinnamon
2 cups good red wine

If you are using fresh cherries, pit them and cook them with a little water and enough sugar to sweeten them. Let them simmer a few minutes until tender but not mushy. Use the canned cherries straight from the can. Place the cherries in a 2-quart pan, add the jelly, the sliced lemon, the cinnamon and the wine. Heat, stirring until the jelly is completely melted. Taste and add more sugar if necessary but don't make it cloyingly sweet. Remove the cinnamon and the lemon slices, chill and serve in small cups. Crisp sweet cookies passed with this make it a delicious light dessert.

VIN AUX FRAISES

You can use fresh or frozen strawberries for this delicious wine. It is a little stronger than the cherry wine: a little brandy is added.

FOR 6 TO 8 SERVINGS:

2 pints fresh or 2 boxes (8 to 12 ounces) frozen strawberries
1 bottle red Bordeaux wine
¼ cup brandy, preferably cognac
Sugar to taste
1 orange

Mash lightly 1 pint fresh strawberries or thaw 1 box frozen ones. Pour on them the wine and the brandy and add sugar to taste. Slice the orange very, very thinly and add also. Leave this mixture to steep for several hours or overnight. Before serving, strain, then add the other pint of strawberries, sliced and lightly sweetened. If you are using the frozen ones, add them still partially frozen. Serve well chilled.

CASSIS—VIN BLANC

A vermouth-cassis or vin blanc-cassis is a favorite summer drink in the Southern part of France. Cassis is black currant syrup. Simply pour a couple of tablespoonfuls in the bottom of a glass and fill with a good, well-chilled white wine or dry vermouth. A white Burgundy is particularly suitable but other white wines will do excellently. Adjust the amount of syrup to your particular taste and that of your guests. Add a twist of lemon peel and serve.

VIN BLANC AUX FRUITS

This is something light for the ladies! Slice 1 orange and 1 lemon very, very thinly. Place in a large pitcher and add about ¾ cup sugar. Allow to stand for a couple of hours or until the sugar has dissolved. Pour in 4 tablespoons raspberry syrup or grenadine (which is pomegranate syrup, by the way!), 3 or 4 cups chilled white wine and a tray of ice cubes (about 12). Stir well and serve. Delicious and not very strong.

VIN CHAUD À LA FRANÇAISE

A glass or cup of this hot red wine is guaranteed to warm you from the tip of your nose to your toes! A marvelous drink to serve after playing in the snow. Be careful, though, it lets itself be drunk quite easily but is quite heady!

6 tablespoons sugar
1 bottle good red Bordeaux wine
1 small stick cinnamon
1 lemon

Melt the sugar into the wine, add the cinnamon stick and a long strip of lemon peel. Heat until slightly frothy on top, stirring until the sugar is dissolved. Pour into glasses or mugs and serve with a paper-thin slice of peeled lemon floating on top.

PORTO FLIP

This is French eggnog. It is extremely easy to make, delicious and much stronger than the American version usually. You need, per person:

> 1 egg yolk
> 1 tablespoon sugar
> ⅓ cup good port wine
> A little grated nutmeg

Mix the egg yolk and the sugar, beating it well. Add the port wine drop by drop at first, stirring very fast so that no lumps form. After the first couple of spoonfuls, you can relax! Shake well and serve with a little grated nutmeg on top. This is very creamy and delicious.

ADVOCAAT

This is a dessert liqueur beloved by the Belgians and Dutch people. You can buy it ready made, of course, but there is something about the homemade kind which surpasses any other. This is definitely potent stuff, a combination of eggs, sugar, brandy or Rum. A small glass of it should revive the dead! Served in very small glasses at the end of a plentiful meal, simply with a few dry sweet cookies, it would make a memorable finish. Besides, it is supposed to aid digestion, though I cannot vouch for this.

When making it, use a glass or unchipped enameled double boiler. Aluminum sometimes alters the color of the eggs.

FOR APPROXIMATELY 3 CUPS LIQUEUR:
> 1 teaspoon cornstarch
> 1 ounce water
> 6 egg yolks
> 1 cup sugar
> 1 pinch grated nutmeg
> 1 pinch cinnamon
> 1 pint (2 cups) good brandy, cognac, rum or kirsch
>   as preferred

Mix the cornstarch with the water into a smooth paste. Add it to the other ingredients, except the alcohol, in the top of the double boiler. Place the double boiler over a fairly high fire and bring the water in the bottom half to simmering, beating the egg mixture constantly with an egg beater. Cook, still beating, until the eggs are thick, light and fluffy. Remove from the fire, cool a little, still stirring once in a while, and gradually beat in the brandy. The result will be a rather thick, unbelievably smooth liqueur. A votre santé!

CAFÉ VIENNOIS

In Belgium, you would have to ask for café Liégeois to get this delicious mixture of iced, strong coffee and loads of whipped cream. The name was changed for patriotic reasons during the First World War.

To make it, start with a pot of strong coffee, about twice as strong as you would usually make it. I hesitate to give you exact quantities, brands and tastes vary so much. Sweeten it generously while it is still hot. Chill it or almost freeze it in a covered container. The container must be covered or you will lose a lot of the coffee aroma. Preferably find a plastic or one that is not metal. Coffee and metal are archenemies in my mind!

Half fill glasses with very finely crushed ice. Pour coffee over this to about 2 inches from the top. Fill the rest of the glass with chilled whipped and sweetened heavy cream, mounding it as high as you can. Serve with straws and long spoons.

ICED TEA

Iced tea is not much used on the continent. The English drink a lot of tea but like theirs hot! However, they have the best tasting tea in the world and whether served hot or cold, it is worth making good tea for a start.

For the best iced tea you ever tasted try this: make a pot of tea using 2 teaspoons or 2 tea bags (but the loose tea is infinitely preferable for flavor) per cup of freshly boiling water. The English specify that you must boil freshly drawn cold water and that the water must always be allowed to come to a rolling boil. Another maxim is that the pot should be brought to the kettle but never the kettle to the pot: it would stop boiling merrily! Let the tea steep for about 3 minutes, then strain over a thinly sliced lemon. Let stand for 10 minutes or so, don't crush the lemon. Pour over lots of ice and sweeten to taste. Hot strong tea iced this way quickly has a marvelous flavor. When I am making it for a crowd, and just the family at my house IS a crowd, I sweeten the hot tea with about 1 cup of sugar to 4 cups tea. Diluted with ice, this is about right for everybody: it makes around 2 quarts.

Index